Onward Christian Soldiers?

Dilemmas in American Politics

Series Editor: **Craig A. Rimmerman**, Hobart and William Smith Colleges

If the answers to the problems facing U.S. democracy were easy, politicians would solve them, accept credit, and move on. But certain dilemmas have confronted the American political system continuously. They defy solution; they are endemic to the system. Some can best be described as institutional dilemmas: How can the Congress be both a representative body and a national decision-maker? How can the president communicate with more than 250 million citizens effectively? Why do we have a two-party system when many voters are disappointed with the choices presented to them? Others are policy dilemmas: How do we find compromises on issues that defy compromise, such as abortion policy? How do we incorporate racial and ethnic minorities or immigrant groups into American society, allowing them to reap the benefits of this land without losing their identity? How do we fund health care for our poorest or oldest citizens?

Dilemmas such as these are what propel students toward an interest in the study of U.S. government. Each book in the *Dilemmas in American Politics* series addresses a "real world" problem, raising the issues that are of most concern to students. Each is structured to cover the historical and theoretical aspects of the dilemma but also to explore the dilemma from a practical point of view and to speculate about the future. The books are designed as supplements to introductory courses in American politics or as case studies to be used in upper-level courses. The link among them is the desire to make the real issues confronting the political world come alive in students' eyes.

BOOKS IN THIS SERIES

Onward Christian Soldiers?

The Religious Right in American Politics

THIRD EDITION

Clyde Wilcox
Georgetown University

and

Carin Larson
Georgetown University

A Member of the Perseus Books Group

Copyright © 2006 by Westview Press, a Member of the Perseus Books Group.

Published in the United States of America by Westview Press, A Member of the Perseus Books Group, 5500 Central Avenue, Boulder, Colorado 80301–2877.

Find us on the world wide web at www.westviewpress.com

Westview Press books are available at special discounts for bulk purchases in the United States by cor- porations, institutions, and other organizations. For more information, please contact the Special Markets Department at the Perseus Books Group, 11 Cambridge Center, Cambridge, MA 02142, or call (617) 252–5298 or (800) 255–1514, or email special.markets@perseusbooks.com.

Library of Congress Cataloging-in-Publication Data

Wilcox, Clyde, 1953-
    Onward Christian soldiers? : the religious right in American politics / Clyde Wilcox and Carin Larson.— 3rd ed.
        p. cm.
    Includes bibliographical references and index.
    ISBN-13: 978-0-8133-4333-4 (alk. paper)
    ISBN-10: 0-8133-4333-X (alk. paper)
    1. Christianity and politics—United States—History—20th century. 2. Religious right—United States. 3. United States—Politics and government—1945-1989. 4. United States—Politics and government—1989-. 5. United States—Church history—20th century. I. Larson, Carin. II. Title.

BR526.W53 2006
320.5'50973—dc22

                                                                                2005030395

The paper used in this publication meets the requirements of the American National Standard for Per- manence of Paper for Printed Library Materials Z39.48–1984.

10   9   8   7   6   5   4   3   2   1

Contents

Illustrations

Tables

Figures

Boxes

Map

Preface

Writing about the Christian Right always brings out the schizophrenic elements in me, as my roots war with my politics. I grew up in rural West Virginia, and many of my family and friends who still live in that area are supporters of the Christian Right. My father was a fundamentalist Sunday school teacher who taught me the Bible and was a fan of Jerry Falwell. My mother was a charismatic who regularly watched Pat Robertson's *700 Club* and who greatly enjoyed a Spirit-filled religious retreat every spring. My great-aunts, to whom this book is dedicated, seldom missed a televised sermon by Charles Stanley.

As a child I attended the Walnut Grove United Methodist Church, a church in the revivalist tradition of Spirit-filled fundamentalism. I was often drafted to play the piano in revival services in small churches in the surrounding area, where I would spend a few hectic minutes trying to determine in which key I could play each song so as to minimize the number of dead keys on the very old, poorly maintained pianos. The people in those churches are fair-minded, warm, and compassionate. I could fill a book with tales of their extraordinary kindness and generosity. Most of them are also very conservative; they oppose abortion, gay rights, government welfare programs, and most other liberal policies. Although I am no longer part of that culture, I respect, admire, and love the people there.

Yet I also came of age politically in the late 1960s and was shaped by the civil rights, antiwar, feminist, and environmental movements. I strongly oppose most of the policy agenda of the Christian Right. I want my daughter and son to grow up in a world in which they have equal access to a wider range of roles than society now provides. I want my gay and lesbian friends to live free of discrimination based on whom they love. I want the public schools to teach my children to think for themselves, to be tolerant of diverse lifestyles, and to know about the latest scientific thinking. Thus my political values are in conflict with my roots, and I engage in much internal debate when I write about the Christian Right.

I hope this internal dialogue has produced a fair assessment of the role of the Christian Right in American politics and the dilemmas it creates for the polity. If the book is balanced, I owe a great debt to John Green, who engaged in a protracted dialogue and sometimes debate through e-mail. John read and commented on the first draft of the book, served as a sounding board for my arguments, and kept me from saying some silly things from time to time. He ran data to help me test some questions I was asking.

A number of other people offered valuable comments. Ted Jelen, Matt Moen, and my wife, Elizabeth Cook, read the entire first edition manuscript and made useful suggestions. Mary Bendyna also read early drafts of some chapters and helped me craft a better book. The second edition of the book owes a great debt to Rachel Goldberg, who served as my research assistant for much of the time leading up to the book's completion. The series editor, Sandy Maisel, and the staff of Westview Press provided invaluable advice and assistance. We would like to specifically thank Steve Catalano, Kay Mariea, and Jennifer B. Swearingen for their contribution to the third edition.

For the third edition, I have invited Carin Larson, a graduate student at Georgetown University, to join me in the revision. Carin and I have written together several times, and her unique perspective also helps me maintain a balance about the movement and its agenda. It has been a pleasure working with her on the book, and I have enjoyed our e-mail dialogues over various issues.

I wrote the first edition of this book while teaching a small seminar on the Christian Right at Georgetown University in the fall of 1995. The thirteen students in that class were a lively group who inspired me to rethink many questions, assisted me in locating important information, and reminded me why I enjoy teaching. Over the ten years since then, I have taught the class several other times, and in many cases had wonderful students whose papers have been influential in my understanding of various issues.

In the summer of 2005, as we were completing the draft of this third edition, Walt Barbee died. Walt had founded Virginia's Family Foundation, described later in this book, and he shared his time and knowledge with me repeatedly over the years, although he knew that we did not share a common outlook on politics. Walt was an ordinary citizen who built a strong statewide organization through his personal skills, his determination, and his personal demeanor—a clear story for all students that individuals can matter in politics. I will miss our lunches, from which I learned a great deal about Virginia politics and the Christian Right.

This book is dedicated to my grandmother, Zoe Wilcox, and her two sisters, Beulah Musgrove and Grace Ice. Although these women lived quite different lives, they shared a lifelong interest in learning and teaching. Their strength, compassion, decency, and love of life inspire me daily.

Clyde Wilcox

My first exposure to American politics came from Focus on the Family and Christian news magazines. I grew up reading about abortion and prayer in schools, thinking little else mattered to the stability of our society. Today I approach the study of the Christian Right with great ambivalence. My ambivalence is a function of my sympathies for portions of the movement's platform—the fight to defend the unborn and the commitment to the traditional family structure—mixed with my understanding of Scripture that leads me to forsake all political warfare for the simple message of salvation through Christ. While I can agree with certain policy positions of the Christian Right, I do not readily endorse the movement as a reflection of biblical Christianity. I fear Christians in this country have Americanized the Bible and limited our scope of influence by equating truth with public policy—or a political party, for that matter. While my political identity and understandings have no doubt been shaped by my religious upbringing, I refrain from making claims about God's will for America—for He has the *whole* world in his hands—and I cringe at the notion that a Democrat cannot be a true believer.

Revising this book has been a great exercise for me as I sort through both the support for and opposition to the social movement as it stands in 2005. I hope the perspective I bring to this edition contributes to the balance my co-author achieved in the previous editions. I am incredibly grateful to him for the opportunity he has given me to participate in this scholarly discussion as well as the challenges he poses, which refine my own faith. I also thank the staff of Westview Press for their kind assistance.

My contribution to this book is in honor of my grandparents, Verne and Ardelle Larson and Helen Ahern-Dyson and in memory of Edward Ahern. I am thankful for their enthusiastic and unconditional support.

Carin Larson

1

....

Introduction:
The Christian Right
in Context

What kind of judges do the liberals want? Those like the ones who allowed Terri Schiavo to be starved and dehydrated to death. Those like the ones who don't believe it should be illegal for abortionists to suck the brains out of nearly-delivered children. Those who believe pornography showing women being raped, mutilated and defecated upon is protected by the First Amendment—but the Ten Commandments are not. Keeping judges like this in power is the real motivation for the blockade of President Bush's judicial nominees.

—Focus on the Family Action e-mail to supporters,
April 28, 2005

On the evening of April 24, 2005, Christian conservatives across the nation participated in Justice Sunday, a simulcast sponsored by Focus on the Family Action and Family Research Council Action, two of the most prominent Christian Right organizations. Held in a megachurch in Louisville, Kentucky, the event was broadcast to several hundred churches by satellite and to thousands of people across the country over the Internet and by Christian radio and television stations. Christian Right leaders urged evangelicals to call their senators and tell them to end the filibuster "against people of faith" (Kirkpatrick and Salvato, 2005).

Behind the podium stood large pictures of court nominees whose confirmation votes had been threatened with a Senate filibuster. Nominees such as Priscilla Owens and Janice Rogers Brown looked somber in the photos, adding to the sense that they were victims of religious discrimination. Holding a Bible in one hand and a gavel in the other, Tony Perkins, president of the Family Research Council said, "As American citizens we should not have to choose between believing and living by what is in [the Bible] and serving the public." Perkins urged attendees and viewers at home to call their senators, whose office phone numbers scrolled across the bottom of the screen throughout the simulcast. James Dobson, chairman of Focus on the Family, expressed outrage over "activist" courts, saying, "There is a majority on the Supreme Court that is . . . unelected, unaccountable, arrogant, imperious, and determined to redesign the culture according to their own biases and values, and they are out of control. I think they need to be reined in." Senate majority leader Bill Frist (R-TN), who was leading the effort to change Senate rules to bar filibusters of court nominees, spoke to the group via satellite. Frist was contemplating a run for president and hoping that participation in the event would gain him the support of evangelical Christian voters in the presidential primaries.

The charge that Democrats were filibustering potential judges because of their faith was designed to fire up Christian Right activists, who would then pressure senators to support President Bush's nominees. The truth was somewhat more subtle; the Senate had already confirmed most of Bush's nominees, and many of those who had been confirmed had the same kinds of religious views as the nominees the Democrats were threatening to filibuster. Owens, Brown, and the others faced filibusters not because of their religious faith but because of their judicial philosophy and their records on abortion, the environment, business regulation, and civil rights. President Bush acknowledged as much in an April 28, 2005, press conference.

Justice Sunday marked a new season of Christian Right activity in the United States. It came only a few months after the 2004 presidential election, in which Christian Right groups played a significant role. Many analysts credited white evangelical voters with returning Bush to the White House and swelling the GOP margin in Congress. Much of the speculation centered on reports of exit polls showing that "moral issues" were highly salient to voters in general and to Bush supporters in particular. Leaders of the Christian Right, claiming responsibility for the "values voters," spent little time celebrating. Focus on the Family e-mailed its supporters this warning soon after the election: "The future of our nation is still in danger. We must be careful to not only protect what has been won, but move forward aggressively, pressing for the pro-family, pro-life and pro-morality agenda we believe in. In other words, we must strike while the iron is hot."[1]

It is unclear whether Christian conservatives can be credited with Bush's victory. The media focused heavily on evangelical voters and on issues such as same-sex marriage in explaining Bush's narrow victory. But media accounts of the influence of the Christian Right have gyrated wildly between underestimating the movement's considerable resources and overstating its numbers and impact. In 1995, most accounts supported the claims by Ralph Reed (then director of the Christian Coalition) and others that the Christian Right helped the Republicans gain control of the House of Representatives for the first time in a generation and win control of the U.S. Senate (Wilcox, 1995). Just three years earlier, many commentators blamed Christian conservatives for damaging President George H. W. Bush's chances for reelection by using divisive and often extreme rhetoric at the Republican National Convention.

In 1980, after Ronald Reagan won the White House with a margin that surprised pollsters, the media credited Jerry Falwell and the Moral Majority with the Republican victory. Journalists "discovered" the strength of the Christian Right, and some painted the Moral Majority as a juggernaut that represented a substantial portion of the American citizenry. But public opinion polls soon revealed that Jerry Falwell was one of the most unpopular men in America, and journalists then "discovered" the weakness of the Christian Right. They painted the movement as small, extreme, and so deeply fragmented that further growth was impossible. By 1983, the media pronounced the Christian Right moribund. In 1984, when Jerry Falwell, Pat Robertson, and their followers were visible presences at the Republican nominating convention, the media rediscovered the assets of the Christian Right, only to rediscover its weaknesses by 1986. Early in the 1988 presidential campaign, when Pat Robertson did surprisingly well in the very early Michigan balloting and placed second in the Iowa caucuses, the media again discovered a hidden army of Christian Right activists. At the end of the campaign, when Robertson had spent more money than any other candidate but won only a handful of delegates, the weakness of the Christian Right was again the story. In late 1988, with a moderate Republican in the White House, Robertson back on television, and the Moral Majority essentially bankrupt, the media wrote the movement's obituary. Journalists were not alone; some scholars saw the movement as moribund at various points in its history and depicted its downfall as inevitable (Bruce, 1988).

In fact, public support for the Christian Right and its issue agenda has probably not changed a great deal since the formation of the Moral Majority in the late 1970s. What *has* changed is the sophistication of movement leaders and the presence of grassroots organizations. Between 10 and 15 percent of whites support the Christian Right and have done so since the formation of the Moral Majority in 1979 (Wilcox, 1992; Wilcox, DeBell, and Sigelman, 1999). Yet the organizations of the Christian Right became more effective in enlisting some of those supporters into activism and in providing informational cues for voting. In doing so, it established itself as a major element of the Republican governing coalition.

The movement has important strengths and weaknesses. It is likely that the fiery speeches by Christian Right leaders at the Republican National Convention in 1992 hurt the GOP in that election and that the quiet mobilization of Christian conservatives in the 1994 elections helped the Republicans win a number of closely contested House and Senate races.[2] The movement has great assets. It has many dedicated, savvy activists who have worked for many years on issues they care about, and a broader base of members and supporters. Most of these supporters attend church once a week or more, which means that they meet face to face several times a month, giving the movement an infrastructural advantage that liberal groups envy.

But many of the movement's leaders are prone to publicly voicing extreme statements, which often result in ridicule of the movement. For example, Jerry Falwell, speaking soon after the terrorist attacks in September 2001, proclaimed on national television: "I really believe that the pagans, and the abortionists, and the feminists, and the gays and the lesbians who are actively trying to make that an alternative lifestyle, the ACLU, People for the American Way, all of them who have tried to secularize America. I point the finger in their face and say, 'You helped this happen.'" Falwell later apologized, but he became the target of angry blogs and television and radio talk show jokes for months. More recently, Pat Robertson called for the assassination of Venezuelan president Hugo Chavez in August 2005. Robertson later insisted that he had been misunderstood, but since he had spoken on national television, a video record of his remarks remained, and his denial did little to quell the international uproar.

What Is the Christian Right?

The Christian Right is a social movement that attempts to mobilize **evangelical** Protestants and other orthodox Christians into conservative political action. Many Christian Right leaders object to the term "Christian Right," which they believe depicts a narrow movement. Some prefer the term "religious Right," which would encompass all "people of faith," including conservative Jews and possibly Muslims. Yet despite the visible presence of orthodox Jews at Christian Coalition conventions, the movement remains concentrated primarily among white evangelical Christians (Green, 1995). Others object to both "Christian Right" and "religious Right" on the grounds that labeling the movement as part of the "Right" implies that it is outside the political mainstream. Ralph Reed, formerly of the **Christian Coalition**, prefers the term "Christian conservative," but many conservative Christians oppose the Christian Coalition and similar organizations. Other Christian Right leaders insist that theirs is truly a "**pro-family**" movement, although the agenda of the Christian Right includes many issues unrelated to the health of American families. Moreover, many liberals believe that Christian Right policies would harm families. We use the term "Christian Right" in this book without any necessary implication that the movement lies outside the American mainstream.

Like all social movements, the Christian Right is composed of social movement organizations, leaders, activists, and members, and it seeks to attract support from a broad potential constituency. Robert Zwier argued that "the primary audience, or constituency, for these groups was the approximately 50 million evangelicals in the country, and in particular the fundamentalist wing of that community. The aim from the beginning was to mobilize a group of people who had traditionally avoided politics because they saw it as dirty, corrupt business . . . by convincing people that political involvement was a God-given responsibility" (Zwier, 1984, pp. 9–10).

Movement leaders were and remain more ambitious, seeking an even larger constituency. Jerry Falwell spoke of appealing to "Catholics, Jews, Protestants, Mormons, and fundamentalists." Ralph Reed and the Christian Coalition made major efforts to expand its appeal to mainline Protestants, Catholics, African Americans, and Jews. In their efforts to ban gay marriage, the Family Research Council and Focus on the Family have reached out to African American, Hispanic, and Korean churches, and even to social conservatives in other faith traditions, including Muslims and Jews (Campbell and Larson, 2006).

It is important to distinguish among movement leaders, movement activists, movement supporters, and the potential constituency of the Christian Right. Media accounts frequently equate the Christian Right with all born-again Christians. Such reports greatly exaggerate the movement's strength, for there are many born-again evangelical Christians in the United States. Many born-again Christians are African American, and their faith leads them to a somewhat different policy agenda than the Christian Right. Among white evangelicals, some oppose the Christian Right, many are neutral toward the movement, a sizable minority are supportive, and a much smaller number are active members. White evangelicals are considered to be the core of the potential constituency of the Christian Right.

The organizations of the Christian Right are national groups, such as **Focus on the Family**, the **Family Research Council**, **Concerned Women for America**, and countless state and local organizations. The movement's leaders include James Dobson, Tony Perkins, Beverly LaHaye, and Gary Bauer, among others. Its activists are those who volunteer their time and money to work for these groups, and its members are those who have joined an organization but do not actively participate. The strength of the Christian Right lies in its activist base. For example, activists have distributed voter guides in churches throughout America, and the information in those voter guides may have influenced people who have never considered joining the Christian Right.

Social movements are decentralized, differentiated, and sometimes disorganized. John Green, a political scientist, observed, "There are many modes of mobilization, many pools of resources, many sources of complaint, differential goals and beliefs, and a wide variety of activities, all occurring more or less simultaneously and more or less spontaneously."[3] Thus, no one organization or spokesperson represents the movement. Although Focus on the Family and leaders such as Pat Robertson and Jerry Falwell receive the lion's share of media exposure, there are many Christian Right activists who are not supporters of these groups or figures, and who would support only part of their policy agenda.

Moreover, the Christian Right has no single agenda but rather a collection of overlapping agendas. Some Christian Right activists focus almost entirely on ending abortions in America; others are concerned primarily with issues surrounding homeschooling. Some are motivated to fight what they call the "radical homosexual agenda," whereas others focus on banning same-sex marriage. Others seek to reduce the amount of sexually explicit material in television, movies, and popular music. Some seek to promote a role for religion in public life: prayer in public schools, nativity scenes on city property, and a public acknowledgment that the United States is a Christian (or sometimes Judeo-Christian) nation.[4] Some activists care about all of these issues and more, whereas others focus on one issue.

As has been the case with other social movements, some elements of the Christian Right have become institutionalized. Focus on the Family began as a Christian ministry seeking to strengthen the traditional family. Initially, the organization stood apart from the political arena, but in 1983 it launched its political involvement by helping to found the Family Research Council, an educational organization in Washington, D.C., that advocates for socially conservative public policy. Later, Focus on the Family partnered with the Family Research Council to oversee the creation of more than thirty state affiliates and then created its own political action committee in 2004. Its state-level affiliates played an important role in legislative battles in several states, including Michigan and Virginia.

Part of the institutionalization process involves training leaders, and even members, in the rules and norms of political action. Leading up to the 2004 election, affiliates of Focus on the Family distributed information to churches and pastors explaining how they could politically mobilize their congregants while losing their tax-exempt status. The material included information on "political lingo" and a "resource arsenal" that explained how they could have "maximum patriotic impact" while working within the constraints of the political system.

Organizational leaders have sought to distance the group from activists who make extremist statements in public and to discipline the organization to behave well in political activity. When newly mobilized homeschool advocates threw ice at speakers at the Virginia Republican nominating convention in 1993, Ralph Reed quickly pointed out that the hecklers were not members of the Christian Coalition but rather backers of home school advocate Michael Farris (Rozell and Wilcox, 1996). State and local Christian Right activists have often been dismayed at the public statements made by Pat Robertson and Jerry Falwell.

While some movement activists have worked to institutionalize interest groups of the Christian Right, others have been involved primarily within the Republican Party and now constitute a major faction of the GOP. Although movement leaders sometimes insist for tax purposes that theirs is a nonpartisan movement, it is clear that the Christian Right is active almost exclusively within the GOP. This was not always the case: The most visible spokesman for an earlier manifestation of the Christian Right in the 1920s was William Jennings Bryan, a perennial Democratic presidential candidate. Moreover, when Pat Robertson first entered politics, he backed a candidate who sought to win the Democratic nomination. In addition, Robertson's father was a Democratic senator.

Yet as the turn of the twenty-first century approached, the movement was so closely identified with the Republican Party that when a Christian activist told a Christian Coalition gathering that his brother was a strong Christian and a Democratic officeholder, he was greeted by stunned silence (Hertzke, 1993). Jerry Falwell left little room for Christians to vote for Democratic presidential candidate John Kerry in 2004 when he spoke to the those attending the Christian Coalition's Road to Victory Conference: "Vote Christian. This means pro-life, pro-family, and pro-national defense. These are second nature to God's people. . . . You cannot be a born-again Christian who takes the Bible seriously and vote for a pro-choice or anti-family candidate."[5]

Christian Right activists flocked to the Republican Party in 1980 as the Moral Majority mobilized for Ronald Reagan, and they participated in even greater numbers in 1988, when Robertson sought the GOP presidential nomination. Some of these early activists retired from politics over the next decade, but others remained active in the Republican Party. By 2004, the

Christian Right was a clearly identifiable faction in the Republican Party at the national and state level. In some states, such as Colorado, the movement divided the party, contributing to a Democratic victory in the state's Senate race. In other states, the movement was part of a larger conservative coalition that worked together to oppose party moderates and Democrats alike.[6]

As a **party faction**, the Christian Right contends with moderates for control of nominations; control in turn leads to access to campaign resources and the party platform. The Christian Right provides the Republican Party with a pool of potential voters and volunteers and a ready communications network and infrastructure. But these resources come with a price. The Christian Right refuses to be taken for granted and uses its leverage as an established voting bloc to move the party's platform to the right on social policy. At a meeting for conservative leaders in 1998, James Dobson threatened to break ties with the Republican Party if it did not back the Christian Right agenda on moral issues: "Does the Republican Party want our votes, no strings attached—to court us every two years, and then to say, 'Don't call me; I'll call you'—and to not care about the moral law of the universe? . . . Is that what they want? Is that the way the system works? Is this the way it's going to be? If it is, I'm gone, and if I go, I will do everything I can to take as many people with me as possible."[7] Catering to Dobson's supporters and the Christian Right more generally, however, does not guarantee success for the Republican Party. In many elections in which Christian Right activists have won their party's nomination, they have lost the general election.

The Controversy

Is the Christian Right good or bad for America? This question inspires answers from Christian conservatives and their opponents that differ radically in substance but are similar in their passion. Among those familiar with the Christian Right, the movement is a source of great controversy.

The Christian Right is controversial for several reasons. First, its central social agenda includes issues that are among the most heated in American politics. Christian Right activists generally seek to sharply limit and eventually ban access to legal abortions, to eliminate all laws that protect gays and lesbians from job and housing discrimination, and to alter the curriculum in the public schools in a variety of areas ranging from sex education to history and sociology to biology and geology. The agenda of most Christian Right groups includes many other issues as well, but abortion, gay rights, and education fuel the greatest enthusiasm. These are issues about which many Americans care passionately and upon which the public is deeply divided. Each issue has spawned well-organized, well-funded interest groups that represent many Americans who oppose the Christian Right agenda.

Second, some citizens object to the general effort to mobilize conservative Christians into political action. They do so for varied reasons. Some believe that America is officially a secular society and that religious values should not play a role in the public debate. For others, religious values have a place in politics, but religious leaders should not become political leaders, and churches should not be the locus of political mobilization. Still others believe that religious values and leaders should play an active role in politics but are offended by claims by the Christian Coalition and others that they speak for all Christians.[8] They argue that the Bible does not contain passages calling for a flat tax or opposing government health care for the poor, positions advocated by Christian Right organizations.

Although Christian Right groups take conservative positions on economic issues, many other Christians take opposing positions, asserting that their views are derived from their religious beliefs. Catholics follow the teachings of their church on the necessity of caring for the poor, and liberal Protestants may point to biblical passages that uphold the virtues of the poor and criticize the behavior of the rich. These Christians object to an organization called the Christian Coalition that presumes to speak for them in politics and to take positions that some Christian Right activists assert are the "true Christian" stands.

Finally, the Christian Right is controversial because of the heated rhetoric that its leaders and especially its most ardent activists sometimes produce. On a variety of issues, Christian Right activists have taken quite extreme positions, and many Americans find their rhetoric to be threatening. Feminist mothers and wives recoiled when newspapers published a quotation from one of Pat Robertson's fund-raising letters in which he claimed: "The feminist agenda is not about equal rights for women. It is about a socialist, anti-family political movement that encourages women to leave their husbands, kill their children, practice witchcraft, destroy capitalism, and become lesbians."[9] Robertson's rhetoric on gays and lesbians has been similarly vitriolic, and some local and state leaders have advocated very harsh punishment of homosexuals.

Many fear that these activists will come to exert undue influence on American politics, through subtle and stealthy political action. Pat Robertson struck fear in the hearts of moderate Republicans when he promised to take over all fifty state party committees and when he wrote that "a small, well-organized minority can influence the selection of candidates to an astonishing degree" (Robertson, 1992). Ralph Reed, in explaining the success of the "stealth" candidates who won election to San Diego's school boards, claimed: "I do guerrilla warfare. I paint my face and travel at night. You don't know it's over until election night" (Blumenthal, 1994, p. 114).[10] One Christian Right activist used a war metaphor to describe efforts to ban same-sex marriage in 2004, saying a "strategic insurgence" is more effective than a "nuke."[11]

Christian Right activists argue, quite correctly, that *all* organizations that raise money through direct mail seek to demonize their political opponents because such appeals result in more effective fund-raising. Indeed, liberal groups such as **People for the American Way** and the **American Civil Liberties Union** (ACLU) make fund-raising appeals that caricature Christian conservatives and seek to heighten fear of the Christian Right. And Christian conservatives argue, again correctly, that political leaders frequently fire up their supporters with bold rhetoric that promises coming victories. Christian Right rhetorical appeals may be no more extreme than those of their political opponents, but they nevertheless make many citizens uneasy.

Of course, controversy is not necessarily a bad thing. If debate over the Christian Right stimulates Americans to deal with their core values and inspires the nation to consider its policies in light of those values, then something worthwhile would be achieved. But critics charge that the Christian Right stirs up intolerance, sexism, and homophobia, and that its involvement in politics is therefore a net detriment to the public discourse.

In the introduction to his thoughtful and balanced book about a legal struggle between Christian conservatives and educators over textbooks used in the Hawkins County, Tennessee, schools, Stephen Bates posed one variant of the dilemma of the Christian Right. "How should a secular, tolerant state cope with devout but intolerant citizens, both in the public schools and in the public square?" (Bates, 1993, p. 12) The answer to this question depends critically on how we characterize the Christian Right—as a defensive movement seeking to protect the religious liberties of conservative Christians or as an offensive movement seeking to impose a narrow morality on all Americans.

Although Christian Right leaders use different rhetorical appeals with different groups, they frequently argue that theirs is a *defensive* movement—one designed to protect their moral values and especially their ability to impart those values to their children. Many see their beliefs and values ridiculed in mainstream media, undermined in schools, and ignored by a consumer culture that promotes a multiculturalism that appears to have no room for evangelical culture. In October 2005, Vision America hosted a "Countering the War on Faith" conference for Christians who were "disgusted by Hollywood's attacks on Judeo-Christian ethics, outraged by media slander of Christians, incensed by judicial assaults on Americans' right to publicly acknowledge God, [and] sick and tired of seeing our children indoctrinated in the homosexual lifestyle."[12]

For its supporters, the Christian Right is an attempt to restore Judeo-Christian values to a country that is in deep moral decline. They quote William Bennett, former secretary of education in the Reagan administration: "We are in a race between civilization and catastrophe. . . . We have record murder and violent crime rates, huge increases in births to unwed mothers, educational decline, broken families. . . . All of this, and we are told that the very religious are those we must fear. Religion is on the side of civilization; more people ought to begin to realize it."[13] Christian Right supporters believe that society suffers from the lack of a firm basis of Judeo-Christian values, and they seek to write laws that embody those values. Ralph Reed maintained that "people of faith are not . . . asking people to subscribe to their theology; they are asking them to subscribe to their public policy views, and to respect their right to participate without their religion being impugned" (Reed, 1994a, p. 41). He argued that the Christian Coalition merely sought to have "a seat at the table," not to dominate discussion around that table. He characterized the agenda of the Christian Right as a mainstream agenda and argued that Christian conservatives want what most Americans want: stronger families, safety from crime, successful schools, and democracy.

Although many movement activists describe a defensive movement seeking to protect religious liberties, other Christian Right activists concede that they seek to apply their moral views to all Americans. Gary Bauer, former head of the Family Research Council and presidential candidate in 1999, noted: "So the question is not whether you legislate morality. The question is whose morality you're going to legislate. Somebody's values are going to win. We just have to have the confidence to get in the public square and say that our values will be best for the country" (*New York Times,* August 17, 1999, A12).

Critics of the movement take a different view and charge that the Christian Right is an intolerant movement seeking to impose a narrow, sectarian morality on America. Some describe the Christian Right as a reactionary movement that would censor books, throw gays and lesbians into jail, and confine women to the kitchen.[14] Soon after the 1994 elections, the Reverend Jesse Jackson charged that conservative white Christians who used the Bible to justify slavery were "the Christian Coalition of the time" and that "the Christian Coalition was a strong force in Germany. . . . it laid down a suitable scientific, theological rationale for the tragedy in Germany."[15] Since the terrorist attacks on September 11, 2001, liberal bloggers have compared the fundamentalism associated with the Christian Right to that of Islamic extremists. One author argues that James Dobson has the "ability to manipulate unsuspecting Americans." She quotes Dobson saying that those who control the education of the country's youth will control the future. She argues that this "is a revelation into the evangelical and fundamentalist mentality. It displays a hunger for mind control of youth, scarcely different from Pakistan and Afghanistan's Islamic Fundamentalists" (Blaker, 2003, p. 7). U.S. Senator Ken Salazar (D-Colorado) called Focus on the Family the "antichrist of the world" after Focus questioned his faith because he opposed President Bush's nominees to the federal courts. He later apologized and retracted his comment saying that he only meant to say that Focus on the Family's actions were "self-serving" (Sprengelmeyer, 2005).

If the Christian Right is a defensive movement that seeks to protect religious liberties of conservative Christians, then there can be no question that it has an obvious place at the bargaining table of American politics. If, on the other hand, the movement seeks to deprive gays and lesbians of their civil rights, to limit dramatically the public and private role of women in society, and to impose a prescientific worldview on public education, then some would argue that its policy demands are illegitimate and outside the mainstream of American politics and therefore should not be part of serious policy discussion.

Ultimately, many Americans fear the Christian Right because they see some movement activists issuing harsh condemnations of Americans whose lifestyles differ from those espoused by conservative Christians. They see local organizations working to remove books from public libraries and to prohibit the reading of *The Wizard of Oz* in public schools because it contains a character who is a "good witch" and activists similarly condemning the Harry Potter books and movies for showing witches and wizards as moral heroes. They see an elected official in Alabama fighting to ban all homosexual authors from school libraries. They hear some of the more extreme movement activists suggesting that known homosexuals be imprisoned, and they watch television accounts of the assassination of abortion providers by those on the fringe of the pro-life movement. To at least some observers, these extremists do indeed echo Nazi persecution of gays and public book burnings.

In the 1980s, Margaret Atwood in *The Handmaid's Tale* wrote of a future in which the Christian Right had triumphed and women were subservient to men. Doctors who provided abortions were executed, and women were taught that rape victims deserved their fate because they had enticed men. Atwood's nightmare world is a far cry from Reed's description of the Christian Right agenda. This disjuncture between the soothing reassurances of Reed and the overheated fears of the Left has made the Christian Right one of the most controversial actors in American politics.

Debates between religious conservatives and other citizens occur in many countries and regions of the world. Catholic conservatives debate moderates and liberals about abortion policy in Ireland and Italy; Islamic fundamentalists debate modernists in Iran and Saudi Arabia; orthodox Jews debate secular Jews in Israel; and Sikh fundamentalists debate Hindu fundamentalists and Muslims in India. Yet to understand the debate about the role of the American Christian Right, it is helpful to consider the American context. This includes America's unique policies on church and state, the religious diversity of the United States, and its tradition of civil religion.

The First Amendment and Church and State

In 2002, the 9th U.S. Circuit Court of Appeals ruled that teacher-led recitations of the Pledge of Allegiance in public schools were unconstitutional because the phrase "under God" impermissibly coerces a religious act by students. In Alabama, Chief Justice Roy Moore was removed from the bench in 2003 after defying a federal judge's order to remove a Ten Commandments monument from the state Supreme Court Building. These events evoked a firestorm of protest from the Christian Right and from moderate Christians as well.

The debate about the role of the Christian Right in America takes place within a larger debate about the role of religion in American politics. The debate is ongoing; it took place in the American colonies before the drafting of the Constitution and the Bill of Rights and has been reignited at various points through U.S. history. At stake are two competing visions for American democracy. One holds that the United States is a Christian nation specially blessed by God; the other maintains that the country should be officially secular, with a strong separation between church and state.

The First Amendment to the U.S. Constitution reads in part: "Congress shall make no law respecting an establishment of religion, or prohibiting the free exercise thereof." The first phrase is generally referred to as the **establishment clause** and the second as the **free exercise clause**. These sixteen words, written more than two hundred years ago, have inspired millions of words in a sometimes heated debate over what these two clauses should mean. Scholars have emphasized the precise wording of the amendment—sometimes focusing on a single word, such as *an* establishment of religion or *respecting* an establishment of religion, or highlighting the contrast between *prohibiting* the free exercise of religion and the stricter *abridging* freedom of speech (Malbin, 1978; Levy, 1986). They have debated the original intent of the founders and whether those intentions should bind a country that is far more religiously pluralistic than it was two centuries ago.

In general, we can distinguish between two positions on each of the two clauses. Those who debate the meaning of the establishment clause generally hold either accommodationist or separationist positions. **Accommodationists** believe that the Constitution merely prohibits the establishment of a national religion. They point out that many colonies had established churches at the time of the founding and indeed for many years afterward. They argue that the First Amendment merely prohibits the government from tilting to one religious group over another but does not mean that the government may not prefer religion generally to nonreligion. In other words, government can endorse religion, but it cannot endorse the Baptist Bible Fellowship.

Although accommodationists claim the government must merely be neutral among religions, the specifics of their arguments usually imply that the government need remain neutral only among religions in the Judeo-Christian tradition and sometimes only among Christian faiths.[16] They quote with approval Alexis de Tocqueville, who wrote in 1835, "Christian morality is everywhere the same. . . . Christianity, therefore, reigns without obstacle, by universal consent; the consequence is . . . that every principle of the moral world is fixed and determinate" (Tocqueville, 1945, pp. 314–315). Thus the Judeo-Christian tradition is seen as giving moral coherence to the nation.

Separationists, in contrast, emphasize the potential of religion to lead to violent conflict. They note that James Madison, an early Federalist leader and later president whose essays on the Constitution are still studied by political scientists and constitutional scholars, listed religion as a potential source of divisive factions in *Federalist No. 10*. In addition, separationists argue that the First Amendment prescribes what Thomas Jefferson later called a "high wall of separation" between church and state. They quote with approval Justice Hugo Black's opinion in *Everson v. Board of Education* (1947): "Neither a state nor the federal government can set up a church. Neither can pass laws which aid one religion, aid all religions, or prefer one religion over another."

Although conservatives frequently portray separationists as hostile to religion, Jefferson believed that religion would benefit from separation. He argued that "true" religion would thrive in direct competition with other religious creeds, whereas "false" religion needed protection by the state (Wills, 1990). Others have argued that religion can better play its prophetic role as critic of the state when there is little entanglement between the two (Jelen, 1991a).

Accommodationists and separationists differ in their views of the proper public role for religion. Most accommodationists think that prayers are acceptable in public schools at graduation ceremonies and sporting events. They favor public displays of nativity scenes at Christmas and other open public support for religion. They argue that as long as these prayers are nonsectarian and a Jewish candelabrum called a **menorah** is displayed along with the nativity scene, the government has not endorsed any particular religion. Few would go so far as to allow Hindu or Buddhist prayers in public schools, however, and this stance suggests there are limits to just how neutral they believe government should be (Jelen and Wilcox, 1995). Separationists would oppose all of these public displays of religion, arguing that any endorsement of religion by government is a violation of constitutional guarantees.

There are also two basic positions on the free exercise clause: One would allow all kinds of religious activity so long as no one is harmed; the other would limit such activities to those within some broadly defined community consensus. **Libertarians** hold that all kinds of religious practices are protected, including those of non-Christian groups. They would support the right of Sikh schoolchildren to wear special religious headgear to school, of Muslim girls to cover their heads in gym class, of Santerians to sacrifice animals to their gods. **Communitarians** would argue that religious freedom for minority religious groups should be limited by community norms. If state law prohibits the use of peyote in an effort to control drug use, then Native Americans should not use it in their age-old ceremonies, and if the U.S. Army denies recruits the right to any special attire, then orthodox Jews should not wear special religious headgear.

Of course, many issues fall between these two clauses, evoking both establishment and free exercise claims. For example, when student religious groups ask to use school property to hold their meetings after school, is this a question of establishment (using taxpayer funds to keep the building open) or of free exercise (allowing students to practice their religion)? Over the past several years, Christian Right groups have increasingly framed their concerns around free exercise issues rather than establishment ones. For example, instead of arguing that all schoolchildren would benefit from a public prayer to begin their school day (an establishment issue), Christian conservatives now argue that children should be permitted to offer up audible prayers (a free exercise issue).

Most Christian Right activists take accommodationist positions on the establishment clause and communitarian stands on the free exercise clause, making them what some scholars have called **Christian preferentialists** (Jelen and Wilcox, 1995). These activists want a public role for Christian symbols and practices but resist the notion of non-Christian groups having equal access to public support. Christian Right leaders, however, frequently endorse a position of **religious nonpreferentialism**, which holds that all religious groups have a place in the public square. Ralph Reed wrote: "America is not solely a Christian nation, but a pluralistic society of Protestants, Catholics, Jews, Muslims, and other people of faith whose broader culture once honored religion, but which today increasingly reflects a hostility toward faith in the public square" (Reed, 1994a, p. 135).

It is important to understand that those who oppose the Christian Right are not universally opposed to religion or even to a role for religion in public life. However, many do oppose the Christian Right because they believe the policies it promotes violate the separation between church and state and might infringe on the free exercise rights of religious minorities. Indeed, some who oppose the Christian Right are themselves devoted evangelical Christians who believe that the movement is mistaken in important ways.

To summarize, those who support the Christian Right see contemporary society as aggressively secular and generally hostile to religious values and expression. Those who oppose the Christian Right believe that the movement seeks an unconstitutional establishment of one set of religious views.

Religion and Politics in America

America is unique among Western democracies in the intensity of its moral politics. Compared with other industrialized democracies, America is remarkable for both its religious diversity and the strength of its religious institutions. Many European countries have established churches, and in those countries the majority of religious citizens—and a sizable number of less religious citizens—are members. Large majorities of churchgoers in the nations of southern Europe are Catholic, and large majorities of those in Scandinavia are Lutheran. Germany is nearly evenly divided between Lutherans in the north and Catholics in the south. In no country are there more than three or four dominant religious groups.

In contrast, Americans belong to an almost bewildering array of churches. Many states and regions have clear religious majorities—Baptists in the South, Catholics in New England, Mormons in Utah—but every state has churches representing dozens of Protestant denominations. Moreover, in urban areas on the East and West Coasts, there are growing numbers of Muslims, Hindus, Sikhs, Buddhists, and others from outside the Judeo-Christian tradition.

Not only is America a religiously diverse country, but it is also one in which religious belief and practice are unusually common. International surveys show that more than half of Americans indicate that God is extremely important to their life, compared with fewer than 30 percent of citizens in France, Italy, Germany, Russia, and Japan.[17] Americans attend church more often than citizens in most other industrialized democracies, pray more often, and read their Bibles more frequently.

Some have argued that it is America's religious diversity that sustains its rich religious life. In nations where one church enjoys monopoly status, that church may grow "lazy" and make little effort to seek new converts. In the United States, in contrast, Baptist, Methodist, Presbyterian, and Assembly of God pastors may compete in a small community for the same potential flock of congregants and therefore try much harder to attract and keep new members (Finke and Stark, 1992, but see Jelen 2004 for an elaboration of the debate). The combination of this religious diversity and intensity creates an atmosphere in which moral issues are hotly contested because there are competing moral visions, each with devoted adherents.

Yet underlying the diversity of American religion is a more general support for its basic civil religion. Religious imagery, language, and concepts pervade public discourse, appear on currency, and are present in the pledge

to the flag. Many Christians see America as somehow chosen by God to fulfill his will. The Puritans frequently likened their new covenant with God to
that of God with Abraham and sought to create "God's New Israel." This in-
fusion of religious belief and national purpose persists today.

Researchers have found that many children and adults alike agree with
statements such as "America is God's chosen people today," "I consider holi-
days like the Fourth of July religious as well as patriotic," and "We should respect the president's authority since his authority is from God" (Wimberly,
1976; Smidt, 1980). In many Christian churches, American flags hang behind the pulpit, beside the Christian flag, and children in Sunday school
classes pledge allegiance to both.

Those who support this **civil religion** generally believe that the president has a moral, prophetic role as well as a political one. Perhaps for this
reason, surveys have shown that Americans would vote for candidates from
many different religious backgrounds, but only a minority would vote for a
candidate with no religious affiliation.[18] President George W. Bush has frequently referred to his faith in television interviews and even in candidate
debates. He has spoken consistently of his faith as a source of strength and
comfort (Larson and Wilcox, 2006). Although Bush is himself a divisive
figure in American politics, a majority of Americans are content with his
religious talk. In July 2003, 62 percent of Americans believed Bush mentioned his faith "the right amount." Only 14 percent of those polled believed he mentioned it too much.[19] President Reagan often used religious
language in his speeches, although he seldom attended church, and President Clinton called for a return to religious values in the public debate.
Such public proclamations of the religious character of the nation are very
much in keeping with its civil religion, and many Christian Right activists
believe that the president has a unique role to play as moral as well as political leader of the nation. This view helps explain the vehemence with which
Christian Right activists pressured Congress to impeach and remove President Clinton from office after it became clear that he had engaged in extra-
marital sexual contact with a White House intern and then lied about it on
national television.

These tenets of civil religion are held by nearly all Christian Right activists and leaders and by many opponents of the movement as well. Civil
religion provides an undercurrent of unity beneath the choppy waters of religious diversity. Yet the precise meaning of this civil religion is contested in
America, with moderates focusing on the melting pot of religious diversity

and the Christian Right centering instead on the idea that Americans are God's chosen people.

The belief that there is a religious character to the American polity has important consequences for Christian conservatives. If America is God's new chosen nation, then Christian Right leaders may be likened to the prophets of the Old Testament, who repeatedly called on Israel to repent. When their warnings were ignored, God inflicted various punishments described in the Old Testament.

Jerry Falwell has sounded this theme:

> The rise and fall of nations conform to the Scripture. . . . Psalm 9:17 admonishes, "The wicked shall be turned into hell, and all the nations that forget God." America will be no exception. If she forgets God, she too will face His wrath and judgment like every other nation in the history of humanity. But we have the promise of Psalm 33:12, which declares, "Blessed is the nation whose name is the Lord." When a nation's ways please the Lord, that nation is blessed with supernatural help. (Falwell, 1981, pp. 24–25)

Many activists see their role as that of "redeeming America" (Lienesch, 1994), calling it to repent for many sins and directing it to the path of salvation. Thus, Christian conservatives interpret elements of America's civil religion as mandating their political activity. Many are reluctant political warriors who feel the need to protect America from policies that might result in a loss of God's favor.

Although most Americans expect their political leaders to express religious sentiments, the public is more deeply divided about whether preachers and churches should be involved in politics. In 2004, the Bush campaign sought to identify liaisons in individual churches who would share membership lists with the campaign for use in political mobilization. This resulted in widespread criticism—even from Bush's supporters.

Nearly one in four Americans would not vote for a minister even if the person were from their party and shared their political views, and a somewhat larger number oppose the involvement of preachers in a variety of specific political activities. Liberals and conservatives alike are more likely to disapprove of political action by religious leaders if they disagree with the substance of the policies. One survey revealed that conservative evangelicals are very supportive of ministers being active in pro-life or antipornography demonstrations but far less likely to approve of involvement to end apartheid in South Africa, whereas liberals are more supportive of antiapartheid activity and less so of pro-life activism (Jelen and Wilcox, 1995).

Both liberal and conservative Christians have been quite critical of the political involvement of churches on the other side of the aisle. Conservative clerics decried the involvement of liberal churches in the civil rights and antiwar movements of the 1960s and argued that preachers should never be involved in politics. When preachers became involved with the Christian Right in the 1980s, it was the liberal pastors who denounced such action as violating the primary mission of the church. In fact, American churches have long been involved in crusades of moral reform, including fights over slavery, racial segregation, abortion, and Prohibition (Wilcox, 2005).

However, some churches defended slavery, alcohol consumption, segregation, and abortion rights, and it is this division among religious institutions that troubles many religious professionals. For every position of the Christian Right, there is a Christian religious body in America that takes a very different view. For this reason, many liberals resent the term "Christian" Coalition, for they believe that the Christian Right movement claims to speak for all Christians but in fact represents the views of only one segment of the Christian community. In light of this, it is not surprising that the Houses of Worship Freedom of Speech Restoration Act—a bill that would allow church leaders to speak on political matters while maintaining their churches' tax-exempt status—has never made it out of committee in the House of Representatives.

The debate over the role of the Christian Right takes place within the context of this uniquely American religious pluralism and civil religion. Christian Right activists proclaim their worldview loudly because it competes with so many different worldviews, many derived from different religious traditions. The activists seek to redeem an America that they view as the new chosen land. Opponents point to the many diverse religious views in America and argue that it is best for the state to leave many moral questions to individual choice and to remain neutral as the many diverse traditions compete for adherents.

A Culture War?

Many Christian Right activists and some social scientists see America engaged in a culture war between highly religious citizens and secular citizens. Slightly less than a quarter of Americans say they attend church at least weekly, and more than a third report that religion influences their daily lives "a great deal." These numbers are far higher than in most other Western democracies and validate claims that America is a highly religious nation. Yet many other Americans have no attachment to religious institutions, never attend church except for weddings and other ceremonies, and report that religion is not important in their lives. Others have only marginal involvement in religion. More than four in ten Americans report that religion provides at best "some" guidance in their lives and that they attend church rarely. This relatively secular set of Americans is seen as being in conflict with those with deep religious convictions.[20]

A noted sociologist, James Davison Hunter, described these two groups as being engaged in a culture war that affects public policy and individual lives (Hunter, 1991). He argued that the conflict is rooted in different worldviews—in different beliefs about moral authority between orthodox and progressive Americans. Although Hunter included many deeply religious Americans in his progressive category, many Christian Right leaders and some scholars have recast his argument as a battle between religious and nonreligious Americans.

Over time, these differences have come to be reflected in voting behavior. According to national election exit polls in 2004, those voters who attended church every week supported Bush over Kerry by 61 percent to 39 percent, and those who never attended church supported Kerry over Bush by 62 percent to 36 percent. In 2004, many religious leaders delivered sermons and speeches on the topic "How Would Jesus Vote?" making it clear that Jesus would cast a vote for Bush. Clearly, some political and religious leaders are cultural warriors, eager to have the national debate center on issues such as abortion, religion in public schools, and same-sex marriage.

Yet the idea of a culture war oversimplifies the dimensions of conflict over social and moral issues. It is clear that secular and highly religious Americans do differ in their views on political issues such as abortion, gay rights, and school prayer, but it is also true that many deeply religious Americans differ on these issues as well. Not all deeply religious Catholics agree on church doctrine, for example. Among Catholics who attend religious services every week, a large majority favor allowing abortion under some circumstances, nearly half favor providing birth control to teenagers, more than 60 percent favor the death penalty, more than half favor allowing doctors to actively end the life of terminally ill patients who request it, and a third think that homosexual sex is sometimes morally acceptable. In each case this position is in direct violation of church teaching.[21]

Moreover, it is not the case that secular Americans are uniformly hostile to religion. One study of attitudes on church-state issues reported that most secular citizens were generally supportive of the rights of religious expression and were actually more supportive of the rights of fundamentalist preachers to speak on college campuses than were white evangelicals (Jelen and Wilcox, 1995). Although there clearly is cultural conflict in America, there are many sides to that conflict, and the Christian Right represents only one of them.

In addition, many Americans are what some have called "noncombatants" in the culture war. A sizable number of Americans would like to restore religious values to public life but resist efforts by Christian Right groups to dictate the nature and meaning of those values. They are not moved by claims of the Left that the Christian Right is a "radical, extreme" movement that constitutes a clear and present danger to America, but they are also unconvinced that American culture discriminates against Christians and that "radical liberals" are seeking to take away religious freedom.

Conclusion and Overview of the Book

These broader contexts help us understand the nuances of the dilemma of the Christian Right. Movement proponents see the Christian Right as a defensive movement that seeks to represent the interests of evangelicals and other orthodox Christians in American politics. They believe that secular Americans are waging a culture war on religious conservatives, undermining traditional values and religious practices. They see the Christian Right as a movement that merely seeks to blunt this secular assault and to protect America's Christian heritage.

Critics of the movement argue that the Christian Right seeks to deny America's pluralism by establishing or restoring an orthodox Christian cultural hegemony. To these critics, the Christian Right represents one narrow segment of Christianity in a nation that also includes Jews, Muslims, Hindus, Buddhists, Sikhs, and secular citizens. They argue that the Christian Right seeks not to bargain at the table but to impose its narrow morality on all Americans. They charge that Christian conservatives would establish a sectarian religion in America and that its adherents are the aggressors in any culture war because they seek to deny reproductive rights to women, civil rights protection to gays and lesbians, and opportunities to women.

In this chapter we have defined the Christian Right and discussed the various constituents of the movement. We have also defined the basic controversy over the role of the Christian Right in American politics and described the context in which that debate takes place. The contemporary Christian Right is in fact the fourth wave of conservative Christian activity during the twentieth century. In the next chapter we place the Christian Right in historical context, compare and contrast the movement with its earlier incarnations, and discuss the target constituency of the Christian Right. Chapter 3 introduces the organizations of the Christian Right and their leaders. It also examines the activities of Christian Right groups, both in elections and in influencing government policy. We conclude the chapter with an assessment of the movement's impact on public policy in America. The dilemma of the Christian Right is explored in greater detail in Chapter 4. We examine claims that the Christian Right has expanded American democracy by politically activating a previously apolitical group of citizens and counter-claims that Christian Right adherents do not share the democratic norms that form the foundation of American politics. In addition, Chapter 4 examines the issue agenda of the Christian Right and analyzes the potential policy ramifications should movement leaders come to dominate American politics. In the final chapter, we consider the future of the Christian Right and its issue agenda.

2

···

Revivals and Revolution: The Christian Right in Twentieth-Century America

If evolution wins, Christianity goes—not suddenly, of course, but gradually, for the two cannot stand together.

—William Jennings Bryan

....

THE FAMILY RESEARCH COUNCIL, Focus on the Family, and Concerned Women for America are only the most recent of many conservative political organizations that have been formed out of the religious enthusiasms of white evangelical Protestantism. Throughout the twentieth century, the energy and influence of the Christian Right have ebbed and flowed. Many organizations claiming to represent the political views of white evangelicals have come and gone, and the latest incarnation of the Christian Right has some important similarities and differences when compared with these earlier movements. To understand fully the Christian Right today, it is important to know more about the earlier movements.

The principal constituency for the Christian Right in the twentieth century has been white evangelical Christians, but within this broad category are many different theological groups, whose members have not always gotten along with one another or supported the same political causes. It is therefore useful to discuss the history of the religious movements that have created these divisions among white evangelicals and whose enthusiasms have frequently led to the formation of Christian Right groups.

The Fundamentalist Religious Revolt

Early in the twentieth century, two religious movements—fundamentalism and pentecostalism—emerged that would later provide the major constituencies for the Christian Right. The pentecostals did not become involved in politics until later in the century, but the **fundamentalist** movement quickly emerged as the vanguard of resistance to theological modernists. At the heart of the debate between fundamentalists and modernists was the way the church should respond to new scientific theories and discoveries, especially Darwin's articulation of the theory of evolution.

During the last decades of the nineteenth century, many of the clergy in the largest Protestant denominations began to embrace modern scientific and social ideas. Leading intellectuals in Protestant seminaries sought to make interpretation of scripture consonant with the new understandings of science. These modernists also emphasized the web of social obligations that the church could fulfill. When some social thinkers transformed Darwin's descriptive theory of natural selection into a prescriptive theory that government should leave those who were less "fit" to their natural fate, many Protestant churches instead preached a **social gospel** of responsibility to the poor and disadvantaged. In this view, Darwin's theory implied that humans were perfectible, and the best way to pursue that perfection was to ameliorate the conditions of poverty and ignorance that helped create imperfection.

This emphasis on the social gospel was controversial, for religious conservatives resisted both the policy implications of these teachings and the shift of focus away from saving souls. The conservatives, who were initially a loose coalition of pietistic revivalists, conservative Calvinists, and other evangelicals, joined forces to publish *The Fundamentals* in 1910, a collection of essays in defense of orthodoxy. Although this collection went unnoticed in the media and among academics, it provided the intellectual underpinnings (and the name) of a new religious movement called fundamentalism. Over the next decade, the split between the conservatives and liberals widened, and in 1919 the conservatives formed the **World's Christian Fundamentals Association** (WCFA). This marked the beginning of a bitter religious battle between the fundamentalists and modernists.

The fundamentalist leadership, including William Riley, Clarence Dixon, and John Straton, instituted a series of more than one hundred conferences in the United States and Canada to preach the fundamentals. The Baptist and Presbyterian churches were deeply divided, and eventually each of these denominations split. The fundamentalists emphasized the need to remain pure and separate from the world—even separate from other nonfundamentalist Protestants.

At the core of fundamentalist doctrine were three ideas (Sandeen, 1970; Marsden, 1980; Jorstad, 1970). First, fundamentalists embraced **premillennialism**, a doctrine about the timing of the second coming of Christ. Premillennialists believed that the world must first worsen, and then an Antichrist would arise who would win power. Eventually, however, Christ would return and summon the faithful in the Rapture. At that time all true Christians, living or dead, would go immediately to heaven, leaving the "unsaved" to endure an unsavory time of tribulation on earth under the rule of the Antichrist. Soon Christ would return to lead the faithful in a successful battle with the Antichrist. Premillenialist eschatology is dramatized in a series of novels by Timothy LaHaye and Jerry Jenkins—*Left Behind* and its sequels, which have appeared on the *New York Times* best-seller lists.

In contrast, the doctrine of **postmillennialism** held that Christ would come again after the millennium, a thousand-year period of perfect peace. The debate between the premillennialists and postmillennialists had been heated in theological circles for some time, but fundamentalist leaders staked a clear position on behalf of the premillennialists.

This seemingly technical doctrinal difference has important political consequences. If Christians must establish the millennium on earth before Christ comes again, then politics becomes an essential Christian duty. Only by improving the state of the world can prophecy be fulfilled and the kingdom of heaven brought into existence. Christians should work for peace and justice in this world in order to hasten the transition into the kingdom. Since human history has never contained anything remotely close to 1,000 years of peace, Christians have their work cut out for them.

If, on the other hand, the world must inevitably worsen until Christ rescues his followers, then politics is a futile endeavor. Moreover, if Christ might come again at any moment and summon the pure to him, then the top priority for Christians must be to remain distinct from the sinful world to avoid temptation.[1] Political involvement might lead to compromise with sin, which would leave the Christian unready for the trumpet call that would signal the second coming. The fundamentalist acceptance of premillennialism therefore created a strong resistance to political involvement that the movement leaders have worked hard at various times to overcome.

The second component of fundamentalist doctrine was **dispensationalism**, the belief that God has dealt with humans under different covenants in different eras. Most fundamentalists believed there were to be seven dispensations, and the world was in its sixth. Because the seventh was the kingdom of heaven, dispensationalism served to heighten expectations that the Rapture, or second coming of Christ, would occur very soon. Dispensationalism is an important source of fundamentalist disputes with pentecostals (discussed later in this section) and thereby undermined the potential unity of the Christian Right in the 1980s (Wills, 1990).

Third, fundamentalists believed that the way to know God's will was to study the Bible, which was the inerrant word of God. Most accepted an even stronger position—that every word of the Bible was literally true. The most politically charged issue at the turn of the century that arose out of the literal interpretation of the Bible was **creationism**—the teaching that the biblical creation story in Genesis is literally true. In the biblical account, the world was created in six days, and Adam was made directly by God out of the dust of the ground, with Eve constructed from one of Adam's ribs. Many fundamentalists believed that the earth was created on October 25, 4004 B.C., a date established in 1654 by Bishop Usher.

Although the literal interpretation of Genesis was once widely accepted among American elites, in the late nineteenth and early twentieth centuries, scientific theories that contradicted this reading gained prominence. Darwin's theory of evolution gained acceptance among biologists; geologists began to read the earth's history in strata of rocks, and most came to believe that the earth was far older than fundamentalist doctrine would suggest; and astrophysicists read the history of the universe from the light of distant stars and argued that the universe is billions of years old.

The heads of seminaries in the modernist denominations attempted to make peace with Darwin by arguing that although God had surely made the world, he did it over billions of years, not six days. They argued that the biblical account was a metaphor, not meant to be taken literally. Fundamentalists rejected the scientific theories, accepting by faith that the heavens and earth were created in six twenty-four-hour days. If the biblical account must be true, then scientific discoveries must be made consonant with biblical truth. In response to scientific evidence that the rocks of the earth were older than 6,000 years, for example, some fundamentalists countered that when God created the earth he pre-aged the rocks, or that the great flood of Noah disrupted the underlying geology of the earth (Brin, 1994; Numbers, 1992).

The fundamentalist movement generated enormous religious energy. Pietistic clergy preached the fundamentals in tent revivals throughout the South and Midwest, and individual congregations sometimes split apart as had their parent denomination. Some of these new churches affiliated with newly formed fundamentalist denominations; others remained as independent fundamentalist churches.

From these doctrinal elements and religious schisms, fundamentalists fashioned their most distinctive characteristic—fervent **separatism**. Fundamentalists emphasized the importance of keeping themselves apart from the impure world and from doctrinally impure Christians as well. They stressed the importance of avoiding extensive contact with "unsaved" Americans, kept to their own churches and social networks, and began to fashion their own communication channels through publications, seminaries, and other means.

Although the fundamentalist movement attracted the most attention, the turn of the century was also the occasion for the birth of **pentecostalism**. As in the case of fundamentalism, pentecostal denominations were created out of schisms within Protestant churches. Whereas the fundamentalists stressed the literal truth of scripture, the pentecostals focused on the immanent power of God and especially of the Holy Spirit in their lives. The movement took its name from the biblical account of the day of Pentecost, the day the Holy Spirit was poured onto the disciples, who then spoke in tongues that people from all nations could understand.[2] In pentecostal belief the Holy Spirit imparts to many an additional blessing of special religious gifts.[3] The most common of these gifts is **glossolalia**, or the speaking in tongues; others include faith healing, prophecy, and being "slain in the Spirit."[4]

The pentecostals shared with the fundamentalists an opposition to modernism and a belief in the inerrancy of scriptures, and many pentecostals at the turn of the twentieth century considered themselves in some ways to be fundamentalists. Indeed, a variety of religious movements at the time endorsed the doctrinal orthodoxy of *The Fundamentals* and shared the fundamentalists' strong rejection of modernism.

Nevertheless, fundamentalist clergy emphatically rejected the pentecostal movement. At the core of the doctrinal dispute was dispensationalism—or rather a dispute about precisely which dispensation was in effect at the time. Many pentecostals believed that the "age of the Spirit" began in the early 1900s and marked a time when Christians should expect to receive spiritual gifts. In contrast, the fundamentalists believed that these gifts were part of an earlier dispensation at the time of the apostles and that speaking in tongues and faith healing were no longer legitimate spiritual practices.[5]

Although fundamentalists and pentecostals shared a large core of doctrine, the differences between them created great hostility. Ruben Archer Torrey, dean of the Los Angeles Bible Institute and one of the most prominent fundamentalists of the period, referred to the pentecostals as the "last vomit of Satan" (Quebedeaux, 1983). Torrey's rhetoric was extreme, but most fundamentalists violently rejected pentecostal practice. The hostility has continued into the present: The fundamentalist leader Jerry Falwell once stated that those who spoke in tongues had eaten too much pizza the night before, and Nancy Ammerman reported that in a fundamentalist

congregation she studied, the pastor warned his parishioners that pentecostals "are allowing Satan to work in their lives" (1987, p. 81).

Why should seemingly minor differences in doctrine between two similar religious movements entail such hostility? There are several reasons.
Most important, the doctrinal differences that may seem minor to those
outside of the evangelical tradition are quite important to those within it.
The fundamentalists insisted on an extreme, pure doctrine and rejected any
deviations from those beliefs. For fundamentalists, salvation came through
the saving grace of the **born-again experience**. Pentecostals believed in additional levels of grace, including a sanctifying grace of the baptism of the
Holy Spirit. Issues such as salvation, grace, and the purity of doctrine are extremely important to evangelicals, and substantive disputes on these issues
ignite much debate.

Second, both movements arose at approximately the same time and com-
peted for roughly the same set of potential members. Fundamentalist pastors worried that they would lose their congregants to a pentecostal church
and thus chose to demonize the competition to help fill their pews. Like
competitors of all kinds, movement leaders chose to focus on the differences
between fundamentalism and related religious movements rather than on
their similarities, partly in an effort to differentiate their product and
demonstrate its superiority.

Finally, there are differences in style that accompany these doctrinal dis-
tinctions and that persist today. Fundamentalists are a serious lot and believe that knowing God's will requires concentrated study of "the Book."
Fundamentalist sermons are laced with scripture: Pastors cite the text to
support their themes and frequently tie together passages from several
books and chapters of the Bible. Congregants read these passages along with
the minister from their well-worn Bibles. In contrast, pentecostals worship
through ecstatic outpourings of spiritual joy, and in their services people
shout, jump, and occasionally fall onto the floor in religious ecstasy. One
pentecostal outpouring in the United States entailed uncontrolled laughter,
which swept the congregation and lasted for some time. Fundamentalists
are uncomfortable with such exuberant worship.

It is small wonder, then, that the serious fundamentalist clergy worried
that church members might be tempted to go down the street to the local
pentecostal church. Yet the fundamentalists were initially far better situated
to mobilize their congregations into politics, for their sermons linked the
inspired word of God to events of the day. A pastor could preach a series of

sermons on a political issue, weaving together divergent scriptural references to support his position, and could finally advocate political action
with some accepted evidence that it was the will of God. In contrast, the immanent religious experience in pentecostal services had no obvious political
meaning and thus was more difficult to mobilize. Early pentecostal churches
focused on spiritual experience, not politics.

Thus, fundamentalists formed the backbone of Christian Right activity
from the turn of the century through the mid-1980s. Only in recent years
have pentecostals and charismatics moved into political action.

The Fundamentalist Political Revolt

The fundamentalist movement generated enormous energy and spawned
the creation of many organizations. In the 1920s this energy spilled over
into politics, as fundamentalist ministers began to challenge modernism
head-on by defending the literal interpretation of the Genesis creation story
against scientific theories. They objected to the teaching of evolution in high
school classes and sought to remove evolution from the curriculum and replace it with the teaching of biblical creationism. Organizations such as the
Bible League of North America, the **Bible Crusaders of America**, the **Defenders of the Christian Faith**, and an offshoot, the **Flying Fundamentalists**, which sent squadrons of speakers throughout the Midwest, all
fought the teaching of evolution in public schools. State-level organizations
formed as well and were active in many states.[6]

The antievolution groups used a variety of tactics in their efforts to pass
state laws banning the teaching of evolution. Their leaders sought to meet
with state legislators to persuade them of the validity of their positions, and
other activists addressed large rallies in an effort to mobilize public opinion.
This mixing of quiet persuasion and public pressure marked the antievolution crusades as one of the most sophisticated of the various waves of Christian Right activity.

Perhaps the movement's greatest asset was William Jennings Bryan, a
frequent Democratic presidential candidate who held leftist-populist economic views but who had ties to the fundamentalist leadership. Bryan became convinced that German militarism was linked to the teachings of
Darwin, and he invested much of his personal energies and reputation on
behalf of the antievolution crusades. In leading the campaign, Bryan was
fighting social Darwinism and, more important, the teachings of the

German philosopher Nietzsche, which he believed had been the impetus for German expansion in World War I (Wills, 1990).

In all, thirty-seven antievolution bills were introduced in twenty state legislatures, but most failed to pass. One bill died in a committee on fish, game, and oysters—apparently referred there because the bill proscribed teaching that humans had evolved from lower organisms.[7] The climax of the antievolution crusades was the famous **Scopes trial**, in which William Jennings Bryan took the stand to defend the fundamentalist view of evolution, only to be humiliated by Clarence Darrow's questioning (see box 2.1). Bryan died soon afterward, and the antievolution crusades lacked a prominent national leader (Lienesch, 1995).

Although the Scopes trial was widely interpreted as a defeat for the fundamentalist leadership, its outcome was more ambiguous. John Thomas Scopes was convicted of teaching evolution, but because of Darrow's efforts to attract great media attention to the trial, the conviction was quickly overturned by the state supreme court—a move that therefore denied Darrow an opportunity to appeal to the U.S. Supreme Court and set a national precedent. Moreover, many textbook publishers, fearing further controversy, removed references to evolution from biology texts soon after the Scopes case. Not until the Soviet Union launched the Sputnik satellite into space in 1957 did evolution again become a major component of high school biology classes, as Americans sought to catch up to the perceived Soviet lead in science and technology.

Many fundamentalists objected to the politicization of their movement, and eventually the crusade became limited to the most extreme fundamentalists and struggled financially (Cole, 1931). As enthusiasm for antievolution activities waned, some fundamentalist leaders began to focus on a different message—anticommunism. Anticommunism was a natural rallying issue for fundamentalists, for many believed that the Bible predicted that the ultimate battle between the forces of Christ and the Antichrist would be fought in Israel, with the latter's forces coming from the land then occupied by the Soviet Union. Communism was a new force in the world in the 1920s, and its militant atheism resonated with this interpretation of scripture.

During the Great Depression of the 1930s and into World War II, many fundamentalist organizations remained active, but their financial base eroded substantially. Some of their leaders drifted into fascism, anti-Semitism, and bigotry (Ribuffo, 1983). The fundamentalist Christian

BOX 2.1   The Great Monkey Trial

Journalists called it the "trial of the century," for it involved a clash of two strong men and, more important, of two strong ideas. In Dayton, Tennessee, John Thomas Scopes stood accused in 1925 of teaching evolution in the public schools. A state law banned the teaching of any doctrine that contradicted creationism, and modernists had encouraged Scopes to teach evolution to provide a test case of the constitutionality of the Tennessee law.

In the sweltering July heat in a time before air conditioning, more than 100 newspaper reporters crammed into the courtroom, leaving only for quick gulps of lemonade from the stands outside. By July 21 more than 3,000 onlookers crowded the aisles and stood huddled outside, listening to accounts carried back from those who stood just inside. A jury of twelve farmers listened carefully to the testimony and to the arguments of two of the era's biggest personalities.

Scopes was defended by Clarance Darrow, the premier trial lawyer of his day. Darrow was a longtime critic of creationism and a proponent of the philosophy of Nietzsche. William Jennings Bryan was a perennial Democratic presidential candidate who opposed the banks and monopolies and advocated inflating the currency to enable farmers and other debtors to pay off their loans with devalued money. Although Bryan's economic views were more leftist than those of any major party candidate in history, he became one of the leading opponents of the teaching of evolution, perhaps because he thought Darwinism and Nietzsche's philosophy had inspired German militarism that led to World War I.

Bryan and Darrow had disliked each other for years, and Darrow had published in the *Chicago Tribune* a long list of questions to Bryan about the Bible designed to undermine the position of biblical literalism. Bryan agreed to prosecute the Scopes case in part because it gave him a chance to take on Darrow. It proved to be a disastrous decision.

Bryan was in poor health, whereas Darrow was fit and energetic. The trial climaxed when Darrow called Bryan to the stand and questioned him about his belief in the literal interpretation of the Bible. Under Darrow's sharp questioning, it became clear that Bryan had not thought carefully about many of the issues of biblical literalism, and in one portion of his testimony he angered fundamentalists by admitting that the earth may have been created over a period longer than six days.

Darrow scored points in other portions of the questioning as well. At two points, he focused on apparent inconsistencies in the Bible. The following transcript omits some repetitive questioning but shows Bryan's difficulty.

Darrow: Did you ever discover where Cain got his wife?

(continues)

(Box 2.1 continued)

Bryan:	No, sir; I leave the agnostics to hunt for her.
Darrow:	You have never found out?
Bryan:	I have never tried to find out.
Darrow:	The Bible says he got one, doesn't it? Were there other people on the earth at that time?
Bryan:	I cannot say.
Darrow:	There were no others recorded, but Cain got a wife.
Bryan:	That is what the Bible says.
Darrow:	Where she came from, you do not know?
Darrow:	Do you think the sun was made on the fourth day?
Bryan:	Yes.
Darrow:	And they had evening and morning without the sun?
Bryan:	I believe it was creation as there told, and if I am not able to explain it I will accept it. Then you can explain it to suit yourself.

SOURCE: *Washington Post,* May 18, 1995, p. A6.

Right continued to preach anticommunism, but this theme lacked strong appeal in the depths of the Great Depression, and the organizations faded into obscurity.

In the aftermath of the Scopes trial and the failure of Prohibition, fundamentalists and other evangelicals retreated from politics in what has been called the "great reversal." Politics was seen as an ultimately futile endeavor. Yet during this period, fundamentalists built Bible colleges, churches, and new organizations, including the **American Council of Christian Churches** (ACCC). The ACCC was vehemently anticommunist, and its leadership even attacked leaders of mainline Protestant denominations for their alleged ties to communists. Its extremism alienated many moderate fundamentalists, who formed in 1942 the **National Association of Evangelicals** (NAE) and launched a movement that became known as **neoevangelicalism.** The neoevangelicals took orthodox doctrinal positions but were more moderate than the fundamentalists, both in religion and politics. Their religious moderation was evident in their rejection of separatism, their political moderation in their unwillingness to label their political opponents as communists.

The Anticommunist Crusades

After World War II, the Soviet Union emerged as the United States' only serious international rival. A number of political figures began to stir fears of domestic communist influence. The most notable was Senator Joseph McCarthy of Wisconsin, who charged that much of America's government was infiltrated by communist agents. McCarthy's campaign helped establish a political market for anticommunist groups, and fundamentalist entrepreneurs formed a set of new political organizations to take part in the anticommunist movement. The **Christian Crusade**, the **Christian Anti-Communism Crusade**, and the **Church League of America** were all formed by leaders of the ACCC and emphasized primarily the threat of domestic communists.

Using radio broadcasts and traveling "schools of anticommunism," these groups focused narrowly on the "Red Menace." These schools did not always emphasize the fundamentalist roots of the organizations and thus attracted not only highly religious fundamentalists who were recruited in churches but also secular anticommunists (Wolfinger et al., 1969; Wilcox, 1992). Regardless of their religious ties, those who attended the anticommunist schools were convinced that communists had infiltrated important national political institutions (Koeppen, 1969; Wolfinger et al., 1969).

The issue agenda was slightly broader than the one pursued by the antievolution groups of the 1920s. The Christian Anti-Communism Crusade officially opposed Medicare (labeling it socialized medicine) and sex education (arguing that it would weaken the nation's moral fiber and make America ripe for communist takeover). These issues were secondary to combating domestic communist infiltration, however, and were always linked directly to the communist conspiracy.

The fundamentalist anticommunist crusades never attracted a wide audience and were not well known even among those conservative fundamentalists most sympathetic to their message. McCarthy's crusade ended in disarray after he attacked the military, but the groups survived McCarthy's demise and signed on with enthusiasm to Barry Goldwater's 1964 presidential bid. After Goldwater's landslide defeat, the fundamentalist anticommunist groups slid into obscurity.[8]

Yet even as the Christian Right of the 1950s faded away, the religious conservatives who served as their target constituency continued to build

infrastructure—Bible colleges, Christian bookstores, and specialized magazines and newspapers (Ammerman, 1987). One of the best-selling books of
the 1970s was Hal Lindsey's *The Late Great Planet Earth,* which mixed premillennialism with far-right, often paranoid, politics. Christian radio and
television programs and stations began to proliferate, providing leading
fundamentalist, pentecostal, and evangelical preachers a wider audience.

The late 1960s and early 1970s also brought rapid growth of the **charismatic** movement in mainline Protestant and Catholic churches. Like the
pentecostals at the turn of the century, charismatics emphasized the importance of the "gifts of the Spirit," and many spoke in tongues or were slain in
the Spirit. Unlike the pentecostals, however, the charismatics did not form
their own churches but instead built an ecumenical movement across denominational lines and established charismatic caucuses within their home
denominations. Charismatic businessmen's groups sprang up, and in many
communities charismatic Catholics, Episcopalians, Methodists, Lutherans,
and others met together in churches and other public places to worship.
Some individual churches within mainline Protestant denominations
adopted charismatic worship styles. The charismatics became an important
source of support for Pat Robertson's 1988 presidential campaign.

The Fundamentalist Right of the 1980s

In the late 1970s, after a period of relative quiescence, a new fundamentalist
Christian Right organized. Two sets of events seem to have precipitated this
third wave of activity. First, a series of local political movements across the
country demonstrated the potential political energy of fundamentalists and
evangelicals in politics. Evangelicals rallied to protest textbooks used in the
Kanawha County, West Virginia, public schools, to help repeal gay rights
legislation in Dade County, Florida, and to oppose the Equal Rights
Amendment (ERA) in many states and cities—in each case showing that
evangelicals can be enthusiastic and effective political actors (Wald, 1992).

In 1976 the presidential candidacy of Jimmy Carter, a born-again
Southern Baptist, provided more proof that evangelicals might be politi-
cized. Carter, Democratic governor of Georgia, was a deeply religious man
who had taught Sunday school for many years, and his sister was an evan-
gelist. Carter publicly called on evangelicals to abandon their historical
distrust of politics, and his campaign mobilized white evangelicals to vote
in greater numbers than in past elections. When conservative leaders real-

ized that fundamentalists and other evangelicals might be induced to become more involved in politics and that it might be possible to mold that political action into support of Republican candidates, they provided resources to help form groups such as the **Moral Majority**, the **Christian Voice**, and the **Religious Roundtable** in 1978 and 1979 (Guth, 1983; Wilcox, 1992; Moen, 1989).

Of all the fundamentalist groups of the 1970s and 1980s, the Moral Majority attracted the most attention. Its leader was Jerry Falwell, a Baptist Bible Fellowship pastor who had built the Thomas Road Baptist Church in Lynchburg, Virginia, from an initial gathering of thirty-five adults into a megachurch with more than 15,000 members.[9] Falwell's televised sermons were broadcast as the *Old Time Gospel Hour* and were carried on more than 300 stations. Falwell was an eager advocate for the Christian Right, appearing on television programs soon after the 1980 election to claim that evangelicals had provided Ronald Reagan's victory margin.

The Moral Majority built its organization primarily through pastors in the Baptist Bible Fellowship (BBF). Falwell recruited most of the organization's state and county leaders through the BBF, and this enabled him to quickly establish organizations in most states and in many counties (Liebman, 1983). When the media "discovered" the Christian Right in early 1981, the Moral Majority appeared on the surface to have a thriving organization.

These ready resources came with a price, however. The BBF pastors were religious entrepreneurs, and a pastor often built a church from scratch from a small circle of friends who first met in the pastor's living room. Many pastors hoped eventually to establish a megachurch as Falwell and some others had done. Most sought to build auxiliary organizations such as church schools. These men were frequently too busy with their religious construction to build a political organization.

Moreover, the BBF pastors were a generally intolerant lot. They were hostile to Catholics, pentecostals, charismatics, evangelicals, and mainline Protestants and not especially warm toward other Baptist churches. Their state Moral Majority organizations seldom had leaders outside of their faith, and those who did serve often felt uncomfortable and unwelcome. Not surprisingly, surveys of state Moral Majority membership generally found that a majority were Baptist, and few, if any, were Catholic (Wilcox, 1992; Georgianna, 1989).

Thus, although the Moral Majority organization looked impressive on paper, in practice most state organizations were moribund (Hadden et al.,

1987). The few state and local groups that were active went their considerably divergent ways, often to the embarrassment of the national organization. In Maryland, for example, the state organization made its stand on the
issue of a beachfront bakery's sale of "anatomically correct" cookies, which
the organization labeled as pornographic. The incident attracted national
media attention and ultimately succeeded in boosting cookie sales.

Robert Grant formed Christian Voice at about the same time, initially
from state-level antigay and antipornography groups in California. Pat
Robertson provided some early funding for the group, which specialized in
producing scorecards that rated the "moral votes" of members of Congress.
Christian Voice established a few state chapters but remained primarily a
national organization.

The Moral Majority, Christian Voice, and other groups of the 1970s and
1980s had a far broader issue agenda than their predecessors. The core
agenda involved opposition to abortion, to civil rights protection for gays
and lesbians, and to the ERA, and support for school prayer and tuition tax
credits for religious schools. But the organizations staked positions on a variety of other issues. Falwell made a highly publicized defense of South
Africa and consistently supported increases in defense spending. The *Moral
Majority Report,* the organization's newsletter, attempted to build support
for conservative economic issues as well, including a subminimum wage, a
return to the gold standard, and cuts in social welfare spending.

Although studies showed that the Moral Majority and other groups had
the steady support of 10 to 15 percent of the public, their fortunes were
more directly tied to the direct-mail revenues that funded the organizations.
By the mid-1980s, it became increasingly hard for these groups to induce
the primarily elderly women who constituted their financial base to part
with their money.

This was true for two reasons. First, Reagan's reelection campaign in 1984
told these conservative Christians that it was already "morning in America,"
and the fuzzy Norman Rockwell images that were the core of Reagan's television advertising sent the message that his presidency had succeeded in
restoring America to its historical values. Reagan's campaign and subsequent reelection made it appear less necessary to send money to "save"
America.

Second, scandals involving televangelists in the latter part of the 1980s
made many more people skeptical about the increasingly frequent appeals
for money. Although these evangelists had not been political activists, their

widely publicized problems hurt fundraising by the Moral Majority and damaged the presidential campaign of Pat Robertson. Jim Bakker was accused of various sexual and financial improprieties, and he eventually served time in prison for fraud. The investigations into Bakker's financial dealings revealed that he and his wife had provided their dog with an air-conditioned doghouse and had gold fixtures in their bathrooms. Oral Roberts's claim that God had threatened to "call him home" if his viewers did not contribute several million dollars to his ministry drew widespread ridicule. A Doonesbury cartoon noted that Roberts's claim, if true, would mean that God was a common terrorist using Roberts as a hostage to extort ransom.

All of this made it difficult for the Moral Majority to raise money through direct mail, and by 1988 it was strapped for cash. The organization was disbanded in 1989. Falwell claimed he quit because he had accomplished his goal, but the key issue agenda of the Moral Majority remained unrealized. Like the other fundamentalist crusades before it, the Moral Majority eventually folded its tent and went home. Since its demise, Falwell has created other smaller organizations which have never managed to gather enough resources to be active in politics.

The Robertson Campaign

In 1987, Marion "Pat" Robertson announced that he would seek the Republican presidential nomination. Robertson was an ordained Baptist minister whose father had served as a Democratic senator from Virginia. Although Robertson had never held elected office, he had been active in Virginia politics for a decade and had built a highly successful business empire.

Robertson's *700 Club* television show was very different from Falwell's fundamentalist sermons. The program was a religious talk show, with a variety of guests sharing their music or testimony with Robertson and Ben Kenslow, his African American cohost. Robertson also regularly provided a conservative analysis of political events in the news.

Robertson was a charismatic, and in the earliest shows he spoke in tongues and healed by faith. Although his later programs did not feature these religious gifts, his audience continued to include large numbers of pentecostals and charismatics. Robertson welcomed guests from many religious traditions, including Catholics, mainline Protestants, evangelicals, fundamentalists, pentecostals, charismatics, and black Protestants. Robertson himself noted his eclectic approach: "In terms of the succession of the church, I'm a Roman Catholic. As far as the majesty of worship, I'm an Episcopalian; as far as the belief in the sovereignty of God, I'm Presbyterian; in terms of holiness, I'm a Methodist; in terms of the priesthood of believers and baptism, I'm a Baptist; in terms of the baptism of the Holy Spirit, I'm a Pentecostal. So I'm a little bit of all of them."[10]

Robertson launched his campaign by gathering some 3 million signatures on petitions asking him to run, and these individuals served as the financial base of his campaign. Most of these contributors were regular viewers of his *700 Club* program, and many made regular gifts of $19.88 as part of the "1988 Club" (Brown, Powell, and Wilcox, 1995). Robertson's first campaign finance report to the Federal Election Commission contained the names of 70,000 donors and had to be delivered on a sixteen-foot truck.

Allen Hertzke (1993) described Robertson's campaign as a populist crusade to return America to a sound moral footing. Robertson decried the failures of the American education system, focusing not only on the teaching of secular humanism and the absence of school prayer but also on the failure of modern education methods to teach "the basics" effectively. He opposed abortion, which he argued was harmful because it reduced the number of babies born, thereby also reducing the number of potential taxpayers that could eventually pay for the retirements of the baby boomers. He touched briefly on the historical Christian Right theme of anticommunism, claiming that missiles were hidden in caves on Cuba, but he focused most of his campaign on domestic politics.

His economic positions were complex and did not fit neatly into the mainstream Republican debates between fiscal conservatives and supply-side economists. He strongly criticized the morality of large corporations that put profits ahead of morals, and the world banking cartel, which he blamed for maintaining tight money that hurt working families. His most controversial stand was his call for a "Year of Jubilee," a year in which debt would be forgiven. Basing his proposal on an Old Testament account of a similar policy in ancient Israel, Robertson argued that the growing mountains of debt (both domestic and foreign) threatened to overwhelm the international economy. By calling for debt relief and looser money, Robertson echoed the earlier populist campaign of William Jennings Bryan but drew the ridicule of the *Wall Street Journal*.

Robertson's campaign got off to a good start. He probably won the first round of balloting in the early multistage Michigan caucus-convention, and he beat George Bush for second place in the Iowa caucuses.[11] But a disastrous series of stories undermined his campaign: He was forced to drop a suit in which he charged that an account of how his father kept him out of combat in the Korean War was libelous; journalists reported that his wife was very pregnant when they married; Robertson claimed that he knew where the hostages were in Lebanon (though he had not shared that information with the government) and that there were secret missile bases in the caves of Cuba.

About the same time, televangelist Jimmy Swaggert was caught in a motel room with a prostitute, and television accounts reminded viewers of Jim Bakker's sex scandal and Oral Roberts's financial demands. Swaggert had supported Robertson, and Robertson initially blamed the scandal on a dirty trick of the Bush campaign, but it was soon revealed that a fellow televangelist had alerted the newspapers to Swaggert's escapades in revenge for an earlier episode in which Swaggert had accused him of sexual impropriety. Taken together, these stories took a heavy toll.

Robertson's campaign also suffered from some of the religious prejudices that limited the appeal of the Moral Majority. Although he made efforts to reach out to Catholics and blacks, neither group voted often in Republican primaries. Moreover, fundamentalists were actually less likely than mainline Protestants to support Robertson, presumably because of disapproval of his pentecostal leanings. Studies revealed that Robertson's support was limited largely to charismatic and pentecostal Christians (Green and Guth, 1988; Wilcox, 1992; Brown, Powell, and Wilcox, 1995).

Robertson lost badly in the Super Tuesday primaries, including in Texas, where he outspent Bush by almost three to one. Ultimately, Robertson spent more money than any presidential candidate in history to that point to garner only thirty-five pledged delegates. Robertson failed to win a single primary and lost badly even in his home state of Virginia.

Yet the Robertson campaign was a vital part of the birth of a new, more sophisticated Christian Right. In many states where Bush won the Republican primary, Robertson's forces continued to work to select delegates to the convention. Ultimately, there were many delegates at the national convention who were pledged by state law to vote for Bush but who supported Robertson. More important, Robertson's Republicans worked to gain influence in and even control of state and local party committees.[12] These activists provided a core of skilled political workers ready to enlist in the next Christian Right crusade.

After Robertson's defeat and the disbanding of the Moral Majority, many observers proclaimed the Christian Right to be defeated, argued that its defeat had always been inevitable, and wrote its obituary.[13] In fact, research showed that support for the movement and its agenda had not declined any more than it had surged in the early 1980s (Wilcox, 1992).

In 1989, Robertson launched the Christian Coalition. In June 1990, the Coalition took out a full-page ad in the *Washington Post* and other national newspapers warning members of Congress to vote against funding for the National Endowment for the Arts. The Christian Coalition threatened to pass out 100,000 reproductions of controversial art by Robert Mapplethorpe and Andres Serrano in districts where members voted for funding. The text of the advertisement told of the kind of organization Robertson was trying to build: "There may be more homosexuals and pedophiles in your district than there are Roman Catholics and Baptists. You may find that the working folks in your district want you to use their tax money to teach their sons how to sodomize each other. You may find that the Roman Catholics in your district want their money spent on pictures of the Pope soaked in urine. BUT MAYBE NOT." Robertson's clear appeal to Catholics and Baptists—two constituencies that did not rally to his presidential bid—signaled a conscious effort to build a broader, ecumenical Christian Right.

The Christian Right, 1920–1990: Continuity and Change

The waves of Christian Right activity between 1920 and 1990 had several things in common. Each was mobilized through infrastructure and communication channels already in place—the WCFA, the ACCC, the Baptist Bible Fellowship and Falwell's *Old Time Gospel Hour* and its contributor list, the *700 Club* and its list of donors. In each movement, anticommunism and education were important elements of the agenda, although they varied in importance.[14] Each was built around one or more preachers who used the technology of the time (mass meetings, radio, television, direct mail) to reach an increasingly broader mass audience.

The first three waves of activity were based in the fundamentalist segment of the evangelical community, and each suffered because of the religious intolerance of fundamentalist leaders. None of the three fundamentalist movements succeeded in building an enduring or even significant grassroots presence, and all faded away when the initial enthusiasm died down. The Robertson campaign, however, made conscious appeals to a wide variety of Christians and even to conservative Jews.

A Second Coming? The Christian Right, 1990–2005

At the end of the 1980s, the Christian Right seemed defeated. Most of the major organizations that had been active in that decade were disbanded or moribund, and the conservative direct-mail industry was crowded and in disarray (Moen, 1994). Yet even as the large national organizations died, movement activists planned a grassroots mobilization of immense scope. The goal was to have activists in place in every precinct in America by the millennium and to influence and perhaps control the Republican candidate-selection process. By the end of the decade, it was clear that this goal would not be achieved, and some observers were again proclaiming the end of the movement.

The most visible organization in the early 1990s was the Christian Coalition. Its former executive director, Ralph Reed, wrote of the need for a new ecumenicism in the movement and appealed directly for conservative Catholics, Jews, and African Americans to join the coalition (Reed, 1994b). The Coalition made a conscious effort to build its state and county chapters around political activists, not preachers, in order to attract members from many religious traditions. The organization distributed materials and held training sessions on how different religious groups can work well together.

Since 2000, Focus on the Family and the Family Research Council have assumed the movement's leadership role. Focus has active affiliates in many states and some counties and has a well-established network of activists who respond to e-mail alerts and other forms of communications. The Family Research Council has been especially active in coordinating opposition to same-sex marriage. However, the same-sex marriage issue has led to the creation of a number of coalitions that extend beyond the Christian Right to include more moderate Catholics, African American pastors, mainline protestants, and others (Campbell and Larson, 2006).

The latest incarnation of the Christian Right has had considerable success in forging ecumenical ties. In Virginia, the state Christian Coalition leader for a time was a Catholic (Bendyna, 1995), and in many other states Catholics and mainline Protestants have served as county chairs. Concerned Women for America had strong support among conservative Catholics in the northern part of Virginia, and Focus on the Family has solid support among many conservative Catholics as well.

Whereas the Christian Right of the 1980s practiced confrontation, the new organizations have used different tactics. Originally, some Christian Coalition candidates ran as **stealth candidates**, hiding their ties with the organization. This brought complaints not only from liberals, who labeled the practice deceptive, but also from some conservative Christians, who charged that the tactic made it appear that Christians were afraid to profess their faith publicly. A Pennsylvania Christian Coalition manual that encouraged stealth candidacies was widely distributed and reprinted in the media, much to the discomfort of the organization's leaders, who argued that the manual was only a draft prepared by an overzealous volunteer.

More recently, the Christian Right has encouraged its activists and candidates to couch their arguments differently for religious and nonreligious audiences. Activists are told to "mainstream the message" by avoiding explicitly religious language in public speeches and by emphasizing positions on taxes, crime, abortion, and gay rights. Although many liberals complain that this tactic is just another form of a stealth candidacy, Christian Right activists respond that all candidates tailor their message to different audiences. Michael Farris, longtime movement activist and director of a group that provides legal protection to homeschool parents, noted:

> Evangelical Christians need to find ways to communicate effectively with different people. They can't just interact among themselves. Many are learning that as they interact in the Republican Party, not everyone understands or accepts the lingo that evangelicals use when talking to each other. . . . I've got to understand the other person if I want to be persuasive. Understanding that person means respecting that other person. I've got to get around other people's mental roadblocks. That means respecting where that person is coming from. That's the way that evangelical Christians can be more effective. It's a growing up thing. That is, being able to disagree with others but still be respectful of their values. That's the trick. Not all of our spokesmen have been very effective at that.[15]

As part of their efforts to adopt the secular language of politics, Christian Right candidates and activists have couched their political arguments in the "rights" language of liberalism (Moen, 1992). Instead of arguing that America is a Christian nation and therefore public schools should begin with a Christian prayer, activists now argue that Christian children have a right to exercise their religious beliefs freely in prayer. Instead of arguing that certain textbooks endorse evil lifestyles, activists now talk of "parental rights" in molding their children's education. Abortion is framed as protecting the rights of the unborn. The substantive solution to these infringements of the asserted rights is identical to those policies advocated by earlier incarnations of the Christian Right, but the justification for those policies is markedly different.

Moreover, many Christian Right activists and candidates have adopted the language of victimization. Although conservatives have long decried efforts by African Americans, women, and gays and lesbians to portray themselves as victims of discrimination, Christian conservatives now purposely use this language. Candidates and groups that attack the Christian Right are now routinely accused of religious bigotry, and Christian Right leaders charge that opposition to their policies comes from those who discriminate against people of faith.

Like the Moral Majority, the Christian Right today has a wide policy agenda that includes domestic policy positions on health care reform, taxes, and crime, but the issues of primary concern to most activists are abortion, education, and a constellation of issues relating to families and sexuality. Yet contemporary Christian Right groups are more clearly political organizations than their predecessors, and they attract a more eclectic set of activists with varying sets of policy concerns.

Many of these activists are also members of local organizations that stress a somewhat different set of issues. The large national organizations frequently provide resources to local activists to form small local groups and help coordinate the efforts of this network of local organizations. Because these groups usually emphasize local issues, they serve as a valuable recruiting mechanism for the Christian Right.

Today Christian Right activists are far more effective than those in the 1980s. John Green, Kimberly Conger, and James Guth said of this transformation after studying Christian Right activists in the 2004 election: "These Christian Rightists appear to be somewhat more pragmatic than their counterparts in the past. Many are adherents of a new civic gospel that justifies political action in defense of traditional morality. And they certainly see politics as a positive and efficacious, probably more so than in the past. This shift in political style may well be the product of the slow and steady integration of the movement into regular politics" (Green, Conger, and Guth, 2006).

Near the end of the 1990s, two developments undermined some of the progress that the movement had made early in the decade. First, the largest national organization faltered. The Christian Coalition lost momentum when Ralph Reed, a savvy political operative with a Ph.D. in history, resigned as executive director and hung out his shingle as a political consultant. His departure destabilized the organization, which had depended on Reed's keen ear for politics to offset Robertson's tendency to engage in extreme rhetoric and spout unexpected proclamations. After Reed's departure, Robertson played a far more active role in the organization.

Ironically, it was Robertson's moderation that led to a series of key resignations by national, state, and local leaders. In late 1998 and again in early 1999, Robertson proclaimed that a ban on abortions was not achievable and that the Coalition should work to limit abortions through additional restrictions and bans on certain late-term procedures. More importantly, in February 1999, Robertson called for an end to efforts to remove Bill Clinton from the presidency. Although Robertson was primarily acknowledging political reality, many activists believed that they had been betrayed—that the Coalition had asked them to commit their resources to removing the president, only to abandon that effort with no warning.

A second, and more potentially important, development is the emergence of a debate among some long-standing movement activists over whether political action is effective. In 1999, as the impeachment effort stalled, Paul Weyrich, a longtime conservative activist who helped form the Moral Majority, announced that the culture war was lost and advised conservative Christians to begin to create alternative cultural institutions and to withdraw from the culture. Two former Moral Majority activists, Cal Thomas and Ed Dobson, argued in a highly publicized book, *Blinded by Might,* that the evangelicals had been seduced by the lure of political power and that they should return to their primary mission of saving souls.

In 2000, the debate over the efficacy of political action was temporarily halted as George W. Bush emerged as a leading candidate for the Republican presidential nomination. Himself a born-again Christian, Bush carefully cultivated Christian Right leaders during the 1990s, after first working to help coordinate evangelical support for his father's re-election campaign in 1992. Bush avoided extreme rhetoric on issues such as abortion and gay rights, but he spoke openly of his faith, of how prayer strengthened him, and on his regular Bible study. To Christian Right activists, the contrast between the sex scandals of the Clinton presidency and Bush's open profession of faith could not have been clearer.

Christian Right leaders put aside differences to work for Bush in the primaries, helping him win crucial victories in South Carolina and elsewhere (Rozell, 2002; Wilcox, 2002). During the general election, the movement worked to help his campaign, but the earlier collapse of the Christian Coalition left the movement without the ability to distribute large quantities of voter guides. Bush narrowly lost the popular vote but narrowly won the electoral vote. Karl Rove, Bush's top political strategist, attributed the narrow margin of Bush's victory to low voter turnout among evangelicals.

In 2003, the Massachusetts state supreme court ruled that the state's constitution required that same-sex couples be allowed to marry. The same-sex marriage issue came as no surprise to Christian Right activists, who had been working on the issue since it first emerged in Hawaii in the early 1990s. But it caught most Americans by surprise, and the Christian Right moved aggressively to define the issue in the public debate and in the election. In a number of states, Christian Right groups gathered signatures to place referenda on state ballots in support of constitutional amendments to ban same-sex marriage, all of which passed handily.

The same-sex marriage issue became a central focus of the Christian Right in 2004 and figured prominently in the fund-raising appeals of the movement (Wilcox, Merolla, and Beer, 2006). The issue also generated new energy among activists and helped to revitalize state organizations, including affiliates of Focus on the Family and even a few state Christian Coalition chapters. In addition, the same-sex marriage issue spurred the formation of new state and local groups and prompted a number of church leaders to enter the electoral arena for the first time. The longer-term implications of the same-sex marriage issue for the movement are discussed in Chapter 5.

The Target Constituency of the Christian Right

The Family Research Council, Focus on the Family, and Concerned Women for America are all social movement organizations seeking to mobilize members of their potential constituency. Like all social movements, they seek to build a common identity, a common set of complaints, a shared belief that the constituency has been unfairly treated by society, and support for collective action. Two important factors that determine whether the organizations fail or succeed are how effectively they mobilize their base and whether they can expand beyond that core constituency.

Most analysts agree that the principal target audience of the Christian Right remains the white evangelical community. In addition, the contemporary Christian Right is targeting conservative Catholics, mainline Protestants, and African Americans.

White Evangelicals

White evangelicals are united by a common theological core: they share a belief in the importance of a personal conversion experience that involves repenting of sin and accepting Jesus Christ as personal savior. Most, though not all, evangelical churches refer to this experience as being "born again."[16] They also agree that the Bible is the inerrant word of God and that Christians should spread their witness and seek to convert others to the faith. Yet evangelicals are also divided by their doctrine, especially on how to interpret the Bible and on how the Holy Spirit operates in their lives.

We might conceive of evangelicals as the broad set of individuals who share the core doctrinal beliefs and of fundamentalists, pentecostals, and charismatics as subsets of evangelicals. Those evangelicals who do not belong to any of these groups are often referred to as "other evangelicals."[17]

Fundamentalists, pentecostals, charismatics, and other evangelicals can be identified in survey data in different ways, and these variations often account for the sometimes conflicting claims made about evangelicals. All groups except charismatics can be identified by the denominations they attend. Those who attend Assembly of God churches are pentecostals, and those who go to Baptist Bible Fellowship churches can be classified as fundamentalists. A denominational definition of evangelicalism helps us focus on the historical and social basis for the movement and on how different denominations have splintered and merged around various interpretations of doctrine.

A denominational definition is useful in that many national and regional surveys include a question about church affiliation, and thus we can use the data from these various surveys to compare evangelicals with other citizens. Moreover, because these types of questions have been asked for many years, we can trace the political behavior of evangelicals. However, a denominational definition is less useful for identifying the theological subgroups among evangelicals. Many fundamentalists attend nondenominational churches, and charismatics are found in all mainline Protestant denominations and among Catholics as well. Some denominations, such as the Southern Baptists, are difficult to classify, since they continue to experience an internal struggle for control between fundamentalists and neoevangelicals.

Moreover, many liberal denominations contain theologically conservative congregations. One of us grew up in the Walnut Grove United Methodist Church in West Virginia. Any denominational coding would place the liberal Methodists with mainline Protestants, but Walnut Grove was and remains an evangelical church, and many of its members would call themselves fundamentalists.

It is also possible to identify evangelicals by their doctrine, as noted by Lyman Kellstedt: "The predominant emphasis of evangelicalism is doctrine. It is 'right' doctrine that self-defined evangelicals look for when they 'check out' a person's Christian credentials" (Kellstedt, 1989, p. 29). The most frequent questions used to identify evangelicals ask whether the respondents have been born again and assess their views of the Bible. Some surveys ask about the practice of spiritual gifts such as speaking in tongues. These measures have the strength of identifying evangelicals in all denominations, although many individuals claim to embrace evangelical doctrine yet exhibit only a marginal attachment to religion.[18]

Finally, some surveys identify evangelicals by inviting them to identify themselves. They ask respondents whether they consider themselves to be evangelicals, fundamentalists, charismatics, and/or pentecostals, in some cases allowing only one positive response, in others allowing respondents to select multiple identities. Such direct questions have the advantage of helping us understand what people mean by these terms, but they also reveal considerable confusion among Americans as to which terms might apply to their beliefs.[19]

Evangelicals differ from other Americans in some important ways. Table 2.1 shows some of the social characteristics of whites who attend mainline Protestant, evangelical Protestant, and Catholic churches and of those who attend no church and do not claim to belong to any denomination. White evangelicals are less likely than other whites to have a college degree and are more likely to have failed to finish high school.

In the 2004 National Election Study data, more than half of white evangelicals attended some college. But white evangelicals are one-third less likely than white Catholics or white mainline Protestants to have a college degree, and more likely than members of these groups not to have finished

TABLE 2.1 Social Characteristics of White Religious Groups

	Mainline Protestants	Evangelical Protestants	Catholics	No Affiliation
Education				
Less than high school	3%	10%	8%	9%
High school	29%	34%	32%	28%
Some college	33%	36%	24%	28%
College degree	19%	14%	23%	20%
Post-graduate	16%	6%	13%	15%
Family income				
Less than $24,999	16%	30%	19%	26%
$25,000–$39,999	16%	15%	12%	22%
$40,000–$59,999	20%	19%	17%	21%
$60,000 and up	47%	36%	52%	32%
Region				
Northeast	8%	6%	35%	29%
Midwest	40%	30%	37%	20%
South	35%	45%	13%	23%
West	17%	20%	16%	28%
Sex				
Female	59%	59%	56%	45%
Age				
18–30	9%	18%	15%	36%
31–45	22%	25%	26%	19%
46–60	31%	30%	29%	29%
61 and up	38%	28%	30%	16%
Religion				
Religion provides a good deal of guidance in life	30%	49%	32%	10%
Prays several times a day	25%	43%	25%	7%
Attends church more than weekly	10%	17%	8%	0%

SOURCE: *2004 National Election Study, whites only.*

high school. This does not mean that evangelicals are all poorly educated; indeed a majority have attended at least some college.

There is an income gap as well, in part because white evangelicals are less well-educated, and in part because women in evangelical households are less likely to work for wages. White evangelicals are also more likely to live in the South, especially compared to white Catholics, who are more likely to live in the Northeast, and the nonaffiliated, who are more likely to live in the West. They are younger than white mainline Protestants but older than their more secular counterparts. Although surveys usually show that white evangelicals are disproportionately female, this was not true in the 2004 National Election Study data. Although women constitute 59 percent of white evangelicals, they constitute a similar percentage of white mainline Protestants and white Catholics as well, whereas men constitute a majority of those with no religious affiliation.

There are important differences as well in the levels of religiosity. White evangelicals are much more likely than white mainline Protestants or white Catholics to indicate that religion provides a good deal of guidance in their lives. They attend church and pray more often than other white Christians. For many evangelicals, their church is their primary social network, and most of their friends attend the same church (Ammerman, 1987). Some fundamentalist churches may even discourage their members from developing close friendships among nonbelievers.

White evangelicals hold more traditional values and are more likely to take conservative positions on social issues. Table 2.2 shows the values and social issue positions of whites who attend mainline Protestant, evangelical Protestant, and Catholic churches and of those with no religious affiliation. White evangelicals are much more likely than all other whites to say newer lifestyles are causing societal breakdown and that people should not be tolerant of those who choose to live by different moral values. They are more likely to value good manners for their children over curiosity, and obedience over self-reliance, than are other whites. They are slightly less likely to think that it is not a problem if people have unequal chances in life, perhaps because they believe that all have an equal chance to go to heaven. But in general, white evangelicals are as supportive of societal equality as other whites.

White evangelicals are distinctly conservative on many social issues. They are more likely than other whites to oppose all abortions and less likely to approve of them under any circumstances. Indeed, white evangelicals are the only group where slightly more oppose abortion always than

TABLE 2.2   Political Values and Social-Issue Positions of White Religious Groups

	Mainline Protestants	Evangelical Protestants	Catholics	No Affiliation
Values				
Newer lifestyles cause societal breakdown	65%	80%	60%	38%
Don't tolerate those with different values	22%	33%	20%	9%
Traits for children				
good manners > curiosity	55%	69%	51%	41%
obedience > self reliance	42%	57%	45%	34%
Not a problem if people have unequal chance in life	28%	35%	32%	22%
The less government the better	56%	55%	43%	45%
Something about America makes ashamed	55%	55%	49%	68%
Love for country extremely strong	67%	74%	63%	37%
Social/Moral Issues				
Abortion				
Never allowed	7%	25%	14%	2%
Always allowed	38%	21%	37%	57%
No government funding abortion	65%	75%	65%	35%
Ban partial-birth abortion	58%	76%	70%	46%
Favor death penalty	82%	82%	69%	67%
Oppose same-sex marriage	57%	82%	56%	38%
No gay antidiscrimination laws	28%	41%	17%	18%
No gays in military	15%	30%	14%	11%
No gay adoption	51%	67%	42%	32%
Rate gays at 0 degrees	7%	21%	8%	8%
Women should not have equal role	8%	12%	6%	4%
Working mothers can't have as warm relationship	20%	34%	30%	28%
Better if woman tends home and man achieves	27%	42%	27%	16%

SOURCE: *2004 National Election Study.*

favor allowing it always. Yet note that support for banning all abortions is still a minority position among white evangelicals. Although one in four white evangelicals would ban all abortions, other questions in the survey show that only one in six want to ban all abortions and also believe that it is extremely important to do so. A large majority of white evangelicals (and indeed all whites) favor a ban on "partial birth" abortion, and a significant majority of white Christians oppose federal funding for abortions for poor women, although whites who are not affiliated with a church support such funding.

White evangelicals are also markedly less likely than other whites to support civil rights for gays and lesbians. An overwhelming majority oppose same-sex marriage, compared with relatively narrow majorities among white mainline Protestants and Catholics and a minority of more secular citizens. But opposition to laws protecting gays from job discrimination and allowing gays and lesbians to serve in the military, though still much higher than among other whites, has dropped dramatically among white evangelicals (and indeed among all Americans) over the past few years. White evangelicals are much more likely to rate gays very coolly—at 0 degrees on a 0 to 100 feeling thermometer—than other whites.

White evangelicals are also more conservative on gender roles. White evangelicals are twice as likely as white Catholics to say that women should not have an equal role in society, yet a large majority favor gender equality. White evangelicals are much more likely than other whites to agree with the statement that it is better if women tend the home and men achieve in the workplace, but even on this position more evangelicals disagree than agree.

White evangelicals are more conservative on other issues as well, reflecting their southern roots and Republican partisanship (see table 2.3). They are more likely to favor increases in defense spending, to favor limits on immigration, and to believe that the Iraq war is worth the cost. However, they are not more likely than other white Protestants to think that the war has decreased the terrorist threat.

On economic issues, white evangelicals are more likely than other whites to support cuts in spending on government programs, to oppose guarantees of jobs and national health insurance, and slightly more likely to think that the rich should pay less in taxes. They are more likely to favor cuts in spending on childcare and science, but not in aid to the poor. Overall, however, white evangelicals are much less distinctive on these issues, and most favor increases in spending on childcare, science, and aid to the poor. On race

TABLE 2.3   Other Issue Positions of White Religious Groups

	Mainline Protestants	Evangelical Protestants	Catholics	No Affiliation
Foreign/Defense Issues				
More defense spending	56%	68%	55%	46%
Iraq decreased terrorist threat	30%	30%	24%	20%
Iraq war worth cost	42%	58%	41%	36%
Decrease immigration	49%	58%	51%	42%
Economic Issues				
Spend less on services	43%	45%	37%	38%
Oppose national health plan	40%	48%	32%	30%
Gov't not guarantee job	56%	60%	52%	40%
Rich should pay less in taxes	10%	13%	10%	13%
Poor should pay less in taxes	33%	43%	48%	47%
Spend less on childcare	5%	11%	5%	8%
Spend less on science	5%	10%	6%	8%
Spend less on aid to poor	7%	8%	8%	11%
Race/Crime Issues				
Government should not help blacks	61%	67%	55%	42%
Strongly favor death penalty	57%	61%	44%	51%
Oppose more federal gun control	45%	61%	36%	44%

SOURCE: *2004 National Election Study.*

issues, white evangelicals are more likely to oppose aid to blacks, perhaps reflecting their southern roots. They are also more likely to strongly favor the death penalty and much more likely to oppose federal gun control laws.

Overall, the data in tables 2.2 and 2.3 show that white evangelicals are not uniformly conservative and that abortion, gay rights, women's roles, and other issues divide the evangelical community as they do the rest of the nation. Thus the target constituency for the Christian Right is not uniformly favorable to the movement's positions. Nonetheless, white evangelicals are the most likely source of Christian Right support, though the data show that possible movement recruits may be found in other faith communities as well.

The data from these surveys suggest that the Christian Right can attract its broadest support among white evangelicals by taking positions that are moderately conservative—allowing abortions under a few circumstances and avoiding any endorsement of gender inequality or discrimination against gays and lesbians in hiring or military service. However, these positions may also fail to motivate the most ardent activists who generally take more conservative positions on these issues.

Within the white evangelical community is a smaller subset of Americans who might be called "core evangelicals." Core evangelicals attend evangelical churches, believe that the Bible is the inerrant word of God, and say that religion offers a great deal of guidance in their daily life. White core evangelicals constitute the target activist base for the Christian Right. Whereas white denominational evangelicals constitute approximately one-quarter of the population, this core group is much smaller—less than 9 percent of the general public. However, the data in table 2.4 show that this core group is significantly more conservative than other white evangelicals. Nearly half would ban all abortions, almost all oppose same-sex marriage, a large majority agree that women should tend the home while men achieve outside the home, and nearly half believe that we should not tolerate those with different values.

Conservative Catholics

Although conservative Catholics did not feel welcome in the Moral Majority, the contemporary Christian Right later made special appeals to them (Bendyna, Green, Rozell, and Wilcox, 2000). There has long been a Catholic Right in America, and some Catholics rallied to the antievolution crusades and to Joseph McCarthy's anticommunism. Catholics were the principal audience for Father Charles Coughlin's ultraconservative radio broadcasts in the 1930s and later were a core element in the John Birch Society.

It is clear that many Catholics support some of the key issues of the Christian Right. The data in Table 2.2 show that a significant minority of white Catholics support Christian Right positions on social issues. The principal issue the Christian Right relies on to win Catholic members is abortion. Catholics are also attracted to the movement's support of Christian schools and its general position that family values and Christian faith

TABLE 2.4   Selected Values and Issues: White and Black Evangelicals

	White Core	Other White	Black Core	Other Black
Newer lifestyles cause societal breakdown	91%	68%	67%	59%
Don't tolerate those with different values	49%	23%	17%	28%
Not a problem if people have unequal chance in life	37%	31%	26%	18%
The less government the better	60%	48%	18%	12%
Traits for children obedience > self-reliance	74%	51%	84%	64%
Abortion never allowed	47%	12%	17%	15%
Ban partial-birth abortion	82%	71%	62%	50%
No gay antidiscrimination laws	61%	27%	31%	21%
No gay adoption	83%	58%	82%	55%
No same-sex marriage	95%	73%	89%	62%
Rate gays and lesbians 0 degrees	34%	13%	28%	11%
Women's place in home	20%	8%	3%	1%
Working mother's can't have as warm relationship	41%	30%	30%	26%
Better if woman tends home and man achieves	62%	30%	29%	21%
Favor death penalty	84%	76%	33%	51%
No aid to blacks	43%	37%	22%	33%
History does not make it harder for blacks to succeed	51%	54%	24%	20%

SOURCE: *2004 National Election Study.*

should be more prominent in public life, and to a lesser extent, to their opposition to gay rights and their support for homeschooling.

Yet despite clear teachings by the Roman Catholic Church, only a minority of white Catholics are strictly pro-life. Indeed, the data in table 2.2 show that pro-choice white Catholics outnumber pro-life white Catholics by more than two to one and that white Catholics are far less supportive of restrictions on gay rights than evangelicals. They are also more supportive of gender equality. Moreover, white Catholics are more supportive than white evangelicals of programs to aid the needy and of civil liberties protection for unpopular groups, and the church is officially opposed to the death penalty—although the data in the table show that a majority of white Catholics disagree with this stance. It seems unlikely, therefore, that the Christian Right can ever hope to win the support of a majority of white Catholics for its broad agenda.

Yet the Christian Right need not attract a majority of white Catholics to be a formidable political force. If it were to attract a majority of white evangelicals, a sizable minority of white Catholics and mainline Protestants, and a significant number of black evangelicals, the Christian Right would be a vital force in American politics. In the past few years, there have been signs that white evangelicals have been more welcoming of Catholics than they once were. Millions of evangelicals flocked to Mel Gibson's film *The Passion* which depicted a very Catholic version of Christ's death and resurrection. Catholics and evangelicals worked together to ban same-sex marriage and to try to keep a feeding tube connected to Terry Schiavo, a Florida woman who doctors had declared to be in a persistent vegetative state. This suggests that conservative Catholics may join the Christian Right in a broader coalition in the future.

Although most national surveys do not contain sufficient numbers of Hispanic Catholics to show in the table, studies have generally shown that they are more conservative on abortion, gay rights, and other social issues than white Catholics. This is especially true of foreign-born Latinos, although many of these are not American citizens and thus do not play a role in electoral politics. Yet Hispanic Catholics tend to be less affluent than white Catholics and are drawn to the Democratic Party on many economic and foreign policy issues (Suro, Fry, and Passel, 2005). Interestingly, it is Protestant Hispanics (especially pentecostals) who are the most supportive of Christian Right policies (Ellison, Echevarría, and Smith, 2005).

White Mainline Protestants

Although the Christian Coalition seldom mentions mainline Protestants as a target for future mobilization, Ralph Reed is a Presbyterian and Oliver North, a Reagan White House official and Virginia Senate candidate, attends a charismatic Episcopal church. There are morally conservative Christians in Presbyterian, Methodist, Lutheran, and Episcopal churches across America, and some already have joined the Christian Right. Many hold orthodox doctrinal views, and some regularly watch televangelists, who provide some of their political cues.

Overall, however, white mainline Protestants are quite moderate on social and moral issues. Although pro-choice white mainline Protestants outnumber their pro-life counterparts by more than five to one, more than half of all white mainline Protestants support a ban on partial birth abortion. And although fewer than half support same-sex marriage, only one in six would ban gays from military service. In regard to gender issues, only one in four agrees that families are better off if the man achieves while the woman tends the home. However, when it comes to economic issues, white mainline Protestants are as conservative as white evangelicals, principally because of their relative affluence. Given their moderate stances on these issues, it is unlikely that a majority of white mainline Protestants would enlist in a conservative moral crusade.

Nevertheless, the data in table 2.2 show that there is support for some Christian Right positions among white mainline Protestants, and in the South a substantial minority of white mainline Protestants support much of the Christian Right agenda. This suggests that there may be room for some mobilization by Christian Right groups that take relatively moderate positions on key issues and stress abstract family values.

Black Evangelicals

A majority of African Americans are evangelicals, measured by either denomination or doctrine. A clear majority attend Baptist churches, believe that the Bible is the inerrant word of God, and report a born-again experience. Substantial numbers of blacks have had the spiritual experiences that are the core of pentecostal and charismatic Christianity. Moreover, blacks practice their religion: they attend church, read their Bibles, and pray more often than whites.

Yet these doctrinal beliefs and religious experiences do not translate into the political orientations held by their white counterparts. Although African Americans and whites read from the same Bible, the meaning of the text is socially constructed in different ways in the two traditions. Most black churches interpret the Bible as a book of liberation, equality, and social compassion. Thus, black evangelicals are more likely than their white counterparts to oppose all forms of discrimination and to favor social programs to help the poor.

Yet many African American evangelicals are quite conservative on moral issues, including gay rights, abortion, and school prayer, and this group would seem to constitute a potential constituency for the Christian Right. Many Christian Right leaders clearly perceive the potential, and Ralph Reed laced his speeches with quotations from Martin Luther King Jr. and often compared the Christian Right with the civil rights movement of the 1960s.

Table 2.4 compares the attitudes of white and black evangelicals, including core evangelicals in both groups, for selected political attitudes. The data show that on some issues, such as gay adoption and same-sex marriage, black core evangelicals are as conservative as whites. Moreover, a narrowly crafted Christian Right agenda that focused on opposition to same-sex marriage, gay adoption, partial birth abortion, and general opposition to "newer lifestyles" would draw support from a majority of core black evangelicals and from a significant bloc of other black evangelicals as well. But on other issues, black evangelicals are less conservative. Although nearly half of white core evangelicals would ban all abortions, this is true for only 17 percent of blacks. More than 60 percent of white core evangelicals oppose laws to protect gays from job discrimination, but this is true for less than a third of blacks, perhaps because the history of racial discrimination sensitizes them to the issue. There are significant differences in attitudes on gender roles as well. Although nearly two-thirds of core white evangelicals say it is better if the woman tends home while the man achieves outside the home, less than 30 percent of blacks agree. More generally, a sizable majority of core white evangelicals agree that "the less government the better," compared with only 18 percent of blacks. Clearly, African American evangelicals see government as a potentially positive force to change society, whereas white evangelicals are generally skeptical of government.

There are also striking differences on two other issues—aid to blacks and the death penalty. —The data show that black core evangelicals are actually more "liberal" than those who do not hold evangelical doctrine or believe that their faith provides a great deal of daily guidance. Black churches frequently condemn racial discrimination endemic in the application of the death penalty, protest racial discrimination in employment and education, and call for government action to redress these inequities. Racial differences among evangelicals on these issue remain large.[20] Racial differences are also evident in the responses to the statement, "History does not make it harder for blacks to succeed." White evangelicals (both core and not) are divided on whether history limits the chances of African Americans to succeed in America. African Americans, on the other hand, are far more likely to believe that historical discrimination remains a barrier to black progress.

There are two important barriers to mobilizing blacks into the Christian Right. First, African Americans are overwhelmingly Democratic, and the Christian Right is active almost exclusively in the Republican Party. In the 2004 National Election Study, only 2 percent of blacks identified themselves as Republicans, while an additional 5 percent labeled themselves independents or leaning toward the GOP. Fully 80 percent identified themselves as either Democrats or leaning toward that party. If the Christian Right chose to pursue a bipartisan strategy, they might win black support for primary election candidates who took relatively conservative positions on social and moral issues, but even charismatic black **social conservatives** like Alan Keyes or J. C. Watts are unlikely to sway significant numbers of blacks to vote for Republicans.

The second major barrier is the Christian Right economic agenda. Most African American evangelicals support government programs, affirmative action, and a progressive income tax. Thus, when Christian Right leaders talk of abortion and school prayer, they may reach a receptive audience in some segments of the African American community. But when they endorse a flat tax, propose spending cuts in national and state programs that provide income, health care, and housing for the poor, and call for an end to affirmative action, they are likely to find few black supporters.

In 2004, the debate over same-sex marriage created a new opportunity for the Christian Right to win support from African Americans. On this issue only, there was substantial cooperation between African American pastors and Christian Right leaders. It seems unlikely that this cooperation will extend to a broader alliance on other issues, but there is clearly a morally conservative group of African Americans who might unite behind some restrictions on abortion, bans on same-sex marriage and adoption, and some other issues.

Putting It All Together:
Issue Groups in the Target Constituency

How likely is it that the Christian Right might make significant gains among white and black evangelicals, white mainline Protestants, and white

Catholics? Tables 2.2, 2.3, and 2.4 show only the percentage of each constituency group holding conservative positions on each specific issue; they
do not show the amount of support for the combined issues in each religious community. Although we can see in table 2.2 that 25 percent of white
evangelicals take a strict pro-life position and 12 percent oppose gender
equality for women, we cannot tell from those data whether these conservative responses come from the same or different people. It may be that 12
percent of white evangelicals oppose both abortion and gender equality, or
it may be that 37 percent hold one or the other of these two positions. Most
likely, the truth is in between.

We can identify those people who hold similar sets of positions using the
statistical technique of cluster analysis. In 2004 there were five different issue groupings among members of the four main constituency groups for
the Christian Right—white evangelicals, white mainline Protestants, white
Catholics, and black evangelicals. Individuals in the first issue group might
be called "consistent conservatives," who are quite conservative on basic values, social and moral issues, economic policy, racial issues, and defense issues. The second group can be labeled "social conservatives." Its members
are especially conservative on issues of abortion, women's roles, and gay
rights and are also somewhat conservative on foreign policy. But they are
moderate to liberal on economic policy and the death penalty.

The third group can be labeled "economic conservatives." These people
are generally moderate on all issues except economics, where they favor
deep cuts in social welfare spending, cuts in taxes, and efforts to balance the
budget. The fourth group might be labeled "moderates." These Americans
take generally moderate positions on all groups of issues. Finally, individuals in the fifth group are consistently liberal on all issues.

Of these five groups, the consistent conservatives and social conservatives
are the most likely converts to the Christian Right. Economic conservatives
tend to be moderate to liberal on social issues and so are unlikely to join a
movement that centers on conservative positions on social and moral concerns. Moderates and liberals are unlikely to join a movement that takes
very conservative positions on many policy areas.

Figure 2.1 shows the alignment of each of the four main constituency
groups of the Christian Right within these five issue groupings. Among
white evangelicals, a clear majority are either consistent conservatives or
social conservatives. This suggests that there is solid potential for the
Christian Right to enlist many white evangelicals in its movement. More

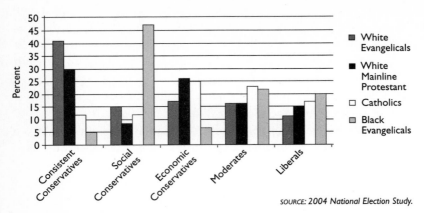

SOURCE: 2004 National Election Study.

**FIGURE 2.1   Issue Grouping Among Christian Right Constituency
                Groups**

than a quarter are moderates or liberals, however, so potential mobilization
has clear limits. Among white mainline Protestants, nearly half are consistent conservatives or social conservatives, so there are real prospects to mobilize in this group as well. Among white Catholics, less than a quarter fall
into these two blocs, so it is likely that Christian Right mobilization will be
limited. African American evangelicals are very likely to fall into the social
conservative grouping, although they are especially conservative only on a
few issues—same sex marriage, partial birth abortion, and gay adoption.
They are liberal on economic issues and the death penalty, so any Christian
Right mobilization of blacks will necessarily focus on a very narrow
agenda. We will return to the question of the potential for future recruitment for the Christian Right in chapter 5.

Conclusion

Although there are potential supporters for the Christian Right among several different religious constituencies, there is opposition to its social agenda
in all groupings as well. Clearly, groups such as Focus on the Family do not
speak for all Christians or even for all white evangelicals, but their social issue agenda does have appeal to many conservatives. If the Christian Right
were to fully mobilize those potential constituents, they would be a powerful movement in American politics.

Well-organized social movement organizations exist that seek to mobilize these potential activists. The next chapter introduces these groups.

3

The Christian Right in American Politics

You are not some small special interest group, that's the
other side. You are America. You are the heart of
America.

—Gary Bauer speaking to more than 100,000 Christian
Right activists at the Mayday for Marriage Rally in
Washington, D.C., October 10, 2004

••

ALTHOUGH THE CHRISTIAN RIGHT movements of the 1920s, 1950s, and 1980s all sought to influence public policy, the contemporary Christian Right is a far more sophisticated movement that pursues a variety of strategies to achieve a variety of goals. The Christian Right seeks to influence Republican nominations and to influence or control the party apparatus, to help the Republicans control the White House and Congress, to achieve legislative victories in Congress and state legislatures, to influence decisions by the U.S. Supreme Court, to win control of school boards in order to influence school curricula, and to win referenda in states and counties to implement its agenda. Movement leaders are very ambitious, and their multi-front initiative is clearly the most sweeping in the history of American Christian conservatism.

In this chapter we first describe the key organizations of the contemporary Christian Right and discuss the special role that each plays in the movement. We then focus on the various political activities of the Christian Right and assess their impact.

The Christian Right in the First Decade of the New Millennium

To understand the activities of the Christian Right, it is first necessary to identify the key actors in the movement. Although it is relatively easy to identify the most important national organizations, defining the precise boundaries of the Christian Right is more difficult. Moreover, much of the action in the 2000s was by state and even local organizations, not all of which had ties to national groups.

Many organizations were active in conservative Christian politics in the 2000s, but three stand out as the largest, most professional, and best organized. Focus on the Family, the Family Research Council, and Concerned Women for America have built sophisticated infrastructures to mobilize and inform their members and bolster state and local affiliates.

Focus on the Family

In the past several years, Focus on the Family has stepped up its political activity to become the Christian Right's dominant organization. Founded by psychologist Dr. James Dobson, Focus on the Family is a media ministry headquartered in Colorado Springs with a budget over $100 million and a staff of more than 1,300. It is aimed at strengthening the traditional family structure through conservative principles, and many of its materials are nonpolitical. Focus's Web site includes advice on discipline for single parents, ideas on how to spice up one's marriage, and reviews of movies and books.

Focus broadcasts a radio program hosted by Dobson that is carried on more than 3,500 radio stations and 80 television outlets in the United States; Dobson also writes a syndicated column that is carried by 500 newspapers (Farrell and Mulkern, 2005). His estimated listening audience includes 200 million people in 99 countries, and the organization sends out 4 million pieces of mail each month (Hedges, 2005). Focus sends books, tapes, and videos to more than 9,000 people daily without charge, although there are suggested donation amounts (Barrett, 1999). It also publishes a number of magazines, which reach some 2.3 million subscribers.

According to the liberal interest group People for the American Way, Dobson is "perhaps the most influential right-wing Christian leader in the country, with a huge and loyal following that he can reach easily through an impressive media empire" (www.pfaw.org). *Time* magazine named Dobson one of the twenty-five most influential evangelicals in 2005. Dobson's rhetoric is uncompromising and ideological and frequently at odds with the pragmatic language preferred by Republican operatives. "My goal is not to see the Republican Party prosper," he asserted, and if the party abandoned its opposition to abortion and gay rights, he has said that he would "do everything I can to take as many people with me as possible." But in 2005, Dobson was the first Christian Right leader to announce his support for President Bush's Supreme Court nomination of Harriet Miers. While many pro-life and Christian Right leaders remained neutral or voiced opposition, Dobson gave Miers an early, if tentative, endorsement, based on personal assurances by Karl Rove, aide to President Bush.

Focus is a tax-exempt Christian ministry, but Dobson has long been politically active. Dobson has been a perennial figure in the halls of Congress, lobbying with other Christian Right leaders. In 1998, he met with Republican leaders after threatening to "go nuclear" by encouraging his followers to sit out the 1998 election. After urging party leaders to focus on issues central to his group's agenda, he told a reporter for *U.S. News & World Report*, "I believe the leadership of the Republican party was listening."[1] His radio programs have long been loaded with political content and have featured Republican policymakers and candidates (Apostolidis, 2000). Republican Tom Coburn appeared on Dobson's program to discuss corruption in Washington, D.C., prior to announcing his candidacy for the U.S. Senate seat in Oklahoma.

Focus has a network of more than thirty-five state affiliates, many of which are also affiliated with the Family Research Council. The state affiliates are involved in public education and lobbying efforts. State affiliates vary in their activity: Some produce ratings of state legislators while others produce research reports on policy issues under debate in their state. These research reports are shared by state organizations, so a report produced in Michigan may be used by Virginia's Family Foundation to lobby state legislators, or it may be sent to activists in several states. In 2004, the Ohio Focus affiliate was a crucial player in drafting the language of the state's constitutional amendment prohibiting same-sex marriage, and in many states the Focus chapter is the most effective Christian Right organization in the state. In some cases, current Focus affiliates were originally formed independently and were later invited to affiliate by Focus officials.

In the past several years, Focus has launched major policy initiatives. In 1999, Focus helped sponsor a large campaign to change public opinion about homosexuality and to promote the "conversion" of gays and lesbians to heterosexuality. In 2004, Focus took the lead in promoting efforts to ban same-sex marriage. The organization also led the call for more conservative federal judges who might interpret the Constitution differently. However, its agenda is broader than these socio-moral issues, encompassing economic policy, environmental policy, welfare policy, and foreign policy.

In 2004, Dobson created Focus on the Family Action, a political action committee (PAC) for the parent organization. The PAC was active in the 2004 election and conducted voter registration drives within churches. The organization supported candidates who opposed abortion rights and same-sex marriage. The PAC mailed letters from Dobson conveying his personal endorsement of candidates. It also distributed model sermons to churches to help pastors advise their congregants on how to properly vote their faith. Focus Action was a sponsor of Justice Sunday discussed in chapter 1. In the 2005 fight over President Bush's judicial nominees, the

PAC ran ads in sixteen states to pressure senators to support the "nuclear option" and bar filibusters of judicial nominees (Farrell and Mulkern, 2005). In late 2005, Focus on the Family Action ran newspaper ads across Michigan condemning Senator Debbie Stabenow (D-MI) for voting against the confirmation of John Roberts as Chief Justice of the U.S. Supreme Court.

Family Research Council

Dobson helped create the Family Research Council (FRC) in 1982, and for a time the FRC was the political arm of Focus on the Family. In 1992 the FRC split from Focus because of IRS concerns, but the two organizations remained linked in many ways. The policy agenda of the FRC is very similar to that of Focus, and some state organizations are affiliates of both. Focus and FRC cooperate closely in their lobbying efforts.

The FRC is now a tax-exempt educational organization that is heavily involved in lobbying national and state governments. As a tax-exempt organization, the FRC cannot endorse or support candidates directly. Instead, it produces policy reports that are designed to shape the policy debate, to help create a legislative agenda for Christian Right activists, and to assist movement activists in lobbying government. It is home to two research institutes built to address some specific core principles: the Center for Human Life and Bioethics and the Center for Marriage and Family Studies.

The Family Research Council played a pivotal role in the formation of the proposed federal marriage amendment in 2004 that would ban same-sex marriage. Positioned in Washington, D.C., the FRC strategically built a coalition to legally define marriage as between one man and one woman at the federal level and also led the Christian Right's efforts to ban same-sex marriage and civil unions in many states in 2004.

In 2003, Tony Perkins became president of the Family Research Council. Perkins is one of the youngest Christian Right leaders currently on the scene and the only one to have held prior electoral office. Prior to heading the FRC, Perkins served as a state representative in Louisiana where he authored and passed the nation's first covenant marriage law. His political skills make Perkins well suited to coalition building in the Christian Right movement, and the FRC is positioning itself as a key player in future Christian Right politics. The FRC has a legislative lobbying arm called FRC Action, which helps coordinate grassroots activities and direct lobbying.

Concerned Women for America

The grandmother of the contemporary Christian Right is Concerned Women for America (CWA). Founded in 1979 by Beverly LaHaye, CWA today resembles in some ways the fundamentalist organizations of the 1970s, as the messages of its direct mail and newsletters are those of a moral crusade rather than a political movement. Yet unlike those earlier groups, CWA has appealed beyond a narrow fundamentalist base; its local chapters include evangelicals, mainline Protestants, and Catholics. Moreover, from its inception, CWA built grassroots organizations such as women's prayer meetings and Bible study groups, unlike most early fundamentalist groups which focused on national direct-mail lists. Indeed, it is not uncommon to find several thriving local chapters without a state chapter to coordinate them. In 2005, CWA claimed to have 500 prayer/action chapters and a membership list of roughly a half million, although some have suggested that the actual numbers may be lower. The special strength of CWA is grassroots lobbying. Its members meet with national, state, and local officials in district offices, write letters, and make phone calls to pressure policymakers.

CWA moved to Washington, D.C., in 1985 and established a national office and lobbying staff, but it remains a decentralized organization. Through matching grants from major corporations, the organization managed to maintain a focused presence in all congressional districts that enabled it to mobilize grassroots action in the 1970s and 1980s (Moen, 1992).

CWA once had a strong legal arm, and it provided legal assistance in many high-profile cases, including the Tennessee school textbook controversy, popularly referred to as "Scopes 2" (Bates, 1993). CWA discontinued its legal efforts for a time but has recently made efforts to rebuild its legal team.

CWA has sought to position itself as the conservative Christian alternative to the National Organization for Women (NOW). On a few issues, such as trafficking in women and, to a certain extent, pornography, CWA actually cooperates with feminist groups. On most issues, though, the group takes strongly antifeminist positions and frequently depicts NOW as its political nemesis and NOW's agenda as being harmful to women. In 2005, in response to the nomination of Harriet Miers, CWA expressed concern that Miers had helped to initiate a women's studies lecture series at Texas Christian University Law School, where "the lecturers have been women who espouse a radical theory of feminism." The group questioned whether Miers might "share the feminist theory that lecturers have presented" (LaRue, 2005).

Over the years, CWA has accumulated a staff of highly skilled women (and a few men) who run CWA's research institutes, publicity operations, and lobbying. Wendy Wright, CWA's executive vice president, has become a strong media presence on national television and radio shows. CWA runs two research foundations: the Beverly LaHaye Institute and the Culture and Family Institute. CWA has also been active in international politics and has been officially recognized by the United Nations as a nongovernmental organization (NGO). CWA has sent representatives to the World Summit for Children and the World Conference on Racism, hoping to shape policy consistent with their core principles (Buss and Herman, 2003).

CWA's founder, Beverly LaHaye, is the only Christian Right leader from the 1970s to have sustained a viable political organization that has become more effective over time. She has become one of the best-known figures of the movement and is the author of many books written for evangelical Christian women. Beverly is the wife of Timothy LaHaye, who is coauthor of the *Left Behind* book series. The series has sold more than 30 million books and made the LaHayes multimillionaires. Timothy LaHaye was instrumental in founding the Moral Majority, and he teaches classes at Jerry Falwell's Liberty University. Together, the LaHayes have made a mark on the contemporary Christian Right movement and have been called the "evangelical power couple . . . [who] rank as four-star generals to many conservative Christians" (White, 2001). Their reputation contributes to the CWA's stature within Christian conservative circles.

The Christian Coalition

In the 1990s, the most visible organization of the Christian Right was the Christian Coalition. Founded by televangelist Pat Robertson from the remains of his failed presidential bid in 1988, the group flourished under the astute leadership of Ralph Reed, a young Republican activist. The organization sought primarily to change policies by changing politicians and spent most of its resources on a massive voter mobilization effort. The organization claimed to distribute tens of millions of voter guides in 1992, 1994, and 1996, primarily in conservative white evangelical churches. The Coalition was more pragmatic than other Christian Right groups and generally supported Republican candidates regardless of their positions on social issues. It fielded an ecumenical and highly skilled lobbying staff in the early 1990s.

When Ralph Reed departed, the organization began a rapid decline. Without the restraining hand of Reed, Robertson quickly was embroiled in a series of controversial public statements that disillusioned key activists. When Robertson announced, without first consulting with state chairs, that it was impossible to impeach Bill Clinton, many resigned. When Robertson later appeared to partially defend China's forced abortion policy in a televised interview, most of the remaining state chairs resigned. With the hiring of Roberta Combs as the organization's president, many of the group's most talented personnel left. By late 2005, the national organization was deeply in debt, and creditors from a number of states were pressing claims. Richard Cizik, director of public policy for the National Association of Evangelicals, proclaimed the organization "moribund" (Duin, 2005).

Yet several state chapters of the Christian Coalition were revitalized in the 2004 campaign and distributed voter guides in battleground states. It is too early to know whether this represents the impact of a highly salient issue (same-sex marriage), a tactical decision by Bush supporters (who helped to fund some of the state efforts), or a genuine resurgence at the state level of what was once the most visible Christian Right group, while the national organization was dying.

Other Organizations

Several other organizations are active, although they lack a strong grassroots presence. The Reverend Donald Wildmon heads the **American Family Association** (AFA), formerly known as the National Federation for Decency. The AFA focuses on organizing boycotts of sponsors of television programs that contain excessive sex or violence or that contain an anti-Christian bias. It also became involved in battles over school curricula. The AFA has a radio program, a foundation, and a legal arm. Estimates of the membership of the AFA vary; it once claimed 650 local chapters across the country and now claims some 19 state affiliates.

The group most active in battles over public school curricula is the **Citizens for Excellence in Education** (CEE), headed by Robert Simonds. The CEE has led the fight against outcomes-based education, the Impressions reading series, and a variety of self-esteem curricula, which the group's activists frequently refer to as teaching witchcraft. It seeks to remove from the public schools texts that teach evolution and that it believes teach secular humanism. It has also been active in working to elect school board members. CEE rhetoric is confrontational; Simonds wrote in a 1994 fundraising letter, "As churches watch from the sidelines, the ungodly elect atheists and homosexuals to school boards and legislatures to enact policies and laws that destroy our Christian children and discriminate against Christian families."

A wealthy but less well-known group is the **Center for Reclaiming America**, an outreach of Coral Ridge Ministries in Fort Lauderdale, Florida. The Center offers training and information to those interested in defending America's Judeo-Christian heritage in the public sphere. It boasts an e-mail network list of 500,000. The group sponsors a Center for Christian Statesmanship in Washington, which hosts Bible study groups and prayer meetings for members of Congress and their staff. The Statesmanship Institute, a part of the center, offers more in-depth training for $345 (Simon, 2005). The Center for Reclaiming America's agenda is broad in scope and aligns very closely with Focus on the Family and the Family Research Council. The organization is headed by Reverend D. James Kennedy. Goals of the organization include opening a lobbying office in Washington, D.C., launching a "strategy institute" to study the tactics of their political opponents, and recruiting one million grassroots activists. It is too early to say whether the group will grow into a major player in the Christian Right movement.

One of the oldest surviving Christian Right groups is **Eagle Forum**, headed by Phyllis Schlafly.[2] Founded in 1972, Eagle Forum was quite effective in fighting the proposed Equal Rights Amendment (ERA) to the U.S. Constitution. Throughout the 1970s, a majority of Americans favored the amendment, but through well-organized grassroots lobbying, Eagle Forum and other groups managed to defeat the amendment in state legislatures across the country. After that, Eagle Forum shrank in size, but it remains active in opposing efforts to add equal rights amendments to state constitutions and in opposing legal abortion. Over the past several years, Eagle Forum has become increasingly involved in education issues. Schlafly is a longtime conservative activist who has spent much of her adult life traveling the country arguing that women should remain at home with their children. While not explicitly opposing President Bush's decision to select a woman for the second Supreme Court vacancy in 2005, the Eagle Forum did not support the selection of Harriet Miers. Executive Director Jessica Echard asserted, "If it's going to be a woman, we expected an equal heavyweight to Ruth Bader Ginsburg and her liberal stance, and we did not get that in Miss Miers" (Baker and Balz, 2005).

The **Traditional Values Coalition**, headed by the Reverend Louis Sheldon, has centered its activity on issues relating to gay rights, although it also takes a pro-life position on abortion and is involved in attempts to alter public school curricula. The group was involved in the Oregon and Colorado initiatives that proposed constitutional amendments to limit antidiscrimination laws against gays and lesbians, and it worked to reject a health education curriculum for California public schools that discussed issues such as homosexuality and AIDS.

A number of groups formed in 2004 around the same-sex marriage issue, most of them coalitions of existing organizations. Two organizations took center stage at the national level. The **Marriage Amendment Project** is a coalition of more than fifty Christian organizations committed to amending the U.S. Constitution, including Focus on the Family, Christian Coalition, and the Center for Reclaiming America. In 2004, the organization coordinated efforts among the Christian Right groups by facilitating meetings of the various leaders, at both the national and state levels. The Marriage Amendment Project has a very small staff and is primarily a coalition of organizations who come together and plan strategy.

The other prominent traditional marriage group is the **Alliance for Marriage** founded by Matt Daniels. The Alliance for Marriage takes a broader approach and seeks to strengthen marriage more generally by supporting public policy that would reduce the tax burden on heterosexual married couples with children and eliminate aspects of welfare programs that penalize married recipients. The Alliance for Marriage has remained somewhat distinct from Christian Right groups thanks to Daniels, who is committed to remaining nonpartisan in his approach to increasing the number of "intact" homes. Daniels went out of his way to recruit an ethnically diverse board of directors, which has contributed to the racial diversity evident in the movement opposed to same-sex marriage.

The Fellow Travelers

Several organizations are best considered as being separate from the Christian Right, although they frequently share resources with Christian Right groups and back the same candidates. Most of these groups take strongly conservative positions on political issues and link those positions in some way to religious belief. Yet most political scientists would not classify them as part of the Christian Right for various reasons.

One religious organization that shares some but not all of the Christian Right's policy goals is the National Association of Evangelicals (NAE), a group which represents 79 denominations and more than 30 million evangelicals. The NAE's mission is primarily religious and includes facilitating cooperative ministry among evangelicals in the United States. Although the NAE serves as something like a trade association of evangelical denominations, the organization has played an increasingly public role in policy issues. In 2005, the NAE brought together evangelical leaders to produce a document titled "For the Health of the Nation: An Evangelical Call to Civic Responsibility." The document outlined NAE's position on general policy issues, many of which overlap those of the Christian Right, and others, such as the evangelical brand of environmentalism known as "**Creation Care**," which do not. Richard Cizik, director of public policy for the National Association of Evangelicals, carried a sign in a pro-life march proclaiming "Stop the Mercury Poisoning of the Unborn"—a clear sign of the NAE's expanded issue agenda (Harden, 2005).

Perhaps the most numerous and intensely organized of the fellow traveler groups are the hundreds of national, state, and local pro-life groups. The National Right to Life Committee and hundreds of other pro-life groups oppose abortion rights and usually tie that position to religious belief. Yet pro-life groups are not generally identified with the Christian Right because a sizable minority of their supporters are not conservatives. In an effort to attract the widest possible audience, most pro-life groups focus their attention solely on abortion and take no official position on any other issue, including contraception, thus allowing liberals who oppose most of the Christian Right agenda to join pro-life groups. The most notable set of liberal pro-life activists come from the "seamless garment" network of organizations that oppose not only abortion but also the death penalty and nuclear weapons and that advocate increased spending on child welfare programs.[3] Thus, although nearly all Christian Right activists are pro-life, not all pro-life activists support the Christian Right. Yet in elections in which candidates take divergent views on abortion, the two sets of organizations often work together, and their activists frequently mingle as they volunteer on behalf of pro-life candidates.

One large and growing segment of the public that provides substantial support to the Christian Right is homeschool advocates. Many Christian conservatives strongly object to elements of the public school curriculum, and some educate their children at home rather than send them to public schools. Like the pro-life movement, the homeschool movement tends to focus on a narrow set of issues to attract a wide diversity of membership. Moreover, there exists a small but important segment of the homeschool community that is politically liberal—indeed, some parents homeschool their children to prevent them from hearing nationalistic and pro-capitalist values in the classroom. Yet the homeschool constituency for the Christian Right is large and growing. In 1993, Michael Farris, a homeschool advocate, successfully mobilized this constituency in Virginia to win the Republican nomination for lieutenant governor before losing the general election.

Farris founded the **Home School Legal Defense Association** (HSLDA), which is a nonprofit advocacy group seeking to defend the right of parents to direct the education of their children as they see fit. Farris is received warmly by Christian Right audiences and spoke at the Christian Coalition's 2004 Road to Victory Conference. HSLDA takes a particular interest in training young evangelicals to be politically active. A division of the organization, Generation Joshua, is aimed at direct political activism. According to its Web site, Generation Joshua equips homeschooled teens with the skills necessary to campaign actively for candidates that have been "prayerfully" selected by HSLDA's board of directors. Homeschoolers worked for President Bush in 2004. "We believe that some day homeschooled young people will help reverse *Roe v. Wade* [and] stop same-sex marriage," wrote HSLDA president Michael Farris in a statement that launched Generation Joshua (quoted in Grove, 2004). All candidate campaign activity is funded by the group's political action committee, HSLDA-PAC.

There is also significant overlap in the membership of the Christian Right and pro-gun groups. The National Rifle Association (NRA) usually has a presence at Christian Coalition meetings—as exhibitor, advertiser, or both. Especially in the South, God and guns are forces often seen moving as one.[4] NRA strategist Chuck Cunningham was once the issues director for the Christian Coalition, and gun control issues appeared on Christian Coalition voter guides during that time. Yet many Christian Right activists, especially in the North, favor gun control, and many NRA activists take libertarian positions on social issues such as abortion and homosexuality.

A number of organizations combine right-wing religion and right-wing politics in ways that most Christian Right activists would find abhorrent. At the fringe of the gun community, the various militia groups that attracted attention after the Oklahoma City bombing frequently proclaim their Christian doctrine, but they are not part of the Christian Right movement, and most Christian Right activists oppose the militia groups. Many racist and anti-Semitic organizations claim a Christian grounding for their views, although their doctrine would be unpalatable to mainstream Christians. The Christian Identity Movement, for example, claims that Jews are the illegitimate spawn of Satan and that whites are the true Israelites (Barkun, 1994). The Christian Right leadership is unanimous in its condemnation of such extremist organizations.

State and Local Organizations

Although national Christian Right organizations attract most of the media attention, each state has unique homegrown groups, which vary in their strength and longevity. In 2004, Christian Right activists in many states created ad-hoc coalitions to help pass amendments to state constitutions banning same-sex marriage. In Ohio, for example, Phil Burress, a longtime Christian Right activist who had run a local antipornography group and later headed the Ohio affiliate of Focus on the Family, started the **Ohio Campaign to Protect Marriage**. In many cases, state and local groups get significant aid from national groups. The American Family Association, for example, sent out mass e-mails to 60,000 supporters living in Ohio to encourage them to sign the petition needed to get the issue on the ballot and to vote in November. Moreover, representatives from Burress's Ohio group met regularly with national leaders from the Family Research Council to discuss strategy.

Other examples of local groups advancing the Christian Right agenda include the **Oregon Citizens Alliance** (OCA), which spearheaded an effort to limit gay and lesbian rights by initiative and referenda.[5] The OCA played an important role in the state's Republican nomination politics for almost a decade and worked with the Christian Coalition and other groups to disseminate information before elections. It disbanded in 1998, but in 2004 a new group, the Defense of Marriage Coalition, formed and was successful in amending the state constitution to bar same-sex marriage. The contrast between these two Oregon organizations is instructive. OCA was primarily the tool of a single political activist and occasional candidate in Oregon, and this limited its possibilities. The Defense of Marriage Coalition, in contrast, sought to mobilize many churches across denominational and racial lines in Oregon and to downplay the personalities of the leadership. State-level organizations in the Christian Right, as in other movements, can flourish or wither depending on their leadership.

Often state groups are formed and then later become affiliates of national organizations. In Virginia, the Family Foundation was created by Walter Barbee out of membership lists of a number of smaller local groups with diverse issue agendas. Barbee had fashioned a statewide organization and raised enough funds to hire a full-time state lobbyist when he was approached by Focus on the Family about becoming a state affiliate. In Michigan, there are several strong, state-level Christian Right groups that have been active for many years, some of which have formed affiliations with national groups (Penning and Smidt, 2006).

In Fairfax County, Virginia, a dispute over the distribution of the gay advocacy newspaper *The Washington Blade* at public libraries led to the formation of a countywide organization. In 1992, Karen Jo Gounaud organized a local group of Christian parents to protest the *Blade* and demand its removal from public libraries. Her organization quickly drew advice and support from sympathetic Christian Right groups and expanded its agenda. The organization also sought to force libraries to provide parents information on the books and tapes their children had checked out and to ban a gay library employee from wearing a pink gay pride triangle on his lapel on the grounds that it advocated a criminal lifestyle.[6] In 1995, she founded Family Friendly Libraries, which incorporated her earlier group and expanded its reach.

The rapid development of this local organization headed by a previously apolitical homemaker is testimony to the solid grassroots networking of Christian Right groups. Gounaud received training from the Christian Coalition at a 1993 political activism seminar held in Manassas, Virginia. She also received advice from the American Family Association and support from key Republican county officials.[7] She soon had a large mailing list, access to a fax network, and other trappings of an institutionalized organization. Her organization is hardly unique, and indeed other local Christian Right groups exist in Fairfax County. Across the country, many counties have affiliates of one or more of the three main Christian Right organizations, affiliates of one or more state-level groups, and one or more unique local organizations.

Christian Right Social Movement Organizations and Leaders: Cooperation and Conflict

The Christian Right organizations described above all share a core of common issues and complaints, but they differ subtly in their explanation of events, in their call for action, and in their issue focus. Social movement organizations and leaders often cooperate on a particular issue, but they also compete; movement organizations seek to mobilize the same pool of potential supporters. That pool is large but finite, and although many activists join more than one group, their average financial contribution may decrease as the number they join increases. In a real sense, Christian Right groups compete for members and money. Perhaps more importantly, they compete for the attention of activists.

Each group offers a subtly different flavor of ideology, explanation, and agenda and seeks to form the movement around that vision. In the 1990s, the Christian Coalition argued the case for pragmatism, for supporting all GOP candidates because the party is more likely to pass legislation favorable to the movement. The Family Research Council and Focus on the Family, in contrast, both promote a more uncompromising view and argue that Republicans have taken the movement for granted because it appears to lack an effective "exit strategy"—that is, the movement cannot threaten to leave the GOP coalition because its members are unlikely to support Democratic candidates, and third party movements are seriously disadvantaged in American politics.

These fundamental differences carry over into legislative strategies, even when groups share similar goals. In 2004, there was disagreement over the wording of a constitutional amendment to ban same-sex marriage. The FRC and Focus both argued that efforts to ban same-sex marriage would be derailed if the amendment also included language prohibiting civil unions. Although the leaders of Focus and the FRC oppose civil unions, they believed that the urgency of banning same-sex marriage necessitated a compromise. In contrast, CWA had long opposed civil unions and argued that the movement should not compromise in their opposition to all homosexual unions. They chose to support only an amendment that banned both same-sex marriage and civil unions.

Movement organizations and leaders do not always agree on the relative importance of various issues. Many Christian Right leaders in 2004 believed that the movement should focus primarily on stopping same-sex marriage because this was a relatively new issue and they feared that gay rights groups might make rapid progress in the near future. Other Christian Right leaders continued to argue that abortion was a more important issue because they believe that abortion involves killing babies. In the end, money and volunteers flocked to newly formed groups that opposed same-sex marriage, and pro-life groups suffered a (perhaps temporary) decrease in resources.

The leaders of Christian Right groups also compete and do not always cooperate. When Pat Robertson ran for president in 1988, Jerry Falwell, head of the Moral Majority, endorsed then Vice President George H. W. Bush. In 1999, when Gary Bauer sought the GOP nomination, Robertson made it clear that he backed Governor George W. Bush of Texas, and Falwell even refused to defuse a rumor linking Bauer with a sexual affair.

This competition is not unusual in social movements—it happened in the civil rights and feminist movements as well. Moreover, competition does not mean that groups do not cooperate on many issues. In the late 1980s it was not unusual to see Ralph Reed traveling the halls of Congress with James Dobson, working together on an issue, even as the men disagreed on general strategy and tactics.

Members and Activists of the Christian Right

Although it is possible to estimate the membership for many of the groups just discussed, it is not easy to estimate combined total membership because many of the same activists have joined several organizations. The Christian Right has formed a variety of organizations that specialize in particular tactics and in particular issues. People most concerned with secular humanism in schools join the Citizens for Excellence in Education; those who want to combat the "radical gay agenda" might join the Traditional Values Coalition; those who wish to engage in electoral mobilization can do so through the Focus on the Family Action; and those who wish to help prepare and disseminate research reports may choose to work for the Family Research Council.

But it is also clear that many Christian Right activists are involved in more than one group, and a core of activists has multiple involvement. Thus, the total number of activists is not as large as the sum of the membership totals of the various organizations. Political scientist John Green, who closely studies the Christian Right, estimates that there may be as many as 4 million Christian Right members nationwide and possibly 150,000 activists who work in politics (Green, 2000).

The activists themselves are generally well-educated, moderately affluent individuals who are distinctive primarily in their high levels of church attendance. They are disproportionately female, for there is a considerable talent pool of conservative Christian wives and mothers who remain out of the paid labor force for religious reasons. Many evangelical women who cannot justify taking on part-time employment find that political action is an important outlet for their energies and abilities.

Organizations communicate with their members in diverse ways. Most groups contact their members regularly by letter, fax, or e-mail, sharing information on pending legislation, the political process, activities of group leaders, and new issues being pursued, and usually asking for financial contributions in the process.

Most organizations also issue action alerts, which inform members of legislation under active consideration by some governmental body. Action alerts include explicit instructions and provide lists of officials to contact and talking points to argue. Most action alerts take the form of e-mails sent out two or three times a day when Congress is in session. These action alerts often contain links to longer Web page accounts, which may in turn contain information on contacting policymakers and links to allow members to contribute to the organization. Christian Right groups often maintain extensive Web pages that provide research reports, video shorts, and information on a range of issues, along with ways to purchase materials and contribute to the groups (see box 3.1).

Once members have been informed about issues, candidates, or events, they frequently share this information with others in their churches who may not be members or even necessarily supporters of the Christian Right. The frequent face-to-face interactions in churches provide an ideal opportunity to disseminate information, and in this way Christian Right arguments and issues have a much greater penetration than mere membership numbers would suggest (Wald, Owen, and Hill, 1988). Individuals who would never support the Family Research Council might nonetheless contact county school officials about the content of sex education classes or vote for a candidate whose views they shared. Moreover, many Christian conservatives receive information from a variety of Christian Right groups, although they are not members, and may use this information to guide their electoral behavior.

Compared with other social movements, such as the feminist and gay rights movements, the Christian Right has not paid particular attention to

BOX 3.1   The Christian Right and Technology

Although critics often charge that Christian conservatives are opposed to any form of modernism, the movement has always used the best technology available to spread its message. In the 1920s antievolution activists used printing presses to distribute fliers, published tracts and special newspapers, and held tent revivals. In the 1950s anticommunist groups used radio to communicate with fellow travelers. In the 1980s the Moral Majority used computers to organize a direct-mail campaign to fund its organization and used television to mobilize its base.

In the 1990s the Christian Right used technology as effectively as any movement in America. Its leaders used radio, television, and direct mail to reach their constituents, but their efforts were even more sophisticated than most. For example, direct-mail appeals were more carefully targeted to supporters based on their past response to solicitations, and cable television provided programming for many market niches.

By 2005, Christian conservative groups had well-established Websites and communicated with their constituents on a daily basis. For example, supporters of the Family Research Council (FRC) can subscribe to "Washington Update"—a daily e-mail that informs recipients of the FRC's position on the day's events in the nation's capital. Other e-mail subscriptions include a Media Update e-mail letting supporters know when FRC will be featured in upcoming news programs, a FRC Prayer Team e-mail, and a Grassroots Alert e-mail announcing local FRC events. Concerned Women for America e-mails weekly "alerts," and Focus on the Family Action e-mails supporters a letter from James Dobson a few times a month discussing current issues and asking for financial contributions.

The Christian Right has successfully used the Internet to mobilize supporters, allowing constituents to "electronically" sign petitions and urging them to e-mail their congressional representatives. The Internet has also allowed Christian Right groups themselves to more quickly communicate with one another.

Web addresses:

Focus on the Family	www.family.org
Focus on the Family Action	www.focusaction.org
Family Research Council	www.frc.org
Center for Reclaiming America	www.reclaimamerica.org
Christian Coalition	www.cc.org
Eagle Forum	www.eagleforum.org
American Family Association	www.afa.net
National Association of Evangelicals	www.nae.net
Citizens for Excellence in Education	www.nace-cee.org
Traditional Values Coalition	www.traditionalvalues.org

(continues)

(Box 3.1 continued)

American Center for Law and Justice	www.aclj.org
Concerned Women for America	www.cwfa.org
Alliance for Marriage	www.allianceformarriage.org
Marriage Amendment Project	www.formarriage.org
Home School Legal Defense Association	www.hslda.org
Family Research Institute	www.familyresearchinst.org
American Center for Law and Justice	www.aclj.org
Susan B. Anthony List	www.sba-list.org

The following are Websites of organizations that oppose the agenda of the Christian Right and monitor the movement:

Interfaith Alliance	www.interfaithalliance.org
People for the American Way	www.pfaw.org
Americans United for Separation of Church and State	www.au.org

recruiting support from university students (Larson and Wilcox, 2005). None of the contemporary Christian Right organizations maintain chapters at college campuses, Christian or otherwise. Concerned Women for America has hosted student prayer groups, but they usually don't survive past the graduation of its leader. The Christian Right appears to be depending upon extra-collegiate programs to develop the next wave of the movement's leaders. Focus on the Family hosts a Focus Institute that includes courses on public policy. The Family Research Council offers an internship program for college students and recent graduates, the Witherspoon Fellowship, which explores the philosophical roots of Christian involvement in the political process. The fellowship attracts students who do not appear as consistently conservative as their parent organization and encourages them to think creatively about policies. A number of Christian Right leaders—Pat Robertson, Jerry Falwell and Michael Farris—have actually started their own colleges with a commitment to teaching conservative principles that may contribute to the future membership of the Christian Right.

Christian Right Action in Electoral Politics

The Christian Right is active in a number of policy arenas and has pursued a variety of tactics to influence different kinds of governmental units. In general, the Christian Right has sought to influence the selection of political elites by working to help favored candidates win party nominations and then by helping them defeat their general election opponents. The movement has chosen a partisan strategy of working with the Republican Party instead of attempting to influence the policies of both parties. It has also sought to influence government leaders, including officials who are not supporters of the movement.

The Nomination Process

Ever since the Christian Right re-entered the political scene in the late 1970s, the groups have worked to help candidates win their party's nomination. In states where nominees are selected in caucuses or statewide conventions, these groups have had considerable success. In Virginia, for example, the Moral Majority sent hundreds of delegates to Republican nominating conventions in the early 1980s, and the Christian Coalition, Family Foundation (the local affiliate of the Family Research Council and Focus on the Family), and CWA did the same in the 1990s. In nearly all cases, the movement has been successful in helping nominate preferred candidates in Virginia. In states where nominees are selected by primary election, however, Christian Right groups have had mixed success (Green, 2000).

Christian Right involvement in nomination politics begins with candidate recruitment. Movement activists sometimes identify potential candidates from within their organizations and churches. They generally encourage a potential candidate to run for some local office and offer an array of services to help persuade the candidate to run. In the 1990s, the Christian Coalition provided training for candidates, their campaign managers, and their campaign finance directors. The Madison Project trains campaign workers and state legislative candidates, and the Susan B. Anthony List trains pro-life women in many aspects of campaigning.

Candidate recruitment provides an invitation to struggle within the movement, for some activists prefer candidates who will take strong, uncompromising positions in support of the Christian Right agenda, whereas others prefer candidates who have a chance of winning. In general, movement leaders prefer the latter; many activists prefer the former. Thus movement leaders may recruit potential candidates who already serve in local or state office and who have demonstrated a strong record of support for Christian Right policies, but who are not themselves members of the movement. These "outsider" candidates have a greater chance of winning than those recruited from within the movement.

Of course, not all Christian Right candidates are recruited by movement leaders and activists. Some evangelicals say they hear a call from God to pursue public service, and over the past decade the movement has produced a number of "self starter" candidates who hear a personal call to run for office. Although these individuals bring a great deal of enthusiasm to their candidacies, they generally bring little else. They lack experience in political office, in assembling electoral coalitions, and in raising money (Green, 2000). Generally they are extremely conservative and often unwilling to compromise their beliefs to win election. Self-starters therefore are prone to extreme statements or actions. For example, when the wife of Minnesota Republican Allen Quist died while pregnant, he had the fetus removed from her body and buried in her arms.[8] The gesture may have won him the undying support of some pro-life activists, but it surely alienated him from the majority of Minnesota voters. In recent years, the Christian Right has begun to work to discourage candidacies by movement activists, preferring instead to back more experienced politicians who would support at least some of the movement's agenda.

After candidates are recruited, the movement can provide many resources for an intraparty nomination, including financial assistance, expertise, and access to a broad communication infrastructure. The most important resource, however, is voter mobilization. Voter mobilization in intraparty nomination contests is useful in all states, but statewide nomination rules make it more valuable in some states than in others. State parties can choose to select their nominees by primary election, by convention, or by caucus, and the Christian Right has far more success in influencing nominations in states that do not use primary elections. Statewide Christian Right groups, including CWA and the state affiliates of the Family Research Council and Focus on the Family, generally put together packets of information on how and where to vote in primary elections, where and when the caucus or convention will be held, and how to register to attend. In the 2004 election, ivotevalues.com offered evangelicals, pastors, and church leaders easy access to such information. This information is crucial in states with caucuses or conventions, where few citizens know how to go about participating in the process. It is less useful in states with primary elections, where it is relatively easy to determine when and where to vote. Included in these packets of information are profiles of various candidates, usually offered without an explicit group endorsement. However, a tacit endorsement is often signaled by the description of issue positions or even by the quality of the photos.

Christian Right candidates may be opposed by party insiders, even if they have political experience. In Colorado in 2004, Republican congressman Bob Schaeffer and businessman Peter Coors squared off for the GOP nomination for the U.S. Senate. Both candidates took pro-life stances, and both endorsed a national constitutional amendment to ban same-sex marriage, but Christian conservatives rallied behind Schaeffer and were skeptical of Coors because his company, a brewery, offered benefits to partners of gay and lesbian employees and had insured abortions under the company's health plan. George W. Bush and other party insiders supported Coors, whose deep pockets were presumably a valuable asset. Coors won the primary election; however, Christian conservatives refused to help Coors in the general election, and he ultimately lost in a close contest (Larson, 2006).

In states with caucuses or conventions, the Christian Right not only can be a major player in nominations but can even dominate the process, for a determined voter mobilization campaign can swamp the opposition. In Virginia's open convention system, for example, Christian Right delegates were in solid control of the nomination process in both 1993 and 1994; however, in an open primary election for a 1998 Senate nomination they lost badly to moderate forces. In Minnesota in 1994, Allen Quist handily defeated the popular moderate incumbent, Arne Carlson, in the state convention. But Minnesota Independent Republicans ultimately selected their nominee by party primary, and Carlson defeated Quist by an overwhelming margin in that larger electoral arena. In 2004, the Christian Right *was* the Republican Party in Iowa, a state famous for its early presidential caucus. The incoming chair of Iowa's Republican Party got his start in Pat Robertson's campaign in the 1980s. Both party candidates and party leaders are chosen in the caucuses. Christian conservatives in the state are known as savvy political operatives who rely on friendship networks to bring about strength in numbers (Conger and Ratcheter, 2006). They rarely lose to moderate forces within the party.

Why is the Christian Right more influential in states with open caucuses and conventions than in states with primary elections? In most states the Christian Right represents a sizable Republican contingent but is clearly a minority. Participating in caucuses and conventions requires more effort than voting in a primary election because caucus and convention meetings sometimes last for hours or even days, and participation requires knowledge of where the local meeting will be held. In states with caucuses and conventions, the Christian Right can win because its activists are more likely to make the extra effort to participate than are party moderates. In states with primary elections, however, voting is relatively easy, and moderate voters generally outnumber supporters of the Christian Right. Thus, the ongoing nomination struggles between Christian conservatives and party moderates often hinge on the party rules that dictate how candidates are chosen.

Because these rules are set by the state party committees, the Christian Right has frequently made efforts to gain working control of state parties. In 1994, *Campaigns & Elections* reported that the Christian Right was the dominant faction in eighteen states and had substantial influence in thirteen others. In 2000, the Christian Right remained dominant in eighteen states, and the number of states where it was influential increased to 26 (Conger and Green, 2002). (See map 3.1.) At the 1995 Christian Coalition convention, Robertson announced that he would not be content until the movement extended its influence into all fifty state committees. Although the Christian Coalition lacks the resources to achieve this goal, other movement organizations and activists continue to seek greater influence in state Republican Party committees.

The Christian Right is influential in state Republican parties in parts of the South and Midwest but is far less influential in the Northeast. In part, this reflects the presence of Christian conservatives, who provide the infantry for the intraparty battle. The Christian Right has also had great success in states in transition from Democratic to Republican majorities, perhaps because they contain fewer entrenched Republican elites who resist its incursion into the party (Green, Guth, and Wilcox, 1998).

In states where the Christian Right has become an important party faction, party moderates and secular conservatives have reacted in diverse ways. Surveys of party activists have revealed that in some states, such as Minnesota and Virginia, the two factions have often expressed mutual hostility, with each preferring Democratic candidates to Republicans from the other faction of the party. In Colorado in 2004, for example, members of the Christian Right actually campaigned against a moderate Republican candidate for the state House of Representatives because she opposed school vouchers. Republican Rep. Ramey Johnson lost her seat to the Democratic challenger by only 41 votes, so clearly the Christian Right campaign cost her

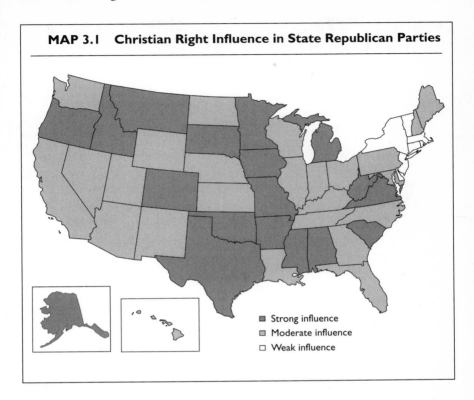

MAP 3.1   Christian Right Influence in State Republican Parties

■ Strong influence
▣ Moderate influence
☐ Weak influence

the seat. After her loss, Johnson said the Republican Party in Colorado is participating in a "circular firing squad" (Bartels, 2004).

In other states, such as Texas and Washington, the factional disputes are more muted. Factional battles are more likely in states where the Christian Right activist core is large but its popular support base is relatively small and in states with convention systems that force activists into face-to-face confrontations (Green, 2000).

In some states, the Christian Right dominates the Republican Party, and moderates complain that their party has been taken over. What does it mean to dominate a state party? In Virginia it means that the state party chair is an ally of the Christian Right and that a working majority of the state central committee is composed of activists in or sympathetic to the movement.[9] The Christian Right also controls many county Republican committees in Virginia, although moderates continue to battle movement activists. In Spotsylvania County, a local Baptist minister mobilized conservative Christians to oust the county committee's GOP chair who had served for ten years and to remove moderates, including the local Republican state senator, from the county GOP board.[10] The Christian Right activists came with a plaque already inscribed thanking the ousted chair for his years of service to the party. In an article in the April 30, 1994, *Richmond Times Dispatch,* Tyler Whitley commented on the struggle: "The old-line group refused to step down, describing the insurgents as 'reactionaries of the fundamentalist right,' and 'rogue elephants.' The state party, however, backs the newcomers." In Campbell County, the committee replaced the ten-year county chair with a nineteen-year-old political newcomer, and later a group of Christian activists ousted the moderate faction from the county board. In these county battles, the support of the state party chair was helpful to Christian Right activists. In most cases, the Christian Right forces remain in control of the party apparatus more than ten years later.

When Christian Right activists become the dominant force in a state party organization, they assume certain responsibilities and gain certain resources. The responsibilities include running the party on an ongoing basis, which requires time and considerable attention. In most states, however, movement activists have found the gains to be worth the investment in time and energy. First, the party has resources to help candidates, and these resources need not be divided evenly among all candidates running. The party makes direct cash contributions, has a corps of volunteers, and has connections with other interest groups that will work for and help fund candidates. Second, the party sets the rules for nominations, and control of the party means that these rules can favor insurgent groups like the Christian Right. Third, the state party writes its own platform, and this constitutes the core of the party's agenda. When Christian Right activists took control of the Washington state Republican Party in 1992, they wrote a platform that included opposition to the teaching of "New Age Movement Philosophy, including reincarnation, mystical powers, Satan worship, etc., as introduced in the textbooks of our education system," opposition to "mind-altering techniques for public school students," and the endorsement of parental control of textbook adoptions.[11] Few party moderates believed that the Washington state public school curriculum taught Satan worship.

In 2004, the Washington state platform was more moderate in tone but still included language reflecting a strong Christian Right influence, including protection of "preborn" life, support for Israel in the Middle East, a definition of marriage as between one man and one woman, and policy that public schools not promote or identify homosexuality as a healthy, morally acceptable, or alternative lifestyle.

In recent years, many state Republican Party platforms have become more moderate. Nevertheless, GOP platforms, which are generally posted on the Internet, continue to reflect the influence of the Christian Right, although party leaders have made efforts to word policy in a way to maximize appeal and minimize extreme rhetoric. This is evident in the following excerpt from the 2004 Washington state GOP platform:

> Ours is a nation created not by force, but by unifying ideals. People came here to be free to worship God as they choose without State restriction. For ours to remain one nation, where the source of our rights derive from God, not the state, we have the duty and obligation to teach our children the profound meaning behind the simple statement of allegiance to our flag and the ideals our nation was founded upon and to which so many have sacrificed their lives.[12]

It concluded, "We strongly support and wish to promote and protect the continued use of the phrase, 'one nation under God' in our Pledge of Allegiance."

The GOP platform in Texas has far stronger Christian Right overtones. In a long document rich in detailed policy prescriptions, the platform addresses almost all issues of importance to the Christian right, along with many other issues of interest to conservatives (see box 3.2).

Presidential Nominations

Presidential nominations are politically distinctive in many ways. They entail national campaigns that are contested state by state, they are lengthy processes that involve a rapid winnowing of the field, and they are extremely expensive. The Christian Right plays an important role in the process of presidential selection because the movement controls state party committees in many states, because some states select among the nominees through caucuses or conventions, and because the movement has ample financial resources to support a candidate.

Although movement leaders backed Ronald Reagan in the 1980 primaries and caucuses, the Christian Right was at the time a fledgling movement, and at least some who would eventually join it were still registered as

---

BOX 3.2   The Texas GOP Platform

Studying state GOP party platforms is one way to assess the influence of the Christian Right. Although some state party leaders have made efforts to phrase platforms in ways to maximize their appeals and minimize extreme rhetoric, other state platforms are more fundamentalist in nature, calling for the criminalization of sodomy and pornography and the required teaching of creationism. The Texas GOP platform includes the following elements, evidence of the Christian Right's presence in the state.

- The Republican Party of Texas affirms that the United States of America is a Christian nation, and the public acknowledgment of God is undeniable in our history. Our nation was founded on fundamental Judeo-Christian principles based on the Holy Bible. The Party affirms freedom of religion, and rejects efforts of courts and secular activists who seek to remove and deny such a rich heritage from our public lives.

- Our Party pledges to exert its influence to restore the original intent of the First Amendment of the United States Constitution and dispel the myth of the separation of Church and State. We support the right of individuals and state and local governments to display symbols of our faith and heritage.

- The Party acknowledges that the church is a God-ordained institution with a sphere of authority separate from that of civil government; thus, churches, synagogues and other places of worship, including home Bible study groups, seminaries and similar institutions should not be regulated, controlled, or taxed by any level of civil government, including the Social Security Administration and the Internal Revenue Service.

- The Party believes that the practice of sodomy tears at the fabric of society, contributes to the breakdown of the family unit, and leads to the spread of dangerous, communicable diseases. Homosexual behavior is contrary to the fundamental, unchanging truths that have been ordained by God, recognized by our country's founders, and shared by the majority of Texans. Homosexuality must not be presented as an acceptable "alternative" lifestyle in our public education and policy, nor should "family" be redefined to include homosexual "couples." We are opposed to any granting of special legal entitlements, recognition, or privileges including, but not limited to, marriage between persons of the same sex, custody of children by homosexuals, homosexual partner insurance or retirement benefits. We oppose any criminal or civil penalties against those who oppose homosexuality out of faith, conviction, or belief in traditional values.

- The Party opposes the legalization of sodomy. The Party demands Congress exercise its authority granted by the U.S. Constitution to withhold jurisdiction from the federal courts from cases involving sodomy.

- The Party demands Congress exercise its constitutional authority to withhold jurisdiction from the federal courts from cases involving sexually-oriented businesses including pornography.

- We urge the Republican Party of Texas to support, financially or with in-kind contributions, only those candidates or nominees of this party who support the entire platform on protecting innocent human life. We urge the members of the State Republican Executive Committee to make such changes to the by-laws of that committee to make this action binding on the Republican Party of Texas.

- We unequivocally oppose the United States Senate ratification of the United Nations Convention on the Rights of the Child, which would transfer jurisdiction over parental rights and responsibilities to international bureaucracies.

- The Party supports parental authority and the teaching of moral values in the home. We oppose school-based clinics and/or youth impact centers located at, sponsored by, or funded by any state agency or public school district, whether or not they dispense condoms and contraceptives or refer, aid, or advise minors to have abortions.

- The Party urges the Legislature to act in 2005 to give the State Board of Education authority to establish textbook adoption standards that allow rejection of textbooks that undermine belief in America and our Constitutional Republic, promulgate anti-American propaganda, and contain unchallenged biased viewpoints.

- To build strong and lasting relationships, we support the requirement that schools teaching sex education must teach directive abstinence until heterosexual marriage with an uninfected person as the only safe and healthy means of preventing sexually transmitted diseases and pregnancies among unwed students. We believe programs should teach the physical and emotional risks of abortion specified in State law and rules. We oppose programs that advocate or legitimize pre-marital sexual activity, advocate condoms and birth control use by unmarried minors, advocate abortions, and condone homosexual, bisexual, and transgender acts and/or lifestyles, and elevate minors' rights to make sexual and health care decisions equivalent to their parents. Sex education classes, if conducted, should be separated by sex.

- The Party supports the objective teaching and equal treatment of scientific strengths and weaknesses of all scientific theories, including Intelligent Design —as Texas law now requires but has yet to enforce. The Party believes theories of life origins and environmental theories should be taught only as theories not fact; that social studies and other curriculum should not be based on any one theory.

Democrats in southern states. In 1984 Reagan ran unopposed, so the first real test of the strength of the Christian Right in nomination politics came in 1988 when Pat Robertson sought the presidency.

The 1988 campaign revealed that the movement had considerable resources. Although Robertson's father had been a U.S. senator and Robertson had been involved indirectly in politics for some time, he lacked experience in elected or even appointed office and was at the time an ordained minister.[13] Despite these liabilities, Robertson's campaign was surprisingly successful. He won most of the states that hold caucuses and raised more money than any previous presidential candidate.

Yet the campaign also showed some of the weaknesses of the Christian Right. Robertson lost badly in all primary elections, despite spending huge sums of money. Religious particularism, especially fundamentalist antipathy toward charismatics, hampered his campaign, and ultimately his support was narrowly based among pentecostal and charismatic Christians. As noted in chapter 2, he made wild statements that attracted widespread derision and in other ways behaved like an amateur candidate.[14]

Robertson suffered because of his lack of experience, general public distrust of preachers who would be president, and religious divisions among his evangelical constituency. Yet when the Christian Right supports presidential candidates who lack these liabilities, it is a formidable force in nomination politics. The movement can provide volunteers, infrastructure, and lots of cash for favored candidates.

In 1996 the movement was courted by several candidates with at least passable credentials as social conservatives. Alan Keyes, Bob Dornan, and Patrick Buchanan all had established records as social conservatives, and Phil Gramm and Bob Dole also made strong appeals. As the campaign unfolded, movement activists divided their votes between Dole and Buchanan. Buchanan's fiery rhetoric excited many of the movement's purists. At one rally he claimed that the founding fathers would have had one response if they had learned that public schools did not teach the Bible but taught about homosexuality: "Lock and load!"

But Buchanan's candidacy came with baggage—many Christian conservatives found evidence of racism and anti-Semitism in his speeches, and others objected to his extreme nativism. Some fundamentalist activists may have opposed Buchanan because of his Catholicism. More pragmatic Christian Right activists backed Dole, whom they saw as the only candidate with a real chance to defeat President Bill Clinton.

In 2000, the field of candidates vying for Christian Right support in the primaries was large. Longtime movement activist Gary Bauer took leave from the Family Research Council to run. Senators Bob Smith of New Hampshire, John McCain of Arizona, and Orrin Hatch of Utah sought the nomination, along with former Vice President Dan Quayle. Perennial candidates Alan Keyes and Patrick Buchanan resumed their quixotic quests. Multimillionaire candidate Steve Forbes, who ran in 1996 as a social moderate, campaigned with the zeal of a born-again social conservative, although many movement activists questioned his sincerity.

Yet party moderates and conservatives ultimately united behind the candidacy of George W. Bush, governor of Texas and son of the former president. By summer 1999 Bush had received more than one hundred endorsements from House GOP members and had the support of most sitting governors as well. Christian Right leaders like Pat Robertson worked openly to help Bush win the nomination, in part because they believed that only Bush could beat Gore in November. Robertson recorded a phone message that was dialed to many registered Republicans in South Carolina that suggested that Bush was a far stronger pro-life candidate than Senator McCain, a move that brought an angry rebuke from the senator.

In South Carolina, Bush spoke at Bob Jones University and failed to use the occasion to chasten the school for its openly anti-Catholic message and its ban on interracial dating. During the primaries, Bush professed that Jesus was his favorite philosopher and the Bible was his favorite book. In private, he reassured Christian conservative leaders in each state of his commitment to Christ and to Christian conservative policies. Overall, Bush campaigned hard for the Christian Right vote, and ultimately it was critical to his primary election victory (Rozell, 2002; Wilcox, 2002).

Incumbent George Bush won the Republican nomination unopposed in 2004, but by 2005 there already were several candidates jockeying for support of the Christian Right. Although it is too soon to know who will run in 2008 and how those candidates will appeal to Christian conservatives, it is clear that the movement will play a key role in the nomination process. Senate majority leader Bill Frist has clearly sought out Christian Right support, appearing at Justice Sunday and later declaring a diagnosis that Terry Schiavo did not suffer from a persistent vegetative state, a statement he has since repudiated. But not all potential candidates will seek Christian Right support. Senator John McCain is currently planning a presidential bid that would likely seek to stake out a moderate position on social issues. McCain would likely attract the active opposition of the Christian Right.

Christian Right activists have also played an active role in drafting presidential nomination platforms. Republicans select delegates to platform committees through procedures that allow organized activists a disproportionate voice, and the movement has "owned" various sections of the platform since 1980. In 1996, Bob Dole worked hard to insert a "tolerance" plank in the platform that proclaimed that the Republican Party welcomed support from those who did not share the pro-life position of the platform. Ultimately he lost this effort. Dole promptly announced that he had not read the platform and did not think he would have time to do so. In 2000 and 2004, Christian Right leaders won key platform victories, such as support for a constitutional ban on same-sex marriage, but they did not press Bush to campaign on abortion or other issues.

General Elections

The Christian Right does not always win its intraparty struggle over nominations, but in the November general election, movement activists usually decide that the Republican candidate is closer than the Democrat to their views and that their policy objectives will fare better in a Congress or state legislature dominated by Republicans.[15]

In the 1990s, the Christian Coalition worked hard for relatively moderate Republican candidates, and most pragmatic activists realize the benefits that come with Republican majorities. In 1996 and again in 1998 the Coalition supported many vulnerable Republican incumbents in the House and Senate, regardless of their ideology, in an effort to help the Republicans retain control of the U.S. Congress. The Family Research Council and Focus on the Family are less pragmatic than the Christian Coalition of the 1990s and do not go out of their way to support moderate Republicans even when they are in a close race with a Democratic challenger. The 2004 Colorado Senate race between Republican Pete Coors and Democrat Ken Salazar is a case in point. Likewise, in the 2004 Pennsylvania Senate race, Focus and the FRC supported the conservative Republican Pat Toomey over the more moderate Republican incumbent Arlen Specter. After Toomey lost, these organizations did not rally the troops for Specter in the general election, and upon his win, they actively opposed his chairmanship of the Senate Judiciary Committee.

Nonetheless, the Christian Right does focus much of its efforts on electing Republican presidents, even moderately conservative candidates such as George H. W. Bush in 1992 and Bob Dole in 1996. These centrists may not be the first choice of movement activists, but they are far more likely to pursue conservative policies than their Democratic opponents. Clinton's veto of a bill banning late-term abortions helped mobilize the Christian Right against him, and its activity was generally more focused on defeating Clinton than on electing Dole.

The Monica Lewinsky scandal in the Clinton administration, coupled with Clinton's victories in many battles with Congress, led many movement leaders and activists in 1999 to believe that a GOP victory in 2000 was essential to the success of their agenda. Moreover, public support for the GOP Congress coming out of the impeachment process was extremely low (Andolina and Wilcox, 2000). As a consequence, Pat Robertson and other leaders worked hard in early 1999 to make George W. Bush acceptable to Christian Right activists; Robertson believed that Bush could win the 2000 general election, whereas other Christian conservative candidates such as Bauer and Buchanan could not. In 2004, Bush had the strong support of Christian Right leaders.

The centerpiece of Christian Right activity in the general election is voter mobilization. Christian Right groups often distribute large numbers of **voter guides** in churches and publish them in religious media. The Christian Coalition voter guides of the 1990s attracted widespread attention; the Coalition claimed to distribute more than 40 million guides in 1992 and more than 30 million in 1996. Christian Right voter guides are supposed to be nonpartisan because of tax law, but in the case of the Christian Coalition there was little doubt that the group backed GOP candidates. In Virginia's 1994 Senate election, for example, the Christian Coalition guide distorted the record of Democratic Senator Chuck Robb and included a very unflattering picture of him (Rozell and Wilcox, 1996).[16] Moreover, the Coalition issued two quite divergent ratings of incumbent Republican Senator John Warner—one in the primary when he was opposed by a social conservative within the party, and another, much higher rating when he ran in the general election against a Democrat. In 1999, the Internal Revenue Service denied the Christian Coalition of Virginia tax-exempt status, but other groups distributed similar voter guides in the 2004 election.

Many pastors in conservative churches allow these voter guides to be distributed before, after, or even occasionally during services on the Sunday before the election. Many pastors make a few brief remarks about the candidates at this time, but some go further. In many cases, candidates are invited to speak directly to congregants, and although pastors are prohibited by tax law from endorsing candidates, they often make it abundantly clear that the candidate has their support.

These voter contact efforts are important because many evangelicals retain a suspicion of politics and a belief that it is better to remain pure than to compromise with "the world." Although it is difficult to assess the scope of these efforts, the 1996 National Election Study revealed that 22 percent of white evangelicals were contacted by a religious group, and 19 percent saw campaign information in their place of worship. Among core evangelicals, 33 percent were contacted, and 29 percent saw campaign information in their churches. These figures are higher than for Americans in other religious traditions and are far higher than for other white Protestants. This suggests that there is substantial voter contact in white evangelical churches, mostly by Christian Right groups and activists. Unfortunately, the National Election Survey did not include these questions in 2004, so we can't determine whether contact by Christian Right groups was more extensive in that presidential election.

Although we cannot measure the extent of voter contact by Christian Right groups in 2004, the collapse of the Christian Coalition nationwide meant that many fewer voter guides were distributed than in the 1990s. As we have described above, Christian Right groups did distribute sample sermons to pastors, and in states with marriage amendments there was extensive church-based mobilization around that issue. Dobson and other religious leaders participated in weekly conference calls with the White House to help coordinate campaign strategies, and some activists found the Christian Right's get-out-the-vote efforts to be much more effective than the Bush-Cheney campaign (Cooperman and Edsall, 2004). In battleground states, Christian Right groups distributed videos and DVDs to pastors featuring Bush's faith, which were frequently shown in churches. Let Freedom Ring distributed a video in Pennsylvania and Ohio that portrayed Bush's faith in a flattering light. In other states, pastors were provided with a copy of the DVD "George W. Bush: Faith in the White House." The tone of the video is captured by the statement on the back cover: "Like no president in the history of the nation, George W. Bush boldly, publicly, and genuinely lives his faith on the job. . . . The Bush administration hums to the sound of prayer. Decide for yourself whether President Bush's faith has been good for America! But whatever you decide, his faith will change and inspire you."

But in 2004, with the Christian Coalition in shambles, the Bush administration believed that the Christian Right would not be sufficient to mobilize evangelical Christians to the extent that they believed necessary to win the election. The Bush team therefore sought to duplicate some of the Christian Coalition's tactics within the presidential campaign and within the Republican Party. The Bush re-election team identified church liaisons that would turn over church membership lists. The campaign then used those lists to contact potential voters and urge them to vote. Although this tactic drew stern rebukes from religious leaders, including many who supported Bush, it did yield valuable lists of potential supporters in several key states. In addition, the Republican National Committee mailed persuasion pieces to potential voters in battleground states, copying themes that had been used by Christian Right groups. In West Virginia, for example, an RNC letter warned that liberals wanted to take away Christians' Bibles.

The Christian Right is also a source of campaign funds for candidates. The organizations of the 1980s used political action committees to raise and distribute money, but throughout the early 1990s the new generation of groups did not form national PACs.[17] Gary Bauer's Campaign for Working Families raised more than $7 million in 1997–1998 and contributed or spent more than $1 million on behalf of federal candidates, including a few Democrats. The PAC also served to help Bauer prepare for his presidential campaign, including paying for consultants and helping him refine his direct-mail solicitation lists. In 2004, however, the PAC had receipts of less than $1.5 million and gave less than $250,000 to federal candidates.

The Susan B. Anthony List is a pro-life PAC that has a special focus on Christian conservative women candidates. Styling itself as a conservative counterpart to EMILY's List, the group recruits, trains, and helps fund pro-life women candidates in both political parties, but it also makes substantial contributions to male candidates. In 2004 the committee made contributions totalling $137,000, most of it to Republican candidates. It also claimed nearly $120,000 in independent expenditures.

Focus on the Family Action has the greatest potential to grow as a political action arm of the Christian Right. To date, the group has focused more on mailing endorsements from Dobson to potential voters than on direct cash contributions to candidates. In 2004, Focus Action spent $256,025 to mail letters offering Dobson's endorsement of socially conservative GOP Senate candidates in four states: Mel Martinez in Florida, James DeMint in South Carolina, Thomas Coburn in Oklahoma, and John Thune in South Dakota.

Another organization that raises and distributes funds for socially conservative candidates is Michael Farris's Madison Project, which contributes money to congressional candidates who support the Christian Right agenda. The Madison Project endorses only pro-life Republicans. The group also trains grassroots volunteer operatives (especially students) and encourages its members to make direct contributions to specific pro-life candidates in close races across the nation.

More importantly, candidates for Congress or the presidency can use mailing lists from Christian Right organizations to send campaign literature directly to members asking for funds. Activists have shown a great willingness to give to candidates who espouse their cause. Many are willing to volunteer time and money, providing candidates backed by the Christian Right with what has been called an "army that meets on Sunday."

School Board Elections

States may dictate that local school board members are appointed or elected, or states may leave these decisions to counties or other local government units. Some states also have elected statewide school boards that set policy for the entire state. The Christian Right has in recent years made a major effort to increase the number of states and counties that elect school boards and to encourage conservative Christians to seek election. School board elections are usually low-information contests; few citizens bother to vote, and those who do typically can recognize only a few names on the ballot. This makes it possible for a well-organized minority to have great success.

Yet in many of these elections, the Christian Right faces well-organized, well-funded opposition from national teachers unions and groups of progressive parents who oppose the Christian Right agenda for public schools. Whenever officials of the National Education Association (NEA) or other teacher groups recognize an attempt by the Christian Right to control a school board, they frequently mobilize supporters in opposition. In many high-profile elections, Christian Right slates have been defeated, including in Virginia Beach, Virginia, home of Pat Robertson's business empire. It is therefore advantageous for Christian Right candidates to avoid recognition by opposition groups, and stealth candidacies persist in school board elections in some areas.

In 1993 the Christian Coalition led a move by conservative Christians to oust Joseph Fernandez, the chancellor of the New York City public schools, and to end a multicultural "rainbow curriculum" that included such controversial books as *Heather Has Two Mommies,* a story about a girl raised by lesbian parents. The Christian Coalition and other groups helped to assemble slates of conservative Christian candidates for many of the city's thirty-two school districts and prepared 550,000 voter guides for distribution in 1,300 white evangelical, Catholic, and black churches (Reed, 1994a). The Christian conservative slates won about as often as those backed by the liberals, and the curriculum was revised under the directorship of a new school board leader (Dillon, 1993a, 1993b; Randolph, 1993).

In one recent study of Christian Right school board candidacies, Melissa Deckman (2004) found that although there have been many candidacies by conservative Christians for school board positions, few candidates reported that they had been recruited by Christian Right groups. Instead, many were motivated by their religious beliefs and concerns over curricular matters—concerns perhaps intensified by information provided by Christian Right groups.

Although Christian Right candidacies are increasing rapidly in school board races, Christian conservative majorities in school boards remain relatively rare across the country. However, a minority of Christian conservatives may work in coalition with other conservative board members to enact policy changes. For example, in Charles County, Maryland, two Christian Right activists hold key positions (including chair) of the school board. Although both have chosen to homeschool their own children rather than send them to public schools, they are working to remove books they consider to be offensive from the curriculum and from optional reading lists.[18]

A string of policy shifts has changed the way evolution is being taught to students in several states. In some states, references to evolution in statewide tests have been scaled back, virtually assuring that it will receive less attention by teachers who generally "teach to the test." In several school districts across the country, evolution is now presented as a controversial theory.

In 2005, opponents of teaching evolution concentrated on promoting the teaching of "**intelligent design**"—a theory that asserts that life on earth is too complex to have evolved through random mutation and must have been designed by a supreme being. The push was aided by President Bush, who stated publicly that he supported presenting both theories to students.

Eighty years after the Scopes "monkey trial," a similar debate about evolution erupted in Dover, Pennsylvania, this time over intelligent design. In 2005, the local school board required biology teachers to read a four-paragraph statement about intelligent design in the classroom that also referred to evolution as a theory with gaps. The school district was the first in the nation to require the teaching of intelligent design. Eleven parents sued the board claiming the requirement was simply a dressed-up form of biblical creationism and violated the separation of church and state. The trial gave advocates of intelligent design, such as scientists at the Seattle-based **Discovery Institute**, media attention and the chance to keep the debate on the agenda. At the time, many legal experts expected the case to go all the way to the Supreme Court.

In 1999, the Kansas statewide school board, dominated by the Christian Right, announced that the state's recommended science curriculum would no longer include core teachings in biology, astronomy, and geology that were inconsistent with creationism. Soon thereafter, moderates won a majority of the board positions. By 2005, however, Christian Right candidates had regained a majority on the board and in November voted to adopt a new standard that although students must understand evolutionary concepts, they should also be taught that Darwin's theory has been challenged by recent findings in biology. The state school board also revised the definition of "science," which no longer includes the search for natural explanations for phenomena. In Dover, Pennsylvania, the school board had sought to teach intelligent design in biology classes, resulting in a court challenge that has not been settled at the time of this writing. In November 2005, the majority of the members of Dover's School board were voted out of office.

The Christian Right as Target: Countermobilization

Although the Christian Right has impressive abilities to mobilize on behalf of candidates in nomination contests and general elections, it also serves as a potent symbol against which to rally secularists, liberals, and even religious moderates. In Virginia in 1994, Christian Right activists won the GOP Senate nomination for Oliver North, only to see him lose despite a nationwide GOP landslide. In Washington state, Christian Right activists helped Linda Smith win the Republican Party primary for a Senate bid in 1998, but she ultimately lost in the general election because many voters saw her as too closely tied to the Christian Right. In California in 1997, Christian conservatives spent time and money helping a socially conservative legislator beat a more moderate candidate in a special primary House election, only to see that candidate lose in a general election that many observers believe the more moderate Republican could have won. In many states, candidates with close ties to the Christian Right have lost when those who oppose its agenda have mobilized to defeat them.

Democratic candidates often attempt to paint Republican candidates as tools of the Christian Right. The Christian Right has dealt with this problem in several ways. Some candidates sought to deflect this countermobilization by hiding or denying their ties to the movement. However, as the movement's more unpopular leaders, such as Jerry Falwell and Pat Robertson, have taken a less visible role, some candidates have instead responded to such attacks with counterattacks accusing Democrats of anti-religious bigotry.

More recently, movement leaders have encouraged candidates to run on a broad array of issues and to speak the secular language of politics at most campaign events. Overall, however, the backing of the Christian Right is a mixed blessing. Candidates do best when they win the support of the Christian Right without being perceived as part of the movement. A candidate who can successfully appeal to Christian conservatives without appearing to most voters to be a Christian Right activist can benefit from the quiet voter mobilization by Focus on the Family and CWA and other organizations without prompting a countermobilization of moderates and liberals. When voters believe that a candidate is part of the Christian Right, however, countermobilization efforts are frequently (though not always) successful.

George W. Bush is a good example of a candidate who has run with the blessings of the Christian Right without prompting a countermobilization. Although liberals and Democrats attacked Bush as a pawn of the Christian Right, a majority of voters saw a candidate who was open about his personal faith but not inordinately influenced by Christian Right leaders. Bush himself intentionally used very ecumenical language in his 2004 campaign, emphasizing his acceptance of all faiths and his willingness to pray with Sikhs and Hindus (Larson and Wilcox, 2006).

Initiatives and Referenda

The Christian Right has also been active in promoting state and local initiatives and referenda, usually on matters dealing with homosexuality. In some cases, these efforts have sought to amend state constitutions in ways that might permanently disadvantage gays and lesbians in the process (Reed, 1998). In Colorado in the early 1990s, Christian Right activists promoted a successful statewide initiative to overturn all city laws banning discrimination against gays and lesbians and to prohibit the state from adopting such laws in the future. The U.S. Supreme Court overturned the Colorado measure by a six to three vote in May 1996, primarily because it would have permanently barred a group from future political participation.

The Oregon Citizens Alliance placed an even more radical initiative on the state ballot in 1992, which was narrowly defeated. It would have included language in the state constitution labeling homosexuality "abnormal, wrong, unnatural, and perverse" and would have required public schools to teach children that homosexuality should be avoided. The year after the defeat of the initiative, thirteen cities and counties in Oregon voted to prohibit antidiscrimination legislation in their local jurisdictions (Gamble, 1995).

Although the leaders of the Oregon Citizens Alliance promised to work to place similar initiatives on the ballot in a number of states in 1994, they were unsuccessful in doing so. In many states political elites maneuvered to keep these issues off the ballot, and in other states the petition drives simply failed to attain the requisite number of signatures.

In Maine a group called **Concerned Maine Families** succeeded in 1995 in gaining ballot access for a referendum that would have prevented the state or any locality from passing legislation to ban discrimination against homosexuals. A similar bill had passed the Maine legislature in 1993 but was vetoed by the governor. Other statewide organizations formed to join the campaign, and Focus on the Family provided some assistance (Hale, 1995). Ultimately, the referendum was defeated 53 percent to 47 percent.

In 2004, the Christian Right movement had great success in amending state constitutions to ban same-sex marriage. In all, thirteen states amended their constitutions by referendum in 2004, including eleven states who voted on the referendum on the day of the presidential election. The Marriage Amendment Project, mentioned earlier in this chapter, helped coordinate strategy between each of the eleven states and the national Christian Right organizations. A total of nineteen states now ban same-sex marriage in their state constitutions. Texas voters passed a ban on same-sex marriage in 2005.

Finally, the Christian Right has worked to pass or oppose initiatives and referenda in other policy areas including abortion, state equal rights amendments for women, and gambling. In 1999, the Christian Right combined with moderate churches and liberals to defeat a lottery proposal in Alabama that would have generated revenues earmarked for public schools.[19]

Lobbying Government

Although much of the focus of the contemporary Christian Right has been on electing socially conservative candidates, these organizations lobby government using the same techniques and tools as other organizations. They approach members of the national executive, legislative, and judicial branches in different ways, seeking to advance their policy agenda. The Christian Right is especially active in lobbying state and local governments.

The Presidency

In every presidential election since 1980, the Christian Right has concentrated its efforts on electing the Republican candidate. There are several reasons for this focus. First, the president has ready access to national media and thus is ideally situated to participate in a moral crusade. The "bully pulpit" is an important resource in efforts to persuade the public of particular goals. America's civil religion seems to require that the president assume the role of national spiritual leader, and if that were to entail assuming a prophetic stance on behalf of a conservative agenda, the Christian Right would surely benefit. Second, the president controls many key appointments in the bureaucracy and therefore has substantial influence on the way the bureaucracy makes rules and interprets laws. Third, the president selects the men and women who fill the nation's judiciary and therefore indirectly shapes the types of decisions made by the courts. Finally, for most of the 1980s, it appeared unlikely that the Republicans could ever capture control of Congress, so the presidency was the only realistic national electoral goal. The Christian Right has lobbied all three Republican presidents since 1980, but it has focused its efforts more on the Reagan and George W. Bush administrations.

In 1980 the Christian Right celebrated the election of Ronald Reagan. Although Reagan was the only divorced man ever to win the White House and seldom attended church services, he ran as a pro-family candidate and openly courted the support of conservative evangelicals. Although he had once, as governor of California, signed the most liberal abortion law in the nation, Reagan ran as a pro-life candidate in 1980, and his supporters promised privately that he would appoint only pro-life judges to the Supreme Court. Reagan supported the elimination of a longtime GOP platform plank endorsing the Equal Rights Amendment and the insertion of a pro-life plank.

Reagan appointed Christian Right activists and supporters to visible posts in his administration. A Moral Majority leader, Bob Billings, assumed a post in the Department of Education, and anti-abortion activist C. Everett Koop became surgeon general. James Watt, Reagan's choice to head the Department of Interior, reportedly argued that the imminent second coming of Christ meant that there was little need to preserve the environment (Wald, 1992). Gary Bauer, who later became head of the Family Research Council and a presidential candidate, served in Reagan's second term as the head of his domestic policy team.

Reagan (and later his successor, George H. W. Bush) also ordered the bureaucracy to interpret laws in ways that pleased Christian Right activists. Perhaps the most famous example was the "gag rule" on abortion, which barred the disbursement of public funds to any family planning organization that discussed abortion with its patients. Moreover, Reagan provided many symbolic benefits to conservative Christians: He addressed pro-life rallies in Washington remotely from the White House and mentioned Christian Right issues in his televised speeches.[20]

Yet ultimately many Christian Right activists became disenchanted with the Reagan administration. They argued that Christian conservatives received primarily symbolic gestures, while Reagan concentrated the energies of his administration on satisfying economic conservatives by providing tax cuts for corporations, and foreign policy conservatives by undertaking a massive military buildup. Reagan's first Supreme Court appointment was Sandra Day O'Connor, who did not vote to overturn *Roe v. Wade,* and his administration did not work to help pass a constitutional amendment that would have allowed prayer in public schools, despite heavy lobbying by the Moral Majority.

This disenchantment grew during the Bush administration, as key Christian conservatives criticized the president's moderation on social issues, exemplified by his inclusion of openly gay activists at the ceremonial signing of the Hate Crimes Act. Michael Farris blasted both the Reagan and George H. W. Bush administrations for giving nothing more to Christian conservatives than "a bunch of political trinkets." He argued that the Republican presidents provided "very little real progress in terms of advancing our public policy goals or getting our kind of people appointed to positions of real influence" (Farris, 1992, p. 43). Although his views represented those of many Christian conservatives, Christian Right activists nonetheless worked hard to re-elect Bush in 1992.

Though Christian conservatives may have been disappointed in the slow pace of policy change in the Reagan and Bush administrations, the election of Bill Clinton illuminated the stark differences between the two parties. Within weeks of his inauguration, Clinton signed executive orders lifting restrictions on abortion rights and appointed feminists to key administration posts. More important, the first major policy challenge for his administration involved the president's effort to lift the ban on gays and lesbians serving in the military. Clinton quickly became the focus of intense Christian Right attacks and a very successful fund-raising foil. Suddenly the Bush presidency seemed like the good old days, and the movement became focused on electing a GOP president. In 1996 the movement worked hard for Bob Dole, and some leaders such as Ralph Reed argued that the GOP should nominate Dole instead of Buchanan (whose views were more compatible with most movement activists) because Dole was more electable.

Soon after Clinton's re-election, the story broke of his affair with a White House intern. Clinton initially denied the story publicly and under oath but eventually admitted to an "inappropriate relationship" with Lewinsky when the evidence of the affair became irrefutable. Christian Right activists and supporters were outraged by what they saw as public immorality by a figure who is supposed to play a key role in American civil religion. Many sermons compared Clinton to immoral kings in the Old Testament, and Christian Right leaders pushed hard on Congress to impeach and remove the president.

Yet the general public did not abandon Clinton, choosing to frame his behavior as personal, not professional. Indeed, popular support for Clinton reached its apex during his trial in the Senate (Andolina and Wilcox, 2000). Eventually Pat Robertson backed away from the impeachment effort, leading many Christian Coalition leaders to complain that the organization had urged them to push hard for impeachment and then had not given them any warning of the retreat from that position.

Christian Right leaders made electing a GOP president in 2000 their top priority, confident that a Republican president would work with the Republican Congress to pass significant portions of their issue agenda.

It is difficult to exaggerate the enthusiasm the Christian Right had for George W. Bush after he won the Republican nomination in 1999. He was immediately viewed by activists as a welcome change from the questionable morality of the Clinton years. Christian conservatives saw Bush as one of their own, in large measure because his personal testimony resonated with the evangelical experience. In his presidential campaign, Bush credited his relationship with Christ for his ability to quit drinking and win public office in the state of Texas. Although previous presidents also have spoken of their faith, Bush intentionally spoke about his faith in a way that would trigger evangelical support. He told Doug Weed, a former pastor and family friend, "As you said, there are some code words. There are some proper ways to say things and some improper ways." He added, "I am going to say that I've accepted Christ into my life. And that's a true statement."[21]

Bush linked his faith to policy positions, especially abortion, on which he did not lay out a concrete position but instead proclaimed his support for a "culture of life." Moreover, in a televised presidential debate in 2000, when asked who his favorite philosopher was, Bush replied, "Jesus, because he changed my life." Pundits were quick to criticize Bush; he was "playing the Jesus card," said *Newsweek* and "running with Jesus" according to the *National Journal.* If it was strategy, it was a successful strategy. The Christian Right pledged their support to Bush in 2000 and contributed to his narrow victory over Vice President Al Gore in a number of swing states.

The Christian Right had great expectations for Bush's presidency, but in many ways their expectations have not been realized. Although Bush had promised to defend a "culture of life," he has not used the bully pulpit to push for restrictions on abortion. He has signed bills sent to him by Congress, such as the Unborn Victims of Violence Act, which allows a pregnant woman's murder to be tried as double homicide in federal murder cases, and another banning partial-birth abortion. However, it is likely that past Republican presidents such as Bush's father and Ronald Reagan would also have signed these bills. Bush also struck a compromise on federal funding for embryonic stem cell research and has threatened to veto any congressional legislation on the question. He also supported the use of federal funds to aid religious charities, and the Bush administration reimbursed religious groups that aided survivors of Hurricane Katrina in 2005. This program did not win universal support from the Christian Right, however, and some who supported the policy complained that the administration preferred to use it as a campaign issue rather than strike a bipartisan compromise. Aside from these minor policy positions, his political agenda has focused more on tax cuts, the repeal of a variety of regulations on corporations, the privatization of Social Security, and the war in Iraq.

On gay rights Bush has been particularly disappointing for many movement activists. He declined to reverse the "don't ask, don't tell" policy that applies to gays serving in the military and publicly announced that his administration would not discriminate against gays and lesbians in hiring. Indeed, Bush hired an openly gay man to head the White House Office of National AIDS Policy to the great ire of the Christian Right.

After some delay, Bush did endorse a national constitutional amendment barring same-sex marriage but allowing civil unions. Yet his endorsement came only after considerable pressure from CWA and other groups; he pointedly avoided mentioning the issue during most of the 2004 campaign. Moreover, although he occasionally used language about the need to defend the institution of marriage, it was activist judges and not "radical homosexual" groups that he identified as the threat. In the third presidential debate in 2004, Bush noted: "I think it's very important that we protect marriage as an institution between a man and a woman. I proposed a constitutional amendment. The reason I did so was because I was worried that activist judges are actually defining the definition of marriage." When asked later in the debate if homosexuality was a choice, Bush replied, "I don't know." Moreover, in other statements, Bush has said that states should be allowed to offer civil unions and other protections for gay and lesbian couples.

Although voter turnout among evangelicals and mobilization within churches played a key role in Bush's victory over Senator John Kerry in 2004, issues of concern to the Christian Right quickly took a back seat to energy policy, the war in Iraq, and Social Security reform in his second term. Many Christian conservatives have protested Bush's lack of support for their agenda in his second term, but support for Bush among the Christian Right's rank and file remains high in late 2005. And if Bush's appointments to vacant positions on the Supreme Court result in a reversal of key Court decisions on abortion and gay rights, Christian Right activists will remember him as one of their strongest supporters in the White House.

It is too early to tell how Bush's nominees will vote, but John Roberts told the Senate Judiciary Committee that he believed in the right to privacy and that he believed that *Roe* deserved great respect as a precedent. And although Samuel Alito had shown in past decisions a willingness to narrow abortion rights, his statements at the time of his nomination suggest that he is unlikely to vote to overturn *Roe*. Christian Right groups were happy with both judges, but their ultimate response will depend on how they vote on the bench.

Congress

The president is the most visible figure in American politics, but Congress drafts and passes legislation, passes the budget, and approves treaties and appointments. No matter how enthusiastically a president may support a bill backed by the Christian Right, there are real limits on his ability to steer it through the legislature. Christian Right groups have fielded full-time congressional lobbyists since 1980, but they have had only limited success.

Until 1995, Christian Right lobbyists faced a Democratic majority in the House of Representatives, and Democrats controlled the U.S. Senate between 1987 and 1995 and again briefly in 2000 and 2001. Democratic Party leaders were not receptive to Christian Right policies, but even the Republican-controlled Senate in the early 1980s defeated a proposed constitutional amendment to allow prayer in public schools and failed to pass the tuition tax credit that Christian Right activists sought.

During the 1980s, Christian Right lobbying was generally unsophisticated and frequently alienated even supporters of the movement's policy goals. This was especially true of the Moral Majority, which succeeded in angering even Republican Senator Orrin Hatch, a conservative Mormon sympathetic to the organization's objectives (Moen, 1989). Once important legislation such as the Equal Access Act was under consideration, Moral Majority activists did not participate in the bargaining as the legislation was being rewritten, and their public comments were widely seen by even their allies as harmful (Hertzke, 1988).

The strength of the Christian Right in the 1980s was clearly grassroots, outsider mobilization. The Moral Majority frequently mobilized its members to bombard Congress with mail and phone calls. Often these appeals were misleading. While Congress was considering legislation to reverse Supreme Court decisions on civil rights, Falwell mobilized his followers by telling them that the bill would classify sin as a handicap and then force churches to hire as youth counselors "active homosexuals, transvestites, alcoholics, and drug addicts, among others" (O'Hara, 1989, p. 13).

In the 1990s the Christian Coalition, Focus on the Family, and Family Research Council proved far more sophisticated than the Moral Majority in their lobbying efforts. All three organizations, along with CWA, were skilled not only at grassroots pressure but also at the subtle art of the inside strategy—contacting and persuading congressional members. The Christian Coalition employed an ecumenical staff of professional lobbyists who established a reputation for providing accurate information, playing by the rules, and building effective if sometimes unusual coalitions. The FRC specialized in providing detailed policy analyses to staffers and sympathetic members.

Concerned Women for America built a special network for more sophisticated grassroots lobbying. Its "535 Program" focused on developing a core group of women to track legislation and the voting intentions of members of Congress. The women would communicate this information to women in each congressional district, and in turn they would contact the member's home office, organize prayer chains, and otherwise focus pressure on the member if needed (Hertzke, 1988; Moen, 1992).

When the new Republican majority took office in the House and Senate in January 1995, Christian Right lobbyists suddenly had access to the majority party. Active evangelical Christians constituted a significant portion of the new GOP majority (Guth and Kellstedt, 1999). Moreover, because many observers credited the Christian Right with increasing turnout among white evangelicals and thereby helping elect Republicans in close contests, Republican leaders openly promised a "payback time" to vote on items from the Christian Right agenda. House Speaker Newt Gingrich promised a vote on a school prayer amendment by July 1995, but he did not deliver on that promise. The first months of the legislative session were taken up with passing the Contract with America and dealing with budget issues, and the Christian Coalition played an active role in helping promote the Contract, waiting patiently until after the House had dealt with these matters before pursuing congressional action on its agenda.

By spring 2000, however, the GOP Congress had given the Christian Right few policy victories. The Defense of Marriage Act (DOMA) was an important symbolic victory for the movement, allowing states to refuse to honor marriages between two gay men or two lesbians performed in another state. At that time, no state allowed gays or lesbians to marry, but by 2004 officials in Massachusetts were performing same-sex marriages, and thus DOMA took on more importance.

With the election of George W. Bush, many activists were hopeful that Congress would move more quickly on key Christian Right agenda items. But by 2005, the Congress had been less accommodating to the Christian Right than its leaders had hoped. Congress had passed legislation that barred partial birth abortion and that made the murder of a pregnant woman during a federal crime a double homicide, but overall the GOP Congress, like the Bush administration, had focused on tax cuts and economic deregulation.

The furor over the Terry Schiavo case in 2005 made clear both the symbolic power of the Christian Right with Congress and its substantive weaknesses. Schiavo suffered a heart attack in 1990 and was diagnosed as being in a persistent vegetative state, a diagnosis later confirmed by autopsy. A legal battle ensued between her husband, who argued that Schiavo had requested that she not be kept alive under such circumstances, and her parents, who maintained that Schiavo had cognitive abilities and would respond to therapy. With legal options exhausted, the parents appealed to Christian conservative leaders and to the federal government.

In March 2005, the Republican-dominated Congress passed a personal bill for Schiavo's parents, allowing them to appeal her case to federal courts. Bush interrupted a vacation to fly back to Washington to sign the bill. But although this was a significant symbolic victory for the Christian Right, its substance was limited by two important points. First, the bill applied only to Schiavo and did not apply to any other individual in similar circumstances. Second, the bill did not change the underlying law, and thus Schiavo's parents' appeal was ultimately refused by federal courts.

Despite the intense mobilization behind an amendment to bar same-sex marriage, the Republican-majority Senate did not vote on it in 2004 or 2005. In 2005, the Republican-controlled House of Representatives passed a bill that would further expand federal funding for embryonic stem cell research, although Bush promised a veto.

During the 2004 campaign, Republican strategists and Christian Right activists endorsed a Houses of Worship Free Speech Restoration Act. The legislation would essentially allow pastors to endorse political candidates from the pulpit without jeopardizing their church's tax exempt status. Current IRS law prohibits tax-exempt organizations from making political endorsements. Even with the FRC, Focus on the Family, CWA, and the Christian Coalition throwing their weight behind it, the House bill received only 178 votes in favor in the 107th Congress.

By late 2005, many Christian Right leaders were disappointed in the progress of their agenda in the Republican-dominated Congress. Some complained that the Congress had increased spending on projects commonly thought of as "pork" and had created large deficits, which they saw as contrary to biblical teaching. Others saw a majority that was focused more on providing the policies that would lead to large contributions from businesses and wealthy individuals—primarily tax cuts and the relaxation of regulations on business—than on social legislation. With former House Majority Leader Tom DeLay under indictment for violating Texas campaign finance regulations and Senate Majority Leader Bill Frist under investigation for insider stock trading, the hope that electing Republicans would create a new climate of moral governance was rapidly fading.

The Courts

Although Christian Right activists have focused much of their attention on electing presidents and members of Congress, U.S. Supreme Court rulings are the most frequent focus of their anger. The 1962 decision *Engel v. Vitale,* in which the Court ruled that daily classroom prayer violated the establishment clause of the First Amendment, and the 1973 *Roe v. Wade* ruling that overturned state laws banning abortion convinced Christian conservatives that they needed to work to change the composition of the U.S. Supreme Court. President Reagan had the opportunity to appoint several new justices, and yet the Court still upheld the basic abortion right in *Webster v. Reproductive Health Services* in 1989. And despite the fact that President George H. W. Bush was able to appoint still more new justices, the Court struck down a "voluntary" prayer at a high school graduation ceremony in *Lee v. Weisman* in 1992. In a further blow to the Christian Right, the Supreme Court ruled in the 2003 case *Lawrence v. Texas* that state laws barring sodomy between consenting adults in the privacy of their homes are unconstitutional.

Many Christian conservatives perceived the Rehnquist Court as a very liberal institution. Although seven of the nine justices were appointed by Republicans, Christian Right leaders hoped and even openly prayed for vacancies on the Court, where moderate justices could be replaced by strongly conservative ones. Pat Robertson attracted controversy in noting that several justices were quite old and some in ill health, and then announcing Operation Supreme Court Freedom, in which he and others would pray for God to create vacancies on the Court that Bush could fill.

President Bush's appointments to the federal trial and appeals courts generally pleased Christian Right leaders. All of his appointees were strong economic conservatives, but many were also strong social conservatives who were pro-life and opposed expanding gay and lesbian rights. The movement was pleased with nominees such as Janice Rogers Brown, Priscilla Owen, and William Pryor. Although Christian Right leaders framed their support for these candidates on their judicial restraint, in fact all social movements (including the Christian Right) are more concerned with results than judicial philosophy. Priscilla Owen, for example, consistently rejected petitions from minors who sought judicial bypass of the state's parental consent law, inviting some sharp rebukes from Alberto Gonzales, a conservative judge who later served as Bush's attorney general. Gonzales characterized her decisions as "activist." This made Owen very popular with the movement, who saw her decisions not as judicial activism but as principled pro-life activism.

In the summer and fall of 2005, two Supreme Court vacancies were created when centrist justice Sandra Day O'Connor resigned and Chief Justice William Rehnquist died. Bush chose John Roberts, an appeals court judge from the Washington, DC, Circuit, to replace Rehnquist as chief justice. Roberts won strong support from Christian conservatives, although some worried about his public statements that *Roe v. Wade* was settled precedent. NARAL and other groups opposed him, but he won confirmation by a wide margin.

Bush selected White House counsel Harriet Miers to replace O'Connor, but Miers's nomination met opposition from conservatives. Some focused on her lack of experience in dealing with constitutional matters, but Christian conservatives worried that she was not a committed opponent of liberal precedents like *Roe v. Wade*. James Dobson of Focus on the Family endorsed Miers after reassurances from White House political director Karl Rove; other Christian Right groups withheld judgment. After criticizing liberals for questioning Roberts on his faith and judicial views, Bush sought to reassure conservatives that Miers attended a pro-life evangelical church. But remarks by Miers that implied a pro-choice position in the 1980s surfaced, and almost immediately some Christian Right groups called publicly or privately for her withdrawal. She withdrew in late October 2005.

Bush next nominated Court of Appeals judge Samuel Alito. Alito's nomination was greeted with enthusiasm by Christian conservatives because of his dissent in favor of spousal notification in abortion. As we completed this book, early writings by Alito appeared to indicate that he was strongly opposed to *Roe v. Wade*, although he sought to distance himself from these opinions. Alito's confirmation hearings were delayed until early 2006. If Alito is confirmed, it would mean that a majority of justices are Catholics for the first time in American history. Meanwhile, six of seven of the continuing Supreme Court justices are over 65 years of age, and the most liberal judge was 85 years old in 2005. This suggests that Bush may have more vacancies to fill.

Christian Right groups have also formed special organizations designed to change public policy through litigation. Pat Robertson formed the **American Center for Law and Justice** (ACLJ) in 1990, and he promotes the group as the Christian counterpart to the American Civil Liberties Union. The

ACLJ is especially active in cases involving church-state issues. The American Family Association Law Center, founded by the Reverend Donald Wildmon in 1990, has been active in cases defending state and local obscenity and sodomy laws and Operation Rescue protesters. The Concerned Women for America also has a small unit that litigates. Michael Farris heads the Home School Legal Defense Association, where he devotes much of his time to defending the rights of homeschooling parents nationwide.

The **Alliance Defense Fund** (ADF) is one of the largest Christian Right organizations committed to working through the courts to ensure religious freedom and defend the traditional family structure. ADF was founded in 1993 by a number of Christian leaders, including James Dobson and D. James Kennedy, and has grown exponentially since then. In 2003, the organization raised $18 million—up from $4.7 million in 1997 (Peterson and Matthews, 2005). ADF has a legal team of 23 full-time attorneys and 750 lawyers working on a pro bono basis, putting in roughly 450 hours a year. Many of their cases involve the issue of gay rights. In 2000, ADF supported the Boy Scouts of America in a U.S. Supreme Court case about whether state anti-discrimination laws applied to this private organization. The Court upheld the right of the Boy Scouts to bar boys who are gay or atheist from joining the Scouts and to bar gay and atheist men from serving as leaders. ADF also worked to invalidate marriage licenses issued to same-sex couples who were married in San Francisco in 2003. In the 2004 elections, ADF promised legal support to pastors who showed videos produced by Let Freedom Ring that highlighted Bush's personal faith, or who gave sermons about the importance of the election and how congregants could vote their values in the 2004 election.

In recent years the number of Christian Right legal groups has grown, and all groups have become more active (Brown, 2004; Hacker, 2005). These groups have frequently engaged in litigation against public school boards. Some cases involve students who were allegedly prevented by school officials from reading their Bibles or praying; others involve public school curricula.[22] Attorneys for these groups frequently argue that their clients have endured discrimination because of their religious beliefs or that their right to free exercise of religion has been denied. In many cases the threat of a lawsuit is sufficient to change school board policy; in others the threat of suit by the Christian Right balances that by the ACLU, and the counterthreats enable board members to vote their own religious preferences.

There are many other conservative legal groups, such as the Rutherford Institute, which take cases of interest to the Christian Right. The Rutherford

Institute provided free legal counsel for Paula Jones in her sexual harassment lawsuit against President Clinton. Although a federal judge dismissed the Jones lawsuit, material from the discovery portion of the case eventually led to the Lewinsky scandal and impeachment. The Rutherford Institute does not as a rule provide free counsel for sexual harassment cases, and most observers believe that the group did so in this case because of the potential political damage to President Clinton.

State and Local Governments

Today Christian Right groups focus much of their attention and energy on state and local governments because many of the issues of greatest concern to the Christian Right are decided at those levels. State and local governments decide what kinds of regulations to impose on Christian schools, what kinds of books to assign in public schools, and whether and how to teach about human sexuality. State governments can impose some kinds of restrictions on abortion access, including banning abortions in public hospitals, insisting that teenage girls obtain parental consent before having an abortion, and requiring doctors to inform women considering abortion about the development of the fetus and about the alternative of adoption. State governments define marriage and consider any other legal protections that might be offered to same-sex or unmarried heterosexual couples.

In many states, Christian Right organizations employ lobbyists and mobilize grassroots pressure on governors, state attorneys general, members of the state legislature, and on local government officials. Frequently, Christian Right groups try to create ties to governors. In Virginia, for example, the Christian Right had strong ties with Governor George Allen (now a U.S. senator from Virginia). Allen's top advisors in education (including the state secretary of education) were Christian conservatives who opposed sex education and favored prayer in schools. His secretary of health and human services was Kay Coles James, a prominent pro-life activist who had worked in the first Bush administration and had blocked the release an AIDS pamphlet aimed at teens because it advocated the use of condoms. The head of Virginia's Family Foundation became the director of the governor's personnel and training operation (Rozell and Wilcox, 1996).

The issues vary from year to year and from state to state (Cleary and Hertzke, 2006). In 2003, for example, Christian Right organizations continued their work in the Virginia legislature, supporting a series of bills related to abortion. They helped to defeat a bill that would have eased the restrictions on access to emergency contraception and succeeded in getting a bill passed that defined the murder of a pregnant woman as a double homicide. The movement also fought successfully for a bill that reinstated Virginia's law banning sodomy (although that law cannot be enforced) and helped to overturn a county ordinance barring discrimination against gays and lesbians. It also successfully backed a broadly worded measure that limited the ability of same-sex couples to enter into any contract that provided any of the benefits of marriage; the measure appears to be so broad that it might well prohibit other kinds of contracts as well. Activists also helped to pass another bill allowing homeschooling parents to choose their own curriculum. They failed, however, in several attempts to restrict or condition abortion, including a measure requiring that a fetus be anesthetized before abortion.

In a striking testament to the limits to the Christian Right agenda, the movement did *not* mobilize when the legislature accidentally reinstated an old law that required Virginia businesses to allow all workers one day off on every weekend for religious observance and family time. The business community quickly mobilized to demand a special session to repeal this law, and the Christian Right did not oppose them (Larson, Madland, and Wilcox, 2006).

To explore the list of policy victories claimed by the Family Foundation of Virginia, see box 3.3.

Christian Right groups also focus on county and city governments. From county government the Christian Right often seeks policies relating to schools and libraries. In many counties, Christian Right groups push for "adults only" sections in public libraries that would include all books they find objectionable; in others, they seek to remove objectionable books and magazines or force library boards to buy materials published by Christian Right organizations. In many counties groups are pushing to install pornography filters on public computer terminals at libraries and public schools. In some counties, Christian Right activists have sought to end after-school child care in the public schools, arguing that such programs make it easier for women to work outside the home.

Conclusion

The Christian Right is composed of a set of national, state, and local social movement organizations that compete and cooperate in political action. These groups vary in their issue agendas and tactics and attract different sets

BOX 3.3 Victories Claimed by Virginia's Family Foundation

The following are examples of legislative victories shared by Virginia's families.

- Passed "Connor's Law," protecting unborn children from acts of violence

  Created a separate legal penalty for anyone who injures or kills an unborn child during an attack on the mother. Legislation gained its name from the murders of Laci Peterson and her unborn child, Connor.

- Banned counterfeit forms of marriage such as "civil unions"

  This law voids any civil union, partnership, contract or other arrangement between persons of the same sex purporting to bestow the privileges or obligations of marriage. Such an arrangement entered into in another state or jurisdiction is void in Virginia and any contractual rights created thereby unenforceable.

- Required parental consent for minor girls seeking abortion

  Requires that one parent give consent for a minor child to have an abortion.

- Increased criminal penalties for possession of child pornography

  Child exploitation is one of the fastest growing crimes in the nation. This law increased the penalty for possession of child pornography from a misdemeanor to a felony in Virginia.

- Limited distribution of chemical abortion pills

  Blocked yearly legislation that would encourage the distribution of the so-called "morning after pill." Pro-abortion groups seek to redefine what an abortion is so that these pills are not regulated as an abortifacient.

- Required posting of national motto "In God We Trust" in public buildings and schools

- Required Pledge of Allegiance in public schools

- Required "Moment of Silence" in public schools

  This law requires that every public school division conduct a moment of silence so each child can meditate or reflect.

- Required Internet filters be placed on public school computers

  Protects school children in Virginia from accidentally or intentionally accessing obscene material while exploring the Internet with a public school computer by requiring that schools install Internet filtering technology.

- Required Informed Consent

  Requires abortion clinics in Virginia to provide information about the gestational development of an unborn child, full disclosure of the abortion procedure and information on alternatives such as adoption at least 24 hours prior to the abortion.

(continues)

(Box 3.3 continued)

- Prohibited same sex marriage

    Considered a "Defense of Marriage Act" (DOMA), this law bans same-sex marriage in Virginia and declares that Virginia will not recognize same-sex marriages performed or recognized in other states.

- Allowed for local option for family life education

    State Board of Education granted

- Outlawed riverboat gambling
- Established education accountability in public schools

    Created Standards of Learning for public schools to improve student outcomes and increase school accountability.

- Reformed welfare

Source: http://www.familyfoundation.org/victories.html, accessed September 10, 2005.

---

of activists. Overall, the movement employs a wide variety of tactics to influence elections and public policy.

The diversity and growing power of the Christian Right are a source of great solace to its supporters but of great concern to those who oppose its agenda. It is precisely because of the growing effectiveness of the Christian Right that the movement generates such controversy. Different conceptions of the Christian Right are explored in the next chapter.

4

....

Assessing the Christian Right

If religious conservatives took their proper,
proportionate place as leaders in the political and
cultural life of the country, we would work to create the
kind of society in which presumably all of us would like
to live: safe neighborhoods, strong families, schools
that work, a smaller government, lower taxes. Civil
rights protections would be afforded to all Americans.

—Ralph Reed, *Politically Incorrect*

At its core, the Christian Coalition seeks an agenda
that threatens liberty. Behind their mild rhetoric lurks
an undeniable truth: Coalition leaders want to create a
Christianized government that criminalizes abortion,
denies gays and lesbians basic rights of citizenship,
and dictates when and how public school children
should pray.

—People for the American Way,
The Two Faces of the Christian Coalition

．．

T HE CHRISTIAN RIGHT IS A DEEPLY controversial element of American politics. Its activists depict a movement that seeks to defend the rights of conservative Christians to freely exercise their religious beliefs, whereas its opponents describe a movement of moral censors who would impose their interpretation of biblical law on all Americans. At their most extreme, these divergent views of the Christian Right paint a picture of stalwart Christians battling satanic forces for the soul of America or of neo-Nazi storm troopers rounding up homosexuals or roasting marshmallows in the flames from the books they have culled from the public library.

Christian Right direct-mail publications sometimes allege that Christians are in imminent danger of being forbidden to carry Bibles to work, to wear a religious lapel pin or necklace, or even to worship on Sunday, that liberals want to take away their Bibles. Christian Right groups have warned pastors that their churches are in danger of losing their tax exempt status and urged them to support a House of Worship Freedom of Speech Restoration Act to protect their freedom of speech. Despite this extreme rhetoric, there is no real controversy about the right of religious conservatives to worship or to mobilize their beliefs into political action. No one is proposing that preachers be forbidden from talking about politics or that Christians be prosecuted and fed to the hungry lions at the National Zoo.

Instead, at the heart of this dispute is whether Christian Right involvement in politics is good or bad for America. The question posed by opponents of the movement is whether the Christian Right is a dangerous force that might eventually undermine constitutional freedoms in an effort to impose its interpretation of biblical law on the United States. The question posed by Christian conservatives is whether government and society are so biased against religious faith that Christians must band together to protect their way of life.

This chapter examines the dilemma of the Christian Right. The first section explores the question of whether support for the Christian Right is rational. Many scholars from the 1950s argued that supporters exhibited pathological personalities or were deeply alienated from society, but more recent scholarship has rejected that view. The next section poses two important questions: Does the Christian Right promote democratic participation, and does it promote democratic values?

The final section considers the policies the Christian Right seeks to implement, using proclamations by movement elites, data from surveys, and in-depth interviews with movement activists. The section includes a discussion of the disagreements among Christian Right leaders and activists on precisely what policies to pursue in each area, and an analysis of what the public thinks of those policy proposals.

Is the Christian Right "Rational"?

When sociologists who studied the Right in the 1950s and 1960s wrote about the movement, they used terms such as "paranoid style," "authoritarian," and "dogmatic." These scholars were generally not focusing on the Christian Right of that period but rather on the more secular organizations, such as the John Birch Society, but they undoubtedly would have used the same terms to describe the Christian Anti-Communism Crusade.[1] Scholars argued that support for the Right in the 1950s came largely from individuals who had personality disorders, who had anxiety about their social status, or who were alienated from society.[2]

It is not surprising that scholars of the 1950s feared the Right and sought to portray its supporters as irrational. The world was still coming to terms with the frightening legacy of the German Nazi Party and seeking to explain how Germany—with its vibrant cultural life and basic democratic institutions—was within a decade transformed from the Weimar Republic into a nation that committed atrocities against Jews, homosexuals, and gypsies. The Nazis began by imposing seemingly minor restrictions on Jews and gradually escalated into genocide. Many feared that a similar dynamic might be possible in the United States.

Moreover, the Right of the 1950s seemed irrational, and its leaders embraced strange conspiracy theories. Great prominence was given, for example, to the role of the Illuminati, a seventeenth-century European Masonic group, in guiding a worldwide conspiracy of Jews, communists, and world bankers. The unlikely collaboration of world bankers and communists is perhaps symptomatic of the bizarre networks envisioned by the 1950s Right.[3]

The explanations for support for the Right offered by sociologists and political scientists of the 1950s focused on social and psychological patholo- gies. Two of these explanations are considered here with respect to the con- temporary Christian Right: that support for the movement comes from individuals who have troubled personalities or from those who are alienated from society. If true, these explanations would have some important impli- cations for any assessment of dangers posed by the Christian Right.

Personality Explanations

A number of social psychologists in the 1960s wrote that support for the Right (and sometimes for the extreme Left) came from individuals with dis- tinctive, distorted personalities. The most prominent charge was that sup- porters of the Right had authoritarian personalities. In a massive tome published in 1950, several psychologists described the authoritarian person- ality as involving displacement of self-hatred into aggression toward out- groups and support for right-wing figures (Adorno et al., 1950). The logic of the argument implies that individuals with authoritarian personalities should have hatred for certain out-groups such as gays, lesbians, and femi- nists and reverence for strong right-wing leaders such as Pat Robertson or radio commentator Rush Limbaugh. Subsequent writers have attributed other personality disorders, especially dogmatism and the inability to toler- ate ambiguity, to supporters of the Christian Right.

Why would the Christian Right appeal to such individuals? Those who argue for a personality link suggest that the Christian Right encourages ha- tred for feminists, gays and lesbians, and other liberal groups, and provides a vehicle for its supporters to enhance their self-worth by fighting against these insidious forces. Indeed, surveys do show that many Christian Right activists view these groups as almost satanic and see their crusade as rescu- ing America from evil (Wilcox, Jelen, and Linzey, 1991).

In addition, the Christian Right offers a straightforward portrait of a struggle between the forces of darkness and light, symbolism that has strong appeal to those who cannot tolerate ambiguity. Such accounts resonate with biblical allusions to the struggle between God and Satan and invite their ad- herents to conceive of conspiracies to explain the apparent collusion among forces opposed to the movement. Finally, authoritative pronouncements from ministers who interpret the inerrant word of God enable the Christian

Right to offer strong leaders who are especially appealing to those with authoritarian personalities.

If personality explanations for support of the Christian Right are true, then the movement might be truly dangerous, full of maladjusted activists ready to follow whatever suggestions they receive from their leaders. Descriptions of recent assassins of abortion providers suggest that there are some individuals at the fringe of the Christian Right and pro-life movements who may exhibit disturbed personalities of a dangerous sort. Other, less frightening disordered personalities doubtless exist. When one of us asked a Moral Majority county chair why he was involved in the movement, he responded in a serious voice that he was worried about "rampant bestiality" in the high schools. His account revealed more about his personality than about the behavior of the adolescent boys in his rural farming community.

All movements, however, attract on their fringe individuals with disordered lives. Anyone who has interviewed activists in almost any political movement can point to a few whose personalities fit these theories—and this holds true for liberal groups such as environmentalists and feminists as well. The real question is whether the Christian Right has any special appeal to such personalities and whether they constitute a sizable number of movement adherents.

One survey of Moral Majority activists in Indiana showed that a sizable minority exhibited signs of authoritarianism and feelings of inadequacy (see table 4.1). A majority felt that strong leaders would be preferable to laws and talk, and more than a third found it inexcusable to disobey an order. Nearly a third felt guilty when they questioned authority, and another 55 percent felt no guilt because they reported they never questioned authority. There was evidence of feelings of personal inadequacy as well. The data show that those individuals with the strongest evidence of authoritarianism were the least active in the Moral Majority, which suggests that the organization succeeded in keeping maladjusted members at the margins (Wilcox, Jelen, and Linzey, 1995).

These results are difficult to interpret without a comparison with the public or with activists in other organizations, and it is likely that some Americans who oppose the Christian Right would give similar responses. Yet the data do suggest that the Christian Right attracts some individuals whose personalities resemble those posited by the social theorists of the 1950s.

Available evidence also suggests that whatever the Christian Right position on groups regarded as sinful or as political enemies, the attitudes are

TABLE 4.1   Personality Traits Among Indiana Moral Majority Activists
(percent of respondents, N = 162)

Authoritarianism

Strong leaders are better than laws and talk	58
Disobeying orders is inexcusable	38
Obedience is the most important virtue in children	75
I feel guilty when I question authority	27
I sometimes question authority	78

Feelings of inadequacy

I do not have much to be proud of	12
I take a positive attitude toward myself	39
I wish I respected myself more	21

Alienation

I am alienated or on the fringe of society	40
I never feel useless since joining the Moral Majority	39
Membership in the Moral Majority makes me feel worthy	43

SOURCE: *Survey data provided by Sharon Georgianna Linzey.*

not generally anti-Semitic or racist. Supporters of the Christian Right are not cooler toward Jews or blacks than other white Americans, and Christian Right activists do not express more negative views toward these groups than other GOP activists.[4]

A number of studies suggest that Christian Right activists show no evidence of having disproportionate personality problems (Wilcox, 1992), but none of the data is definitive. In our judgment, based on in-depth interviews with activists in the Christian Right, environmentalist, feminist, and other movements, most Christian Right activists are as well adjusted as most activists in other movements. At minimum, it is fair to say that a majority of Christian Right activists show no evidence of personality disorders.

What is striking about Christian Right activists, however, is the extent of their fear of their political opponents. The rhetoric of many Christian Right leaders, especially in fund-raising appeals, portrays a coalition of liberals, feminists, gays and lesbians, and others bent on destroying America and on limiting religious freedom for Christians. Although the feminist, environmental, and civil rights activists we have interviewed dislike their political opponents, Christian Right activists are far more likely to truly despise their opponents (Jelen, 1991a). The vehemence of some movement members can be quite strong, especially in their hatred of gays and lesbians. In Fairfax County, Virginia, liberals who testified at library board meetings in favor of allowing distribution of a gay newspaper reported being pushed, shoved, and spat at, and some received death threats (Rozell and Wilcox, 1997). Coupled with the repeated death threats against abortion providers in the United States and the killings of several doctors, it is clear that the fringe of the Christian Right and related organizations includes some dangerous citizens.

Of course, pushing, shoving, and even death threats are not unique to the Christian Right. Indeed, Christian Right activists in Maine organizing a referendum against gay rights reported receiving death threats. There is no evidence that the Christian Right is especially prone to violence; rather, political groups of all types that engage in direct action over emotional issues attract some activists who cross the line of acceptable behavior. And violence is more likely if an activist fears or despises those on the other side—emotions more common among Christian Right activists.

Alienation

A second, related explanation offered by sociologists for support for the Christian Right has been that mass society has produced a substantial number of isolated individuals who lack attachments to extended families or to social institutions or groups. These rootless individuals are thought to be attracted to organizations that have strong leaders and provide the opportunity to interact and form ties with like-minded citizens. Conover and Gray (1981) argued that such individuals are easily mobilized by political groups: "Without such organizational involvement in their lives, people are thought to grow restless and alienated. . . . Such individuals are 'easy prey' for right-wing movements" (p. 4). If this explanation is true, then the Christian Right may have attracted a core of activists who have few community ties to constrain their behavior.

In fact, most Christian Right activists are strongly attached to social and political groups. Nearly all are deeply involved in their local churches, which can provide an all-encompassing social network replete with many close friends.[5] Most are members of other conservative political groups, and many are members of professional and civic groups as well (Rozell and Wilcox, 1996).

Among small Republican donors in 2000, for example, the average member of a Christian Right group was a member of 3.3 different *types* of political groups in addition to Christian Right groups. Among donors of larger amounts, Christian Right group members were also members of 6 other types of groups.[6]

Data from a number of surveys show that core evangelicals and Christian Right supporters are involved in more organizations than other Americans. Yet the alienation explanation does seem to fit descriptions of extremists who take extralegal actions, including killing abortion providers. These assassins are generally marginal members of groups and have frequently been expelled from their churches and from Christian Right and pro-life groups.

Group Membership as a Rational Choice

In contrast, political scientists beginning in the 1980s have generally dismissed these psychological explanations of Christian Right activism and focused instead on explanations that center on religion and politics. Most see the Christian Right as similar to all social movements, attracting primarily those individuals who share a common religious and political worldview (Wilcox, 1992). In this sense, joining the Christian Right is as rational for Christian conservatives as is joining the Sierra Club or National Organization for Women for environmentalists or feminists.[7]

Those who support the Family Research Council or similar groups do so because these groups articulate their religious, moral, and political sensibilities. Most activists in the Christian Right are orthodox Christians with very conservative political views. The Christian Right appeals to them because it connects their religious beliefs with their political positions.

Nevertheless, evidence that support for the Christian Right is rational does not mean that the movement is not dangerous or is good for America. Well-adjusted, rational citizens can limit the civil liberties of others and even destroy democracies. To know whether the Christian Right is good or bad for America, we must consider its support for civil liberties and its policy agenda.

The Christian Right and American Democracy

Critics of the Christian Right charge that it is a dangerous movement that would undermine basic civil liberties, strip rights from unpopular cultural minorities, and possibly impose a right-wing theocracy on America.[8] Of course, what appears dangerous to one American may seem

perfectly reasonable to another. Direct-mail appeals by groups that oppose the Christian Right routinely begin with a warning in bold red letters that the Bill of Rights is in danger, and the fine print reveals that this
danger is from a proposal to allow a moment of silence at the beginning
of public school sessions in which children could pray if they wished, or
meditate on a book or video game they had seen if they preferred. To
some, such a moment of silence is seen as the dangerous first step down a
slippery slope toward a theocracy; to others it is a basic element of religious freedom. To a pro-choice activist, the Christian Right is dangerous
because it seeks to limit sharply women's reproductive freedom; to someone opposed to abortion, the abortion providers are a danger to "unborn
children."

Supporters of the movement claim that the Christian Right enhances democracy by mobilizing previously apolitical Christians into active citizenship. Opponents argue that the Christian Right is dangerous because its
activists do not share basic democratic norms and are not supportive of basic civil liberties. There is some truth in both claims.

Democratic Participation

Many theorists hold that democracy works best when all groups participate
fully in a range of political activity. The American political system is frequently described as pluralistic—a system in which multiple, competing
social and political groups bargain together within the framework of government to set public policy. When a group is disenfranchised for whatever
reason, the voices of its members are not heard by the political system, and
the policies produced by that system will not reflect their preferences. This
is especially troubling if the members of a group hold distinctive policy positions, for if they do not participate in politics, their views do not even
help shape the debate, much less public policy.

Evangelicals, pentecostals, and especially fundamentalists have traditionally been less likely to participate in politics than other citizens. In the 1972
National Election Study, white evangelical voters turned out at a rate nearly
17 percent lower than other whites, and in 1984 the gap was still 13 percent.
One reason white evangelicals vote less often than other whites is that they
have lower levels of education and income, but that is only part of the explanation. Even among those with the same level of education—for example,

evangelicals and nonevangelicals who have college degrees—evangelicals vote less often than other whites.

Evangelicals have traditionally been less active in politics because their religious doctrine holds that Christians should not compromise with the secular world but should remain apart from it. This is especially true for fundamentalists, whose separatism is more extreme than that of other evangelicals. The fundamentalist organizations of the 1980s faced a substantial barrier in mobilizing their constituency, precisely because many activists believed that politics was a dirty business that would inevitably corrupt those who engaged in it. One survey of members of the Indiana Moral Majority revealed that fully one-quarter had been taught to shun politics, and more than two-thirds believed that "this world belonged to Satan." Although these activists were involved in a political organization, 42 percent were bothered by that involvement in politics, and an additional 15 percent had been bothered at one time. Fully 96 percent believed that Christ could come again at any time, an idea that made voting in the next election seem considerably less urgent.

Yet the National Election Studies show that evangelical turnout rate began to approach that of other whites in the years when the Christian Coalition and other groups mounted massive voter registration and turnout drives. In 1992, when the Christian Coalition claimed to distribute 40 million voter guides in evangelical churches, white evangelicals voted only 5 percent less often than other whites. In 2004, the gap was less than 2 percent.

Core white evangelicals have a distinctive set of policy preferences. Table 4.2 shows the key values and policy preferences of white evangelicals who attend evangelical churches, believe the Bible is the literal word of God, and say that religion has a great deal of influence on their lives as compared with all other white Americans.

There are two important points to be made from these data. First, the core constituency of the Christian Right holds positions that are quite different from those of other whites. More than 85 percent of core white evangelicals would restrict abortion access to no more than those "traumatic" circumstances of rape, incest, and danger to the life of the mother; this view is held by half as many other Americans. The differences are also quite large on gay rights and on the role of women. Second, even this relatively narrow core constituency does not exhibit overwhelming support for an extreme Christian Right agenda. Most of these core white evangelicals would allow

TABLE 4.2   Issue Distinctiveness of Core White Evangelicals

	Core White Evangelicals	Other White Americans
Don't tolerate those with different values	48%	18%
Newer lifestyles cause breakdown	91%	59%
Abortion		
Never allowed	47%	10%
Health, rape and incest only	39%	30%
Ban partial birth abortion	82%	61%
Rate gays at 0 degrees	35%	10%
No gay antidiscrimination laws	61%	21%
No gays in military	43%	17%
No gay adoption	83%	47%
No gay marriage	95%	56%
Working mom cannot establish as warm a relationship	41%	28%
Better if woman tends home and man achieves	62%	25%
Woman's place is in home	20%	6%

SOURCE: *2004 National Election Study. Core White evangelicals are members of evangelical churches, attend services regularly, and hold evangelical doctrine.*

abortions under some circumstances, would allow gays and lesbians to serve in the military, and favor equal rights for women.

If white evangelicals have traditionally been less likely to participate in politics, and if they hold a distinctive set of issue positions, then a social movement that mobilizes them into political action might produce a more balanced and fruitful policy debate. There is ample evidence that government is responsive to those groups that participate in politics, and thus as white evangelicals become more active in politics, it is likely that policy outcomes will change.[9]

The Christian Right and Democratic Values

The American political system was designed to work by negotiation and bargaining. Factions within each body of Congress must bargain with one another, the House must bargain with the Senate, and the Congress must bargain with the president. Many social and political groups help to foster democratic values by helping their citizens understand opposing points of view, by developing political skills, and by inculcating the norms of democratic civility. But not all do, and some believe that groups like the Christian Right that focus on social identity are the least likely to help their members develop civic virtues (Warren, 2000).

Many critics of the Christian Right charge that it is precisely those values of bargaining and compromise that are lacking among movement activists. Instead, they charge, the Christian Right voices a moral certitude that brooks no disagreement. When activists believe that their political activity is helping to work God's will on earth, then the other side of the political discussion is distinctly not doing God's will. Flyers distributed in Virginia before the 1992 presidential election warned churchgoers that "a vote for Bill Clinton is a vote against God." In 2004, the pastor of one North Carolina Baptist church endorsed George W. Bush from the pulpit and told Kerry supporters to "repent or resign" from the church. Nine members of the church resigned in protest.

One northern Virginia Republican related that when he appeared at the local caucus to help select Republican candidates for a state legislative race, a Christian Right activist asked him which candidate he was supporting. When he said he was supporting the moderate, the activist replied, "You must not be a Christian, then." The moderate Republican, who had taught Sunday school for many years in a Methodist church, was understandably appalled.

This certainty that the Christian Right is doing the will of God has obvious implications for how activists interpret the work of their political opponents. Most orthodox Christians believe that Satan is a real force in the world and is the cause of much of the social disintegration that they perceive as pandemic in America. In one survey of Moral Majority activists in Indiana, 99 percent strongly agreed that "the devil exists," nearly three in four agreed that "this world belongs to Satan," and fully 92 percent agreed that any attack on private schools "is an attack by Satan."

Among small Republican donors to the 2000 presidential candidates, for example, half of all Christian Right group members agreed with both of the following statements: the attack on Christian schools is an attack by Satan, and God works today through parties and candidates. If Satan is leading the opposition forces, and God is working through your party, it might seem less necessary to be civil or tolerant of your political opponents.[10]

These beliefs were not confined to the fundamentalists of the Moral Majority. One of the most frequent themes of Christian Right direct mail in the 1990s was that public schools teach "witchcraft." The label has been especially applied to guidance counselors who attempt to implement programs that improve student self-esteem or to help students clarify their values. Such rhetoric makes political compromise difficult, for orthodox churches preach the importance of resisting the wiles of the devil, and the Bible counsels "suffer not a witch to live."[11]

It is not surprising, then, that many Christian Right activists believe that the way to deal with opponents of their policy goals is to defeat them, not to compromise with them. At the Christian Coalition's Road to Victory conference in 2004, Jerry Falwell said, "Let's save America! Forget the hypocrites on the left." Falwell's rhetoric does not suggest a willingness on the part of Christian Right activists to engage in conversation with their political opponents.

More than three-fourths of respondents to the survey of the Indiana Moral Majority disagreed that compromise was necessary. Among members of Christian conservative groups who attended the Virginia Republican conventions of 1993 and 1994, only 43 percent agreed that compromise was sometimes necessary in politics, and nearly half agreed that on most matters of public policy, there was only one correct Christian view. Among political donors in 2000, however, there was more support for political compromise. Nevertheless, a majority of small Christian conservative donors agreed that on most matters there is a single correct view, and more than 80 percent agreed that their involvement in politics had led them to believe that some political views are wrong and dangerous.

Table 4.3 shows the attitudes of small Republican donors toward the 2000 presidential candidates. The data show that a large majority of Christian Right activists believe that the attack on Christian schools comes from Satan and that God works through elections and political parties. Only a small majority can understand why anyone would take a different position on abortion, and nearly half think there is a single correct view on most political issues. Finally, few believe that we should be tolerant of those who live by different moral standards.

The survey of Republican presidential donors asked whether members of various groups should be allowed to demonstrate *if there was no threat of violence,* or should be allowed to teach in public schools *assuming that they showed professional conduct.* Table 4.3 shows that substantial majorities of

TABLE 4.3 Democratic Values Among Small Republican Presidential Donors in 2000

	Member of Christian Conservative Group (N = 389)	*Not a Member (N = 1046)*
Attack on Christian Schools is by Satan	68%	50%
U.S. Christian nation, should make laws consistent with Bible	79%	44%
God works through parties and elections	66%	37%
Can understand why others disagree on abortion	56%	83%
Compromise is important part of American politics	61%	84%
On most issues, one correct view	49%	19%
Should be tolerant of others who live by different moral standards	29%	58%
Demonstrate		
Feminists	78%	87%
Environmentalists	84%	91%
Atheists	71%	82%
Homosexuals	57%	80%
Teach		
Feminists	46%	75%
Environmentalists	63%	83%
Atheists	44%	69%
Homosexuals	30%	64%

SOURCE: *Survey of Republican presidential donors of less than $200 in 2000 elections.*

Christian Right members and nonmembers would allow members of these groups to demonstrate in the community, although a more narrow majority of Christian Right donors would allow homosexuals to demonstrate.

When it comes to teaching in public schools, however, Christian Right activists show surprising levels of intolerance. More than half would not allow feminists or atheists to teach in public schools, more than two-thirds would bar homosexuals, and more than one-third would bar environmentalists. Further research is needed to probe the extent of this intolerance in education. In future studies, we will explore whether Christian conservatives would bar feminists from teaching in the early grades only, or in all public schools. We will examine whether they would bar them from teaching history only, or also algebra. And we will seek to learn how many would fire existing feminist teachers, or simply block hiring of new teachers.

There is additional evidence that the norms of political tolerance have not yet been well learned by Christian Right activists. One large study of religious activists found that Christian Right members most often identified liberal groups such as the National Organization for Women, the American Civil Liberties Union, and People for the American Way as the most dangerous to the country, and they were not especially willing to let members of such liberal groups take part in the political debate. Only 61 percent would allow them to speak in their communities, 57 percent would allow them to run for public office, 53 percent would allow them to demonstrate, and a disconcerting 14 percent would allow them to teach in public schools.[12] In contrast, although religious liberal activists frequently named the Christian Right as the greatest threat, they were far more willing to accord its adherents basic civil rights.

Research has shown that fundamentalists, pentecostals, and evangelicals—the target constituency of the Christian Right—are less tolerant of those with different political views than are other citizens: They are less willing to allow atheists, homosexuals, socialists, militarists, and racists to speak in communities, teach in colleges, or have their books available in public libraries (Wilcox and Jelen, 1990). This lack of tolerance is directly related to religious doctrine and especially to the belief in the inerrancy of the Bible. Although religious liberals and secularists may believe that all voices should be heard and tested in the marketplace of ideas, fundamentalists and other evangelicals believe that they already have the inerrant truth and that other ideas are simply wrong. They are therefore less likely to be willing to allow those ideas to be voiced because they might confuse or tempt vulnerable Christians. One study concluded, "It is not religion per se that generates intolerance, but fundamentalist theological perspectives. . . . Thus, the very motivation for [fundamentalist] political action reduces the civility of their work" (Green et al., 1994, p. 191).

The substantial support for denying cultural liberals and secularists the right to speak, to run candidates, to demonstrate, and especially to teach in schools is troubling. If Christian Right activists were to gain control of the American political system, it is possible that civil liberties for at least some Americans would be limited.[13] As we argue in the next chapter, it is unlikely that the Christian Right will gain that type of political power, but it is significant that many Christian Right activists do not accept the civil-liberty norms of other political activists.[14]

One important reason that Christian Right activists are more willing to deny civil liberties guarantees to liberal and secular groups is, as we noted above, that they perceive these groups to be a major threat to America. This is not surprising given the tendency of especially the fundamentalist wing of the movement to see political battles in eschatological terms. The theology of fundamentalists and pentecostals tends to view the inevitable unfolding of history as a conflict between the forces of God and those of evil.

This perception of threat is exacerbated by direct-mail publications from Christian Right groups, which darkly warn of threats and conspiracies by liberal groups. One newsletter from the Family Research Council, for example, charged that proposed rules by the federal Equal Employment Opportunity Commission (EEOC) would lead to prosecution of Christians if they wore religious jewelry, kept religious artwork on their desks, shared their faith with others during work breaks, or had a calendar with religious themes on their bulletin board.[15] One fund-raising letter that was mailed to one of us by Concerned Women for America warns on its cover: "The Holy Bible declared 'Hate Speech'? It could happen if Ted Kennedy and Hillary Clinton get their way." The cover features a cover of a Bible, with big letters that warn, CENSORED: CONTAINS HATE SPEECH.[16]

Of course, all direct mail warns of the dangers of not immediately sending twenty-five dollars, and liberal groups frequently warn of great dangers to America if the Christian Right were to "win." Yet survey data show that Christian Right activists perceive a greater threat from their political enemies than do religious liberals and that they are more likely to want to limit the civil liberties of groups that they see as threatening. Consequently, Christian Right activists are more likely than others to want to deny their opponents basic civil liberties.

These data provide some support for the alarmist view that the Christian Right might pose a danger to civil liberties. Two factors may mitigate that danger, however. First, Christian Right activists, like all Americans, have internalized abstract basic democratic values and a great respect for the Constitution. They therefore hold two conflicting values: support for freedom and equality, on the one hand, and a willingness to act to protect America from moral decay, on the other. This ambivalence is not uncommon—most Americans hold conflicting values on many issues. But if an actual law were proposed to limit free speech rights, at least some activists would doubtless pull back because of their commitment to the abstract ideal.

Second, the mere process of involvement in politics might instill in Christian Right activists a greater willingness to compromise, and help to humanize their political opponents. Many political theorists have argued that the very process of participating in politics effects personal transformations among citizens. By engaging in political discourse and action, Christian conservatives may enhance their political abilities, especially what some have called their "deliberative capacities" (Warren, 1993; 1996). John Stuart Mill argued that participation provided moral instruction because the citizen is forced to "weigh interests not his own; to be guided, in case of conflicting claims, by another rule than his private partialities; to apply, at every turn, principles and maxims which have for their reason of existence the general good" (Mill, 1862, p. 89). Samuel Barber suggested that by debating together, citizens discover their common humanity (Barber, 1984). They may also increase their overall support for the political system and their trust in government. One study of participation in urban areas concluded that increased participation led to greater efficacy, information, and tolerance for diverse viewpoints, especially among those with lower levels of education and income (Berry, Portney, and Thomson, 1993).

Pluralists also have argued that active involvement in interest group politics tempers political passion and increases the commitment to democratic norms, such as bargaining and compromise. An activist from the Family Research Council may work with a member of the National Rifle Association to support Oklahoma Senate candidate Tom Coburn, for example, and come to understand the latter's libertarian views on social issues. If that NRA member is also a member of the Sierra Club, repeated interactions may sensitize the Family Research Council activist to the logic of environmental activists.

If these theorists are correct, the mere process of political engagement may lead to greater tolerance among Christian Right activists and greater support for democratic norms. As Christian Right activists bargain with moderate Republicans in party meetings, they learn the value of compromise. As they spend time in face-to-face dialogue with moderates, they may discover they share a concern for their children, for their communities, and for their country. As Christian conservatives enter public office, they will be forced to bargain with Democrats and in the process learn that liberals may share many of their concerns, if not their policy positions.

In Virginia, there is some indirect evidence that this process may be under way. Within the Christian Right, century-old hostilities between fundamentalists and Catholics have weakened considerably as members of these two religious groups work together stuffing envelopes and planning strategies. One Catholic activist in Fairfax County found he was welcome in the home of fundamentalists who never would have spoken to him a decade before. Another Catholic activist spoke of the way women in the Farris campaign exchanged their views on religion and politics and of how each side came away with a renewed respect for the other's faith (Rozell and Wilcox, 1996).

Moreover, among Christian Right members in the Virginia GOP, those who have been active in politics the longest are the most willing to compromise and the least likely to believe there is one correct Christian view in politics (see figure 4.1). Those who have been newly mobilized are far more likely to reject the necessity of political compromise and to believe there is one correct Christian view than are those who have been active for ten years or more. Presumably, two separate processes are at work: Those who remain in politics learn the norms of the process, and those who cannot compromise leave the political arena. It seems likely that some Christian Right activists from the 1980s are no longer involved in Republican politics because they were unwilling to compromise. Debra Dodson noted that "the unconventional, anticompromise style may be ill suited to sustain involvement in heterogeneous organizations that must legitimize compromise" (Dodson, 1990, p. 138).

It is by no means certain, however, that continued political involvement will lead all Christian conservative activists to greater tolerance and pragmatism. It is instructive that between a quarter and a third of longtime activists in Virginia reject compromise and believe that there is only one correct Christian view on political issues. These two beliefs go hand in hand, for it is difficult for people to compromise when they are certain theirs is the one "Christian" position. One study of longtime Democratic activists concluded that although party activity may socialize many "unconventional activists" into traditional norms, others of these activists may remain involved in the party despite their failure to adopt the norms of intraparty bargaining and compromise (Dodson, 1990). This appears true for the Christian Right as well.

The Christian Right Agenda: Is It Radical or Mainstream?

The Christian Right, like all social movements, is characterized by decentralization and has competing leaders and social movement organizations, each

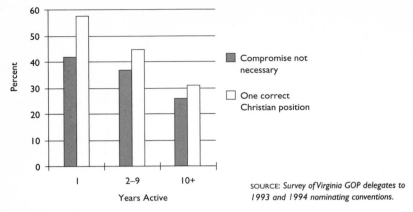

FIGURE 4.1   Norms of Compromise by Years of Activism Among Christian Right Republicans

with somewhat different complaints and policy solutions. Nevertheless, it is possible to speak of the agenda of the movement while mindful that all activists do not support all aspects of that agenda and that different sets of activists may have different policy preferences within each policy domain.

Abortion

Almost all Christian Right activists believe that abortion is murder, and they ardently seek to ban most or all abortions. One survey of contributors to Pat Robertson's presidential campaign found that over 91 percent agreed that abortion should be banned (Brown, Powell, and Wilcox, 1995); in another survey of members of Christian Right groups at the 1993 and 1994 Virginia Republican nominating conventions, 82 percent agreed that abortions should be prohibited (Rozell and Wilcox, 1996).

Most activists regard abortion as the slaughter of innocents and would therefore ban abortion altogether except in those few instances when the life of the mother is truly in danger. Many would not allow abortion even then and would argue that God should make the ultimate decision.[17] For a few committed activists, abortion is murder, and abortion providers are murderers who should be treated as such. One prominent fundamentalist Bible study guide, in its discussion of Exodus 21, reached the dubious conclusion that the Bible called for the death penalty for abortion providers. During his 2004 Senate campaign in Oklahoma, Tom Coburn (R) said it would be appropriate for abortion providers to receive the death penalty if abortion were made illegal.[18]

It is a measure of just how strong the pro-life consensus is in the Christian Right that some activists will voice their reservations on the issue only off the record. One activist in Ohio asked one of us to turn off the tape recorder and to promise never to reveal her responses to other Moral Majority members; she then said that she supported an exception for rape because she had been raped a few years earlier and had worried for weeks about a possible pregnancy. Another Virginia man with a wife in uncertain health privately endorsed an exception for maternal health, but he too repeatedly asked that we tell no one else in the movement of his views.

These activists may not be as isolated as they think, for a survey of Indiana Moral Majority members in 1982 found that nearly one in five approved of abortions in cases of rape, and more than half approved of abortions when the woman's life was in danger. A survey of the membership of Concerned Women of America conducted in the 1980s showed that 65 percent of the organization's members would allow abortions to save the life of the mother, and 21 percent would additionally allow abortions in cases of rape and incest (Blakeman, 1996). These exceptions provoke heated debates in Christian Right circles, and the movement does not want those debates to be held publicly. Perhaps for this reason, Christian Right speakers use consensual language such as "protecting the life of the unborn" rather than focusing on any specific exceptions that should be granted.

Although most Americans are uncomfortable with abortion, they are also uncomfortable with allowing the government to determine when women may obtain them. Surveys consistently show that only a minority of Americans favor banning all abortions, and they are far outnumbered by those who favor allowing abortions for all adult women (Cook, Jelen, and Wilcox, 1992).[19] The public is divided between those who would restrict abortion to the "traumatic" circumstances of danger to the life or health of the mother, rape, and fetal defect and those who would allow abortion in most circumstances. Even among regular church-attending Catholics and white evangelicals, there is not a majority who would ban all abortions.

The Republican Party embraced a pro-life plank in its 1980 presidential platform and has kept it in all elections since; in some elections this has hurt Republicans (Abramowitz, 1995), and in others it has possibly helped them, especially when Republicans have managed to frame elections around "partial birth" abortion instead of whether abortions should be generally legal.

There is a strong consensus in America in favor of some restrictions on abortion (for example, requiring teenage girls to notify a parent before having an abortion or requiring a woman to wait twenty-four hours before the procedure is performed), and strong support for banning some types of abortions, but there is strong opposition to banning all abortions. Candidates who support an outright ban on abortions lose if the election turns on that issue (Cook, Jelen, and Wilcox, 1994).

Some movement leaders appear to believe that it is better to elect candidates who will impose modest procedural restrictions on access to abortion than to fight elections over an abortion ban and lose. Movement activists are sharply divided over strategy on abortion—pragmatism or purity. Many Christian Right leaders promote the former in the belief that it is possible in the United States today to win passage of restrictions on abortion access but it is not possible to ban abortions. In a November 4, 1993, appearance on ABC's *Nightline*, Pat Robertson explained: "I would urge people, as a matter of private choice, not to choose abortion, because I think it is wrong. It's something else, though, in the political arena to go out on a quixotic crusade when you know you'll be beaten continuously. So I say let's do what is possible. What is possible is parental consent."[20]

Christian Right leaders have generally not protested George W. Bush's avoidance of the abortion issue during his two presidential elections. Bush has spoken vaguely of a "culture of life" and has denied that he would impose a pro-life litmus test for potential Supreme Court justices. President Bush did sign the Unborn Victims of Violence Act, which made any federal murder of a pregnant woman a double homicide, although the law has little reach since nearly all murders are prosecuted under state, not federal, law. He also signed a bill into law that bans partial birth abortion, although he has not asked Congress for additional legislation. In 2005, the Christian Right was praying that new justices on the Supreme Court would finally overturn *Roe v. Wade*, which prevents state governments from banning abortions. If this were to occur, then the regulation of abortion would return to the states, and abortion would be banned in some states, allowed under some circumstances in others, and allowed without restriction in others.

Education

Education issues rival abortion and gay marriage in their ability to mobilize Christian Right enthusiasts. In Ohio in the early 1990s, the group advocating for Christian schools was far larger than the Moral Majority. In Virginia, Michael Farris surprised many observers by mobilizing thousands of home-school advocates to attend the 1993 state Republican nominating convention and select him as nominee for lieutenant governor.

At the heart of the Christian Right criticism of American education is the charge that it promotes anti-Christian values and threatens the ability of conservative Christians to inculcate their values in their own children. The specifics of this critique are diverse. Many argue that the schools promote a religion called **secular humanism**, a doctrine that places humans at the center of the universe with no room for God. Others single out multicultural curricula, which promote tolerance for non-Christian lifestyles. Still others decry classes that invite students to clarify their values, for they fear that this activity may lead some to reject their orthodox Christian views. Many Christian Right activists focus their attention on school psychologists, who they believe "brainwash" students away from their Christian values. All bemoan the absence of prayer and religious content in the schools.

For some Christian Right activists, the public schools are a lost cause, and Christian parents must educate their children at home or in religious schools. Michael Farris, for example, exasperated after a court ruling against parents who sought to remove their children from parts of the public school curriculum, proclaimed, "It is time for every born-again Christian to get their children out of public schools."[21] The alternatives promoted by the Christian Right are religious schools, often associated with fundamentalist or Catholic churches, and homeschool education.[22]

Christian Right activists who promote homeschooling and Christian schools have their own agenda. The central objective is tax relief, for they resent paying taxes to support public schools and then paying to educate their children outside those schools. They also vehemently resist state regulation of the content of this education or regulation of the credentials of those who teach it. All enthusiastically support proposals for tuition tax credits and especially for educational vouchers, which would give each family a voucher to be used to purchase whatever kind of education the family desires.

Other activists keep their children in the public schools and fight battles to alter the curriculum. In 2005, Christian conservatives put significant money and effort behind a push to teach "intelligent design" as an acceptable scientific alternative to evolution in public school textbooks. Others seek to teach creationism instead of evolution, to teach only the virtues of abstinence in sex education classes, and to teach the Bible as literature. Others attempt to excuse their children from reading certain books or attending sex education classes. Most seek to include prayer in public schools, although some would have only a moment of silent prayer, others a voluntary spoken prayer, and a small minority a mandatory spoken prayer. All seek more local control of the school curriculum, since a small number of motivated activists can often greatly affect the outcome of educational battles at the local level. Most Christian Right organizations have opposed efforts to establish national educational standards, although George W. Bush's strong support for the No Child Left Behind Act have left some of them uncertain about federal standards. Many activists believe that these programs would establish a national curriculum that promotes secular humanism and values clarification.

Many Christian conservatives believe that education policy at the national level is set by a group of liberal counterculture activists whose values are outside of the American mainstream. On the campaign trail in 1999, presidential candidate Patrick Buchanan got great cheers from Christian Right activists by railing against policymakers from the Department of Education who wore "beads and sandals," a reference to the attire of the "hippies" of the 1960s. Because these liberals are seen as dominating the education establishment, activists believe that it is essential that Christian parents get some control of local school boards. As a result, the number of Christian Right candidacies for school board races is increasing rapidly (Deckman, 2004).

Among members of Christian Right groups who attended Virginia Republican nominating conventions in 1993 and 1994, 80 percent believed that the government should promote homeschooling and that the public schools should be required to teach creationism as an alternative to evolution. Nearly two-thirds of those who gave money to Pat Robertson's presidential campaign favored a mandatory prayer in public schools.

Some elements of the Christian Right agenda for education are quite popular with the public; others strike most Americans as extreme and perhaps dangerous. A clear majority of Americans favor a moment of silence during which children can pray if they wish, though most Americans oppose a chosen, spoken prayer in schools. A majority of Americans also favor teaching creationism along with evolution, but surveys have not asked respondents whether they would want both theories taught as being equally plausible. And a majority of Americans want high school sex education courses to encourage abstinence and discourage homosexual behavior. Nonetheless, a substantial majority of Americans favor teaching about birth control in classrooms and teaching ways to prevent the spread of AIDS and other sexually transmitted diseases. They also want their schools to encourage independent thinking on politics, economics, and moral issues.

Opposition to Gay and Lesbian Rights

For the past twenty-five years, Christian Right groups have made opposition to gay and lesbian rights a central part of their policy agenda and a key theme in their direct-mail fund-raising efforts. With the legalization of same-sex marriage in Massachusetts in 2003, however, the issue moved to the top of the movement's agenda (Wilcox, Merola, and Beer, 2006). Many saw same-sex marriage as undermining the very fabric of civilization and, in the words of Dr. James Dobson, hurtling the nation toward Gomorrah. Christian Right activists interpret the Bible to say that God destroyed Sodom and Gomorrah for their rampant homosexuality.

However, same-sex marriage is far from the only issue on the Christian Right agenda. Christian Right activists perceive that educators, the media elite, and other liberals are trying to legitimate a "radical homosexual rights agenda." One Christian Right direct-mail appeal charged that liberals would seek to mandate that churches and schools hire "known, practicing, soliciting homosexual teachers" and teach children in public schools how to engage in homosexual behavior. One document distributed by Christian Right groups on the internet warns that "one of the primary goals of the homosexual rights movement is to abolish all age of consent laws and to eventually recognize pedophiles as the 'prophets' of a new sexual order."[23] None of the gay and lesbian rights activists whom we have interviewed have ever listed this as a goal of their movement.

Christian Right activists believe that homosexual conduct is sinful. For many, it is far more sinful than adultery or fornication, what political scientist Ted Jelen has called "an inconceivable sin"—that is, one that Christian Right activists cannot imagine tempting them. Many activists know conservative Christians with gay or lesbian children—indeed one son of a prominent Christian Right leader came out in the early 1990s. But the Bible promises that children raised in the faith will not stray from it, and this leads many activists to believe that gays and lesbians seduce heterosexuals and that the gay and lesbian lifestyle is powerfully attractive. As a result, activists oppose any public legitimation of homosexuality. They object to sympathetic portraits of gays on television, in books, and especially in the classroom. Some have gone so far as to seek to remove from school libraries any books that mention homosexuality without condemning it, under the assumption that if adolescents are exposed to even the idea of homosexuality, they will be strongly drawn to experiment.[24]

In addition, Christian Right organizations universally condemn any national, state, or local laws that prohibit discrimination against gays and lesbians in housing and employment. Currently, in many states it is legal to fire an employee discovered to be gay, regardless of the quality of the person's work, and to refuse to rent to or in some cases even to evict gay and lesbian tenants. In some states, and an increasing number of cities and counties, laws that ban such discrimination have been adopted. The Christian Right fights such laws.

The antidiscrimination laws are usually referred to within the movement as conferring "special rights" on gays and lesbians. Some Christian Right activists seek to frame their opposition to laws protecting the civil rights of gays and lesbians as an effort to protect the rights of conservative Christians. Tony Marco, a leading strategist in the movement to limit gay and lesbian rights through amendments to state constitutions, has argued that "law [should not] constrain Christians or anyone else from exercising where appropriate their freedoms . . . , i.e., not forcing them to hire or promote anyone based solely on their alleged homosexual orientation" (cited in Morken, 1994). Thus, when gay and lesbian activists seek to pass laws to protect themselves from job discrimination, Christian Right activists respond that such laws would force them to hire gays and lesbians in violation of their religious beliefs.[25]

Many Christian Right activists argue that homosexual *behavior* is sinful but that Christians should "hate the sin, love the sinner." They strongly reject the implications of recent research that there may be a genetic component to homosexuality and believe instead that sexual orientation is entirely a voluntary choice.[26] The group Christian Regeneration Ministries seeks to "convert" gays and lesbians to heterosexuality, and many Christian Right activists believe that such ministries offer a "solution" to the "gay problem." In 1998 and 1999, Focus on the Family and other Christian Right groups launched a massive campaign to promote conversion of gays and lesbians (Millsaps, 1999). The "Truth in Love" campaign had several goals: to redefine the public debate on homosexuality, to remind movement activists that they were to love gays and lesbians and try to lead them to salvation, and to convince gays and lesbians to attempt to change their lifestyle. Focus on the Family has an ongoing ministry called "Love Won Out," which also seeks to convert gays and lesbians to a heterosexual life.

Other activists clearly hate the "sinner" as well. One segment of the Christian Right is strongly homophobic. When Mark Rozell and one of us surveyed Republican activists in Virginia, some Christian Right activists penciled in vicious comments beside our questions about gay rights. Three quoted Old Testament proscriptions of homosexual behavior that mandated death by stoning for homosexuals. These activists were a minority and were in fact more than matched by others who wrote in nuanced comments that they merely wanted to stop public displays of homosexuality, not to ferret out closeted gays and lesbians. At the MayDay for Marriage Rally in October 2004, one participant told one of us how he had taken his son to a gay pride parade in Pittsburgh the previous weekend so he "could learn the enemy." The survey of Virginia Christian Right activists showed that a substantial minority agreed that "sodomy is a crime, and known homosexuals should be prosecuted (Rozell and Wilcox, 1996). Among small GOP presidential donors in 2004, nearly half agreed that known homosexuals should be prosecuted. Taken together, these anecdotes and data suggest that a majority of Christian Right activists are not homophobic, but that some are.

In 1999, many gay and lesbian activists charged that inflammatory rhetoric by the Christian Right contributed to an atmosphere of homophobia that led to a series of hate crimes, including assaults and murders. In response, the Moral Majority founder, Jerry Falwell, staged a public meeting with gay and lesbian evangelicals (including his own former ghostwriter) and promised to change the language in his fund-raising appeals. But Falwell later accused gays and other cultural liberals of helping bring about the terrorist attacks of September 11, 2001, and used anti-gay themes in his fund-raising appeals.

Although there is a consensus among Christian Right activists that the culture should not promote homosexuality as a legitimate lifestyle, there are divisions in the movement about just how central the issue should be to the Christian Right agenda and how far to go in discouraging homosexual conduct. Among Christian Right activists who attended Virginia Republican nominating conventions in 1993 and 1994, nearly 90 percent opposed allowing gays and lesbians to teach in public schools, and nearly a third favored prosecuting known homosexuals. Yet more than 40 percent opposed such prosecutions. Fully 98 percent of members of the Indiana Moral Majority wanted to fire public school teachers if they were discovered to be homosexual.

In 2005, a substantial majority of Americans opposed same-sex marriage, although when given a choice between allowing marriage, civil unions, or no recognition, half chose either marriage or civil unions. In some states such as Massachusetts, which has allowed same-sex marriage for more than a year, a narrow majority now supports same-sex marriage, and in other states such as California the public appears to be evenly split. In many deep southern states, in contrast, the public is overwhelmingly opposed.

The same-sex marriage issue is relatively new to the policy agenda. On other issues, public attitudes have become rapidly more liberal over time. Whereas allowing gays and lesbians to serve in the military divided the nation in 1992, by 2004 a substantial majority favored allowing them to serve. Large majorities also favored antidiscrimination laws. Half favored allowing gays and lesbians to adopt children, up from 25 percent less than a decade earlier (Wilcox, Brewer, Shames, and Lake, 2006). Yet many Americans remain uncomfortable about homosexuality, and some tell surveys that they find homosexuality disgusting.

Traditional Families

Many Christian Right leaders refer to their groups as pro-family, for obvious reasons. Families are positive symbols to Americans, and most people, liberal or conservative, believe that the policies they favor would help American families. Many Christian Right activists go further and advocate policies that would promote "traditional" families. The central issue is the role of women in society and the rights of children and parents.

The ideal family for many Christian conservatives is a married couple with children, the father working for wages outside the home and the mother working as a homemaker. Christian Right activists charge that government policy encourages women to work, both by providing tax breaks for child care for working mothers and by allowing homemakers to contribute only a small amount toward individual retirement accounts (IRAs). Moreover, they charge that high taxes are the primary reason that women enter the workforce, and many argue that lowering taxes would encourage women to stay at home and tend to their children.[27] Many are critical of county-funded after-school child care, charging that it encourages women to work outside the home.

For some fundamentalists and other conservative evangelicals, the Bible prescribes specific roles for women and men in families, with the man as the head of the household (Ammerman, 1987). Women and men are thought to have different abilities and strengths, which make each specially suited to certain tasks. Televangelists frequently preach on the theme of a woman's role in the family as mother, homemaker, and supporter of her husband and as one who submits to her husband. Some Christian Right activists take this division of labor very seriously: Among the delegates who supported Michael Farris in his bid for the Virginia GOP nomination for lieutenant governor were a number of men whose wives were not delegates because they believed that this was not a proper role for women. Instead, many of these women arranged for baby-sitting for other Farris delegates. Fully a third of Farris delegates believed that men are better suited for politics than women, and 90 percent of the members of the Indiana Moral Majority indicated that they believed in male-dominated families.

A larger number of Christian Right activists believe that women should play an active and equal part in politics but that because they also have special abilities as mothers, they should remain in the home while their children are young. Among Christian Right delegates in the Virginia GOP, a substantial majority believed that women who worked outside the home could not establish as warm and nurturing a relationship with their children as those women who stayed home full-time. It is small wonder that housewives and those who worked only part-time in the paid labor force constituted a substantial majority of women who were Christian Right delegates.

Christian conservatives also object to any government interference in how they raise their children, including in matters of discipline. Although many fundamentalists and other evangelicals believe that God has prescribed physical punishment as the optimal form of discipline, courts in many states are drawing increasingly strict definitions of child abuse. The Christian Right objects to such limitations and also seeks to overturn state laws and policies that might force disturbed children to receive counseling or that might remove children from homes under a variety of circumstances. Michael Farris has written a novel depicting the dangers of such laws when the state tries to remove a child from a Christian home because of an anonymous accusation of child abuse. A few Christian conservatives have also objected to laws that specifically criminalize spousal abuse, including rape within marriage and spousal beating, and have urged the government to stop funding spousal abuse centers.[28]

An overwhelming majority of Americans agree that America would be better off if there was more attention to family values. Yet most also support an equal role for women in politics and in the larger society. Fully 91 percent of respondents in recent surveys indicate that they would vote for a woman for president if she was from their party and shared their views. There is also substantial support for gender equality in families: A clear majority of Americans disagree that the man should be the achiever outside the home while the woman takes care of the home and family and that the husband's career is more important than the wife's career. A majority believe that working mothers can establish just as warm and secure a relationship with their children as can homemakers and that preschool children do not suffer if the mother works. Yet a sizable minority of Americans disagree on these issues and believe that mothers should remain at home, especially before their children enter school.[29]

The pro-family label of the Christian Right deeply angers liberals, who complain that many of the economic policies advocated by Christian Right leaders, including privatizing welfare programs and reducing spending on Medicaid, hurt working families. They also complain that the Christian Right's definition of a family is far too narrow and that single mothers and nontraditional families can provide loving environments for children. Finally, they argue that the Christian Right's strong opposition to gay and lesbian rights and the opposition by some in the movement to laws that protect women and children from physical abuse clearly harm some members of some families. A bumper sticker frequently seen in the Washington, D.C., area is "Hate Is Not a Family Value." As Focus on the Family has become more powerful, a new bumper sticker advises Christian Right activists to "Focus on Your Own Damn Family."

Pornography

Conservative Christians have long sought to limit access by children and adults alike to erotic literature and images, and the Christian Right today wants to restrict the distribution and possession of "pornography." The greatest issue for many activists is the easy access to hard-core pornography provided by the Internet. Many parents worry that their children will stumble across hard-core images or video by accident or will search for it on a whim and be exposed to harmful materials. Most groups advocate stronger legislation on child pornography and have backed proposed legislation to ban pornography from the Internet. In addition, countless local groups seek to remove books and newspapers that they find offensive from their public libraries and to stop the sale of adult magazines in their community.

It is often argued that pornography is difficult to define but easy to recognize. This may be true in some instances, but pornography is also in the eye of the beholder, and Americans in general vary widely in what they label pornographic. Some find *Playboy* magazine pornographic. Others might reserve such a label for *Hustler,* and still others might object only to hard-core Web sites that actually depict sexual acts. Some feel library books that sympathetically portray a lesbian romance are pornographic, and others object to any books that contain pictures of nude men or women, even reproductions of paintings in art books.

Christian Right activists are also divided on these matters and advocate different policies. Some would limit all kinds of erotic materials and ban not only their production and distribution but also their ownership. Others would limit only the sale and distribution of hard-core sexual materials, such as XXX-rated movies and magazines and Internet pictures that depict explicit sex acts. Still others seek primarily to keep adult materials out of the hands of children.

The public is ambivalent about limitations on pornography. A majority favors banning the distribution of pornographic materials to those under eighteen, and a sizable minority favors banning distribution to adults as well. Majorities believe that sexual materials lead people to commit rape and lead to a breakdown in public morals, but a majority also believe that sexual materials provide an outlet for bottled-up sexual urges.

Interestingly, the pornography issue is one on which the Christian Right finds common ground with many feminists, who believe that sexually explicit films and magazines exploit women and may lead to sexual violence. But many libertarian conservatives oppose the Christian Right on this issue, holding that adults should have the right to read whatever they choose. Proposals by the more ideological elements of the Christian Right movement to remove any book from the public library that describes a sexual encounter, including many best-selling novels, lead many to charge that the Christian Right is a movement of book-burning moral censors.

A Christian Nation

Christian Right activists believe that the United States is a Christian nation and that its laws should reflect God's will. Some go further and believe that the country is specially chosen and blessed by God, but that if national policies do not conform to God's laws, he will punish the nation much as the Old Testament describes his punishment of Israel. At the 2004 Christian Coalition Road to Victory conference, Alabama Governor Mike Huckabee, a Baptist minister, compared the state of the United States with that of Rome before its fall and urged attendees to weep for the "sins of the country."

Christian Right activists seek to restore a more public role for religion in general and Christianity in particular in American life. Most Christian Right activists believe that their religion is denigrated by modern society, government, and the media and that God will not continue to smile on a nation that marginalizes Christianity. They note that born-again Christians constitute more than one-quarter of the national population but do not appear as sympathetic characters on network programming, in movies, or in mass media.[30]

The Christian Coalition's **Contract with the American Family** included as its first plank a proposed Religious Equality Amendment to the U.S. Constitution. The Christian Coalition's pamphlet on the contract cites a variety of "wrongs" the amendment is intended to correct, many stemming from misinterpretations by overly zealous school administrators of court rulings about separation of church and state. The pamphlet cites several examples: a schoolgirl in Nevada banned from singing "The First Noel" at a Christmas pageant; bans on religious celebrations in Scarsdale, New York, public schools; children told they cannot read the Bible in study time; nativity scenes barred from post offices; and courthouses banned from displaying the Ten Commandments.

Most activists clearly intend for prayers in schools to be Christian prayers and the public displays of religion to be Christian ones. Although many Christian Right activists would allow displays of the menorah in December and might accept secular symbols such as Santa Claus as well, they are primarily interested in displays of the nativity scene. Some will even privately admit that they are not especially comfortable with displays of the menorah, much less a statue of Buddha or Vishnu, on the courthouse lawn, and that if the price of displaying the nativity scene is to also allow displays of the Buddha at a later time, they might prefer that neither be displayed.

Because of this, many opponents charge that the Christian Right seeks to create a truly "Christian nation," in which religious minorities would be at best marginalized and perhaps forced to participate in Christian religious activities. The leadership of the Christian Coalition has gone to great lengths to calm such fears; Ralph Reed denied explicitly that the group sought to establish an exclusively Christian nation and pointedly included Jews and occasionally Muslims as the "people of faith" discriminated against by American culture (Reed, 1994a).

Yet not all Christian Right activists are so inclusive. Research shows that evangelicals (and others) are uncomfortable with public displays of non-Christian religion and are especially unwilling to have their children exposed to such displays in the classroom. As noted previously, nearly two-thirds of Robertson's donors supported a mandatory spoken school prayer, as did a third of Christian Right activists at the Virginia Republican conventions. For many activists, imposing Christianity on nonbelievers merely increases the odds that their souls will spend eternity in heaven.

In Arizona, Christian Right activists who attended a Republican state convention passed a floor resolution declaring that the United States was a Christian nation and that the Constitution created "a republic based upon the absolute laws of the Bible, not a democracy."[31] The Texas Republican Party platform also declares that this is a Christian nation, as noted in Chapter 3. The Reverend Tim LaHaye, a prominent movement writer, has repeatedly argued that humanists are not fit to hold positions of government and should be removed.

At the fringe of the Christian Right is a group of theorists who adhere to the doctrine of **Christian reconstructionism**. Also known as dominion theologists, kingdom theologians, or theonomists, these reconstructionists are postmillennialists who believe that Christians must work to recover control of America from the forces of Satan in order to establish the millennium and allow Christ to come again. To do this requires that society be reconstructed from the ground up, generally in keeping with Mosaic law (the laws of Moses) as detailed in the first five books of the Bible.

Rousas John Rushdoony, the most influential reconstructionist thinker, has said that a reconstructed America would have no room for Jews, Buddhists, Muslims, Hindus, Baha'is, or humanists. There might not even be room for nonreconstructed Christians, for Christian reconstructionists seek to dominate society. According to Gary North, a leading reconstructionist writer, it is important to adopt the language of liberalism until the reconstruction has begun, but after that time, there is no reason to tolerate dissent.

Perhaps most controversial is the reconstructionists' call for capital punishment to be meted out according to Mosaic law—to those who murder, commit adultery, engage in homosexual behavior, act incorrigibly as teenagers, blaspheme, or commit acts of apostasy. North has claimed that death by stoning not only is an important part of the Mosaic code but also has certain advantages: Stones are plentiful and cheap, no single "killing blow" can be traced to any individual, and group stone-throwing underscores the community norms being enforced.[32]

It must be noted that Christian reconstructionists are but a tiny fringe of the Christian Right, but their arguments are being increasingly incorporated into mainstream writing, including in books by Pat Robertson (Shupe, 1989). This does not mean that many Christian Right activists advocate stoning incorrigible children, but it does indicate that serious discussions are taking place among some Christian Right activists of how to go about restructuring society to conform with biblical law.

Public opinion polls suggest that Americans are generally supportive of a greater role for religion in public life and are at least somewhat willing to accommodate the needs of non-Christian groups. Large majorities of Americans favor a prayer to open sessions of Congress and before high school sporting events, a moment of silence in schools, displays of nativity scenes and menorahs on public land, allowing student religious groups to meet on school property, and teaching creationism in addition to evolution in schools (Jelen and Wilcox, 1995).

Yet focus groups conducted by Ted Jelen revealed a more complex picture. Most of those who participated in these groups were initially unable to imagine why issues such as prayer in schools were controversial. When asked how children from minority religious traditions might react, they suggested nonsectarian prayers. When asked how Buddhist or Muslim children might react, they expressed more discomfort but indicated that these children could simply leave the room. Yet when other participants pointed out that this would stigmatize the students, many became uneasy. And when Jelen suggested that a truly neutral prayer might need to rotate across religious traditions, no parents were willing to have their children sit through a Buddhist prayer (Jelen and Wilcox, 1995).

Nonetheless, the Christian Right's agenda on public accommodation of religion is generally popular—more so than any other issue cluster. Once again, however, the policy proposals of the more radical elements of the movement frighten not only Jews and other non-Christians but many evangelicals as well.

An Economic Agenda?

The Christian Right in the 1920s did not focus on economic issues, although it embraced William Jennings Bryan, perhaps the most liberal presidential nominee in the twentieth century, as their standard-bearer. Beginning with the fundamentalist groups of the 1980s, howerver, Christian Right leaders have tried to develop an economic agenda. Although the target audience for the movement is less affluent than other Americans, various Christian Right groups have endorsed subminimum wages, a return to the gold standard, protectionist trade policies, privatizing the welfare system, cuts in Medicaid and other social spending, a flat income tax, and the end to the estate tax (which conservatives call the "death tax"). The Family Research Council, for example, claims that it is "dedicated to lower taxes, less wasteful spending, and the principles of rational and limited government. The current tax system is too complex and discriminatory and needs simplification so that it works for families, not against them."[33]

A number of internship and summer programs offered by the organizations discussed in chapter 3 address economic issues and provide a biblical justification for a free-market society. Summit Ministries, a Christian worldview training center for high school and college students, assigns a reading that cites a passage in the New Testament—Acts 2:44–45—as an endorsement of capitalism: "And all that believed were together, and had all things common; And sold their possessions and goods, and parted them to all men, as every man had need." The author concludes from this passage, "The student will recognize that whenever modern capitalism is practiced 'with a heart' it showers blessings of wealth, generosity, good will, and happy living on every community it touches" (Larson and Wilcox, 2005).

The economic elements of the Christian Right agenda have received a mixed reception among movement activists. There is a sizable core of movement activists who agree with conservative economic policy positions and back the expanded agenda with enthusiasm. Others agree with the policy positions but feel uncomfortable advocating them within the context of organizations that claim a Christian mandate. These activists argue that the social issue agenda on abortion, gay rights, and school curricula should be central to the movement. Others are neutral toward the policies and take a pragmatic stand: They will support the policy concerns of economic conservatives if the economic conservatives will in turn back the social agenda of the Christian Right.

Yet a number of activists are troubled by the economic positions of the Christian Right. One Catholic activist in northern Virginia told one of us that she interpreted the Bible to indicate a great sympathy for the poor and that cuts in welfare spending might lead to more abortions by poor women. Another activist told one of us that he believed the Christian Right had become too enamored of policies to help the rich, although Christ had warned that "a rich man shall hardly enter into the kingdom of heaven. . . . It is easier for a camel to go through the eye of a needle than for a rich man to enter into the kingdom of heaven."[34]

Surveys show that white evangelicals have a mixed reaction to the economic agenda of the Christian Right. Calls to eliminate welfare and to scale back other poverty programs appeal to the economic individualism rooted in the Calvinist heritage of evangelicals, but even those who take conservative positions on these issues do not see them as essentially religious questions. Other white evangelicals favor government action to provide aid to the poor. It should be noted that a significant minority of evangelicals favor greater government action to help the poor. Most prominent of these is the Sojourners, a pro-life evangelical group that emphasizes Christian obligation to help the poor. In response to the devastation of hurricane Katrina in September 2005, the Sojourners declared: "The poverty we have witnessed in devastated Gulf Coast communities is morally unacceptable. It's time to take action, starting with a renewed personal commitment to overcoming poverty in America."[35] They called on evangelicals to fast and pray that the United States would commit more resources to the world fight against hunger.

The economic agenda may pose a barrier to greater expansion of the Christian Right among Catholics because their communitarian ethic does not mesh well with calls to cut back on programs that provide food and health care for the poor. Moreover, many Catholics believe that the danger of such cuts increasing abortion among poor women is sufficiently great that they oppose any reductions in aid for the poor. The economic agenda is an even greater barrier to mobilizing black evangelicals, who generally support government aid to the poor.

In 2005, Christian Right groups mostly opposed environmental policies, although they did not spend much energy on them. Premilleniallists have frequently argued that there is little need to conserve the environment, for Christ will come again soon. In testimony before Congress in 1981, then-Interior Secretary James Watt stated that "God gave us these things to use. After the last tree is felled, Christ will come back" (quoted in Harden, 2005). Christian Right leaders like Michael Farris have called for the repeal of the Endangered Species Act. But some evangelical leaders have supported environmental protection policies, including the National Association of Evangelicals, which has called for a program of "Creation Care" to distinguish itself from more secular environmentalists. This creates the possibility that Christian conservatives might break with the business community within the Republican coalition on some issues. Moreover, there have been negotiations between Christian Right activists who oppose cloning and environmentalists who oppose genetic modification of foods, in order to form a coalition on some issues (Hula, 2005).

The Agenda as Defensive Action

The core elements of the Christian Right agenda can be seen as reactions against the social change of the past several decades. The successes of other groups—of feminists on abortion and gender equality, of gays and lesbians in gaining social and legal acceptance, of the environmental movement in protecting endangered species, of educational reformers in promoting courses to help children think about values and improve their self-esteem—have sparked a reaction by conservative Christians who preferred the policies of the past. The progress made by liberal groups in these policy areas threatens the worldview of conservative Christians and appears to them to have been possible only because of an almost conspiratorial alliance of liberal forces. For this reason, many Christian Right activists refer to even their policies on abortion, gay rights, and the environment as defensive.

Indeed, many argue that this agenda is necessary to protect their children and families from dangerous temptations. Yet feminists, environmentalists, gays and lesbians, and educators see these same policies as an attempt to impose an outdated lifestyle on all citizens. One bumper sticker common in the Washington, D.C., suburbs captures this sentiment: "IF YOU OPPOSE ABORTION DON'T HAVE ONE." Gays and lesbians who face discrimination, insults, and even hate crimes see the Christian Right's efforts as an attempt to force them back into the closet. Gay and lesbian couples who wish to marry cannot understand how granting them a day with a wedding cake would endanger marriage for Christian conservatives.

For each element of the Christian Right agenda, the policies advocated by movement moderates hold appeal for at least a sizable minority of Americans. Those policies advocated by the more ideological elements of the movement attract support from only a small minority, however, and are passionately opposed by a large number of citizens. Policies advocated by the more ideological fringe of the Christian Right frighten most Americans and provide the evidentiary basis for the most extreme stereotypes of movement activists.

The extreme positions and statements of the fringe elements of the Christian Right movement are not unusual, for all movements attract members who vary in their ideological purity and their willingness to compromise. The civil rights movement in the 1960s attracted pastors who preached nonviolence and Black Panthers who distributed coloring books showing black children killing police officers. The environmental movement includes those who seek to lobby Congress to protect wilderness areas and those who advocate destruction of the equipment used by those who would ravage the earth. Yet anyone evaluating the Christian Right must ultimately choose which of the various factions within the movement is likely to dominate in the future, and much depends on that answer.

Conclusion

Is the Christian Right a democratic force that is engaging a previously apolitical segment of the public in political action, or is it a dangerous force that will limit civil liberties? In this chapter we have posed several questions in an effort to address this larger issue.

First, is support for the Christian Right concentrated among individuals with authoritarian personalities? Although sociologists of the 1950s posited that supporters of the Right must have dysfunctional personalities or be deeply alienated from society, there is little evidence that this is true for the Christian Right. Instead, support for the movement appears to be a politically rational choice of conservative Christians to join groups that will advance their favored policies. Like all social movements, there are maladjusted citizens in this movement. And compared to other social movements, the Christian Right seems to have more members who believe that their political opponents are dangerous.

Second, has the Christian Right expanded the pluralist system in America by mobilizing previously apolitical groups? The evidence suggests that the target constituents of the Christian Right have historically been less likely than other citizens to participate in politics and that they do hold distinctive policy views. Should the Christian Right finally succeed in mobilizing these citizens into politics and in securing for them a voice in policy discussions, the policy debate will be more inclusive.

Third, do Christian Right activists advocate limiting civil rights? Here there is cause for concern. Many Christian Right activists would extend basic civil liberties to their opponents, but many would not. Nearly half of Christian Right activists in the 2000 presidential donor survey would arrest known homosexuals, and more than half oppose hiring feminists in public schools. Many others oppose laws that make it easier for women to find employment outside the home or that would bar discrimination against gays and lesbians in the workplace. In each case, movement extremists advocate policies that would result in a severe curtailment of civil liberties, and a majority of activists would limit the lifestyle options of cultural liberals.

Finally, is the agenda of the Christian Right a mainstream agenda, as movement leaders claim, or a radical one, as the movement's opponents charge? Here again the answer is complex, for in each policy area movement pragmatists propose policies that have at least some broad appeal, and movement ideologues propose policies that frighten and repel many Americans.

Thus, the answer to the question of whether the Christian Right is good or bad for America depends on what role the movement plays in the future and which faction within the movement comes to dominate. In the next chapter we consider the future of the Christian Right.

5

··

The Future of
the Christian Right

The conclusion is that the New Christian Right will fail
. . . both to re-Christianize America and to prevent
further displacement of the values which its supporters
hold dear.

    —Steve Bruce, *The Rise and Fall of the New Christian Right*

The Christian Right has been adaptable and innovative.
It will do well in the twenty-first century precisely
because it will discover ways to balance its increasing
political moderation with its fixed religious principles.

                      —Matthew Moen,
      "The Christian Right in the Twenty-First Century"

Aᴀꜰᴛᴇʀ Cʟᴀʀᴇɴᴄᴇ Dᴀʀʀᴏᴡ ᴇᴍʙᴀʀʀᴀssᴇᴅ William Jennings Bryan in the Scopes trial, many observers thought fundamentalism was finished. H. L. Mencken, writing in the *Baltimore Sun*, described fundamentalists variously as "yokels," "half-wits," "gaping primates," "anthropoid rabble," "morons," and "inquisitors" and predicted their eventual extinction. After the trial, it was accepted wisdom that the fundamentalists had lost their battle with modernism and would be forever vanquished by progress and science.

This prediction proved to be far from the mark. In 1981 journalists declared that the fundamentalist Moral Majority was one of the most important forces in American politics and that its agenda was soon to be realized by the newly elected Republican president and Senate. When Pat Robertson launched his presidential bid in 1987, some sociologists argued that he might win the presidency because of the vast numbers of evangelicals, fundamentalists, and charismatics who would rally to his campaign.

These predictions were also in error, for the Moral Majority accomplished little, and Robertson lost badly. In 1989 it appeared that the third wave of the Christian Right had spent its energies and that evangelicals would again retreat to privatized religious faith. Moral Majority's founder, Jerry Falwell, was immensely unpopular, and his organization was bankrupt. Pat Robertson had been embarrassed during his campaign and was trying to salvage his television empire from its dire financial straits. Many predicted that the Christian Right was defeated and that evangelicals would again retreat into their private religious world.

In the early 1990s, many predicted that the Christian Right would soon take over the Republican Party entirely and begin to influence national politics in a major way. By 1999, some were proclaiming the death of the movement that just a few years earlier they had described as a juggernaut.

After the 2004 election, many journalists credited "values" voters with providing George W. Bush's victory margin, and some strategists advised

Democratic candidates to moderate their positions on abortion and gay rights. Democrats began to reframe their issues with morality language.

Less than a year later, however, Bush's approval ratings had reached a new low in the aftermath of hurricane Katrina and with the escalating casualties in the war in Iraq. House Majority Leader Tom DeLay, a strong spokesman for Christian Right policies, had to resign his leadership post after he was indicted for campaign finance violations. Senate Majority Leader Bill Frist, who had been catering to Christian Right leaders, was subpoenaed by the Securities and Exchange Commission for alleged insider trading. And White House strategist Karl Rove, who had been the key liaison from the administration to the Christian Right, was under investigation by prosecutors looking into the "outing" of a CIA operative.

Moreover, after a year in which thirteen states had amended their constitutions to bar same-sex marriage, the state legislature of Connecticut approved civil unions in that state, the legislature in Massachusetts voted not to amend the state's constitution to bar same-sex marriage, and the legislature of California voted to permit same-sex marriage. Although the governor vetoed the legislation in California, these actions represented the first time that elected bodies had created same-sex marriage laws, or even laws permitting civil unions. Many Christian Right leaders began to worry publicly that they would lose the long-term battle to stop same-sex marriage, although they remained confident of short-term victories in other states.

Clearly, predictions about the future of the Christian Right have great potential to embarrass those bold enough to venture them. For many of the fundamentalists and pentecostals of the Christian Right, the twenty-first century promises great hope. Many believe that the new millennium will usher in the biblical millennium, in which Christ will come again. Pat Robertson has modestly predicted the second coming of Christ on April 29, 2007—Robertson's seventy-seventh birthday.[1] Others predict that the United States will continue what they see as a gradual slide into moral breakdown.

Political scientists differ considerably in their views of the future of the movement. Credible scholars predict the "inevitable failure" of the Christian Right, but others foresee considerable growth and institutionalization for the movement. These disparate evaluations reflect different assessments of the strengths and weaknesses of the movement and, in some cases, some wishful thinking by its opponents and supporters.

In this chapter we consider two specific questions about the future of the Christian Right and then risk some tentative predictions about the movement in the twenty-first century.

Can the Christian Right Expand?

Surveys in the 1980s showed that the Moral Majority commanded the support of approximately 25 percent of white evangelicals, most of them among the fundamentalist wing of the community. In contrast, the July 2005 Pew Forum on Religion and Public Life survey found that 71 percent of white evangelical Protestants rated the "Christian conservative movement" as very favorable or favorable.[2]

Pentecostals and neoevangelicals did not rally to the Moral Majority because of the religious prejudice of its state and local leadership, and it made few inroads among white mainline Protestants, Catholics, or black evangelicals. But the Christian Right has succeeded in broadening its religious coalition and may be poised to extend its gains with conservative Catholics. Among movement activists, there is strong evidence that the Christian Right has begun to bridge the religious chasms that so severely limited the potential of the Moral Majority. For example, in 2005, state efforts to ban same-sex marriage attracted a religiously ecumenical and racially diverse coalition (Campbell and Larson, 2006). Conservative Protestants and Catholics achieved such a high level of camaraderie on issues such as abortion and marriage that two historians asked, "Is the Reformation over?" (Noll and Nystrom, 2005).

Surveys indicate that the Christian Right today is far more ecumenical than in the past. Among Christian Right presidential donors, for example, nearly half were evangelical Protestants, but a quarter were mainline Protestants and another quarter were Catholic.[3] Surveys of delegates to state Republican conventions in the 1990s showed that the religious coalitions of the Christian Right varied by state. Only a third of Christian Right activists in Florida were evangelical, compared to half of those in Texas and Virginia. Pentecostals made up 5 percent of Christian Right activists in Minnesota, and 20 percent of those in Washington. A third of Christian Right activists in Minnesota were Catholic, compared with only 7 percent in Texas.[4]

Thus, one may conclude that the Christian Right is reasonably popular among white evangelicals and has attracted activists among white Catholics and mainline Protestants as well. What are the real limits to its potential expansion? Could the movement capture the support of a majority of Americans? Could it rally black evangelicals to its cause?

In part, the answers to these questions depend on whether pragmatists or ideologues come to dominate the Christian Right. Should pragmatic elements succeed in promoting a moderate agenda, they might be able to rally significant numbers of Americans to their cause. Should the more ideological elements prevail, few outside of the core constituency of the Christian Right will be attracted to the movement.

The best way to demonstrate this point is to examine support for key elements of the Christian Right agenda among various religious constituencies. Consider, for example, five issues on the Christian Right agenda: opposition to all abortions, opposition to partial-birth abortion, opposition to same-sex marriage, opposition to laws protecting gays and lesbians from job discrimination, and opposition to gay and lesbian adoption. Only 4 percent of the public supports the Christian Right position on all five issues, so a movement that insists on a broad agenda that all members must support would be vanishingly small. But 80 percent of the public supports the Christian Right position on at least one of these issues. Fully 25 percent of the public supports the Christian Right agenda on same-sex marriage, partial-birth abortion, and gay adoption, and 40 percent support the agenda on same-sex marriage and partial-birth abortion.[5] Therefore, a movement that focused only on narrow range of issues with public backing would constitute a substantial minority of the public.

Consider the abortion agenda. If the movement focused only on partial-birth abortion, it would have the support of 62 percent of Americans. However, most activists would not be content with banning only one late-term abortion procedure, because it would prevent few abortions overall. Only 13 percent of the general public in the 2004 National Election Study favored banning all abortions, but an additional 32 percent favored restricting abortions to cases involving rape, fetal defect, and protection of the health of the mother. Together these groups constitute 45 percent, a bloc that is close to a majority of the public. Thus, if the movement pursued an agenda of strongly restricting abortion but allowing abortion in those cases that most Americans approve, it could win broad support. Nonetheless, many movement activists believe that abortion is wrong even when a woman has been raped or a fetus is defective and would probably object to those exceptions.

Of course, not all potential members of social movements pay close attention to the nuances of the issue positions of such movements. Scholars have shown that many citizens evaluate social groups based on their relations with other groups and not on the details of their agenda (Sniderman, Brody, and Tetlock, 1991). Thus, white evangelicals and others may evaluate the Family Research Council as a group that represents conservative Christians and is opposed by feminist, gay rights, secular, and other liberal groups. They may know little about the specific positions of the organization beyond the impression that it takes conservative stands on social and moral issues.

No social movement reaches its entire potential audience. There are barriers to mobilizing conservative Catholics, different barriers to enlisting white mainline Protestants, and very different barriers to mobilizing black evangelicals. Different strategies might be needed for each target audience. The Christian Right faces internal dilemmas in choosing its strategies. And Christian conservatives face a dilemma as well in deciding whether to participate in the Christian Right.

Dilemma 1: Moderation in the Defense of Virtue?

We have shown above that the movement can attract its largest possible constituency by staking moderate positions on most issues. The Christian Right has done this in recent years on abortion, seeking not to amend the Constitution to bar all abortions but to enact restrictions on abortions at the national and state level. Although most activists would prefer to ban most if not all abortions, the movement has instead sought to pass laws requiring that teenage girls get their parents' consent before having an abortion, requiring that women wait for a certain period to think over the abortion decision, requiring doctors to tell women various things about abortions (some of which are not consistent with the majority position among the medical profession), requiring that fetuses be anesthetized before an abortion, and defining the murder of a pregnant woman as a double homicide. By focusing on restrictions to abortion rights rather than an outright ban on abortions, the Christian Right has won the support of a broader segment of the population for its policies. Similarly, instead of seeking to ban the teaching of evolution, some Christian Right activists have sought to teach that evolution is simply a controversial theory and that intelligent design is a competing theory. Focus on the Family and the

FRC took a more moderate approach in seeking to ban only same-sex marriage in a national constitutional amendment and not civil unions as well.

A moderate strategy has the potential to appeal to many Americans. Although few favor banning all abortions, many support some restrictions and a sizable majority supports a ban on "partial-birth" abortions. Teaching intelligent design along with evolution wins the support of a majority of Americans, but banning the teaching of evolution does not.

Moderation might also mean adopting a more diverse set of policies instead of focusing narrowly on policies relating to sexuality. The National Association of Evangelicals 2005 document on civic responsibility is a good example of an expanded issue agenda. The document calls for bans on same-sex marriage and embryonic stem-cell research, but it also calls upon evangelicals to seek justice for the poor and to protect the environment, issues not normally considered to be extreme or even conservative.[6]

Although the moderate approach has the advantage of broad appeal, moderation does not inspire activists to devote their evenings to the cause. When Pat Robertson called for moderation on abortion, many activists left the Christian Coalition. The loud applause at the 2004 Christian Coalition convention for speakers who took strong positions on abortion and defense suggests that the activists of the movement are not entirely happy with moderation. And there is also less support for a broader agenda among many activists. Armstrong Williams, the only African American to speak at the conference, received only weak applause when he asserted, "We should be just as strong against racism as we are against abortion and gay adoption."

The danger of the moderate strategy is that the movement may win a larger audience but lose one of its key assets—the enthusiasm of its volunteers. Activism is not common in America, and most citizens can find more enjoyable things to do after a hard day at work or with their children than stuffing envelopes or working fax machines. Moderation is seldom a rallying cry for social movements, and this is especially true for the Christian Right. Many Christian Right activists see themselves battling for the soul of America, but they may be less willing to engage in combat for goals that they perceive as involving too much compromise.

Many activists argue that it is better to "fight a good fight" than to compromise with the world.[7] They support the ban on late-term abortions but think that this is only a tiny victory and prefer that the movement work publicly to ban all abortions. They seek a spoken school prayer rather than a moment of silence when students might pass notes or plan their after-school activities. They want to enforce laws against homosexuality rather than merely keep gays and lesbians from adopting children. In Massachusetts in 2005, conservative Christian activists in the state legislature voted against an amendment that would have banned same-sex marriage but allowed civil unions, preferring instead the stronger amendment that banned both, but which had practically no chance of passing.

An examination of Christian Right direct-mail appeals shows that the financial constituency of the movement prefers the strategy of ideological purity. One fund-raising professional who has mailed to Christian Right lists on behalf of conservative presidential candidates told one of us that the only way to raise money from these activists is to promise to pursue vigorously an uncompromising ideological agenda.

The solution to this dilemma for the Christian Right may be specialization. Several smaller groups that specialize in particular issues (such as Citizens for Excellence in Education) can make extreme rhetorical appeals and take highly ideological positions—and thereby maintain morale among the activists. With the collapse of the Christian Coalition, however, there is now a major void in the movement. Most other social movements have spawned large, moderate organizations in addition to smaller, more narrowly focused, and extremely ideological groups.

Dilemma 2: The Republican Big Tent

The second dilemma for the Christian Right is whether to concentrate its efforts solely within the Republican Party, or pursue a more nonpartisan stance, or form a third party. Currently the movement is concentrated almost solely in the Republican Party, and it controls many state party organizations. The parade of presidential hopefuls at the Christian Coalition convention in 1999 demonstrated that many expected the Christian Right to play an important role in the 2000 elections and that it would be difficult for a candidate to win the Republican nomination or the general election without the movement's tacit approval. This will probably be the case in 2008 as well.

But the marriage between the Christian Right and the Republican Party has not always been a happy one. Many party moderates resent the influence of the Christian Right in candidate selection and in party platforms, and many Christian conservatives resent the history of party moderates who have refused to endorse Christian conservative candidates who win intraparty struggles. The passionate struggle over the 1996 presidential nomination platform suggests that these two party factions do not always get along. George W. Bush has managed to bring together the factions, as Ronald Reagan did before him, but not all candidates are able to appeal to both sides.

In general, abortion has been a litmus-test issue in presidential politics in both parties. In 1998, Jesse Jackson and Richard Gephardt became pro-choice to run for the presidency as Democrats, and George W. Bush became pro-life as a Republican. In 2000, John McCain was angered by attacks on his record on abortion, for he had an almost perfect pro-life record with one exception: He had voted for the use of fetal tissue in research on cures for Parkinson's disease, which killed his friend Morris Udall. This one defection from pro-life orthodoxy was enough to unleash anti-McCain mailings in the South Carolina primary, which pictured a fetus urging voters to support Bush over McCain.

More recently, many Republicans have argued that the party is a "big tent" with room for both pro-choice and pro-life candidates and activists, for both moderates and Christian conservatives. The Christian Coalition was willing to set up a booth under that big tent and worked on behalf of moderately pro-choice Republicans against more strongly pro-choice Democrats. But others in the movement point out that the tent has exits, and they have vowed to leave the party rather than support pro-choice candidates. In 1999, Patrick Buchanan bolted the GOP for the Reform Party, arguing that the Republicans were indistinguishable from Democrats on most issues. Christian conservative Senator Bob Smith from New Hampshire also briefly left the GOP. Others remain in the party but refuse to support compromise policies: Republican Tom Coburn from Oklahoma, elected to the Senate in 2004, is considered a "maverick" who ignores the party line when voting on issues related to his Christian faith.

Uneasy relations between parties and social movements are common; a mutually satisfactory relationship must be negotiated, for they have different goals and resources. Social movements have voters, activists, money, and means of mobilization. Parties have easy access to the electoral ballot, an even larger set of supporters, and experience in running and winning campaigns. Social movements would like to use the party machinery to elect their candidates and use the party platform to advance their policy goals.

Parties would like to use the activists, money, and communication channels of social movements to support their regular candidates.

By pursuing its policies within a single party, the Christian Right has also risked losing its prophetic voice on policy. After supporting Bush strongly in the 2004 election campaign and in many cases implying that he was called by God to be president, the movement had little distance to criticize the administration's policies with respect to the torture of prisoners. By embracing the Republican majority in the House and the efforts by Tom DeLay to create the majority, Christian Right leaders had little ability to condemn his flouting of campaign finance law. This problem exists for all social movements that work within a single political party; for example, feminists found it difficult to criticize Bill Clinton's affair with Monica Lewinsky, although the power imbalance in their relationship would have troubled most feminist theorists.

Indeed, in the early 1990s, feminists and African Americans also threatened to launch independent candidates or start third parties if the Democrats did not accede to their policy demands. In neither case was the threat taken especially seriously, and no one expects the Christian Right to bolt the Republican Party.

But there is a possibility that this troubled marriage might end in divorce. After more than ten years in control of the Congress, the Republican majority has yet to pass much of the Christian Right's social agenda. The Republican Congress has passed frequent tax cuts for businesses and wealthy Americans and has repeatedly voted to appease corporate interests by rolling back regulations that protect workers, public health, and the environment. But its efforts on behalf of the core Christian Right agenda have been limited and symbolic. This was most evident in the fight over whether to continue life support for Terry Schiavo; Congress passed a bill that applied only to her case and made no effort to make broader policy. If the next Republican presidential candidate is less supportive of the Christian Right agenda than George Bush, some activists might bolt the party.

If the Christian Right did leave the Republican Party, it could choose to work within both parties to influence candidate nominations, or it could pursue a more nonpartisan strategy. Such a course would have the potential to attract a wider audience, including more conservative Catholics and especially African Americans. The success of the Christian Right in assembling a large coalition in the fight against same-sex marriage in 2004 shows the potential of a nonpartisan strategy. Indeed, a bipartisan Christian Right might well have a greater policy impact than the current incarnation entrenched within the GOP.

Dilemma 3: Do I Stay or Do I Go?

Christian conservatives face a larger dilemma—whether to continue building a social movement that is primarily political or to concentrate instead on building infrastructure and alternative institutions within their own religious community. In 1999, Paul Weyrich announced that the culture war was lost. "If there really were a moral majority out there, Bill Clinton would have been driven out of office months ago," he said. "It is not only the lack of political will of the Republicans, although that is part of the problem. More powerful is the fact that what Americans found absolutely intolerable only a few years ago, a majority not only tolerates but celebrates." Weyrich argues that the Christian Right's cultural agenda cannot be accomplished through politics. He argues instead that Christian conservatives withdraw from the culture and build alternative institutions to promote and protect their values.

In 1999, former Moral Majority activists Cal Thomas and Ed Dobson produced a book titled *Blinded by Might* that argues that Christian conservatives became obsessed with political victory and in the process abandoned some of their core principles (Thomas and Dobson, 1999). They suggest that conservative Christians should not withdraw entirely from politics but that they should focus on their primary goals of winning souls for Christ and of changing the culture through persuasion.

If Christian conservatives abandon the Christian Right early in the new millennium, it might appear to signal the end of the latest wave of the movement. If past experience is any guide, however, evangelicals would continue to build alternative institutions and infrastructure. Moreover, the movement could emerge stronger if it engages the culture more broadly and is not so strongly tied to any one party.

Thomas and Weyrich suggest that evangelicals begin to persuade the public of the validity of their positions, using reason and not political power. Thus conservative Christians could attempt to persuade citizens that abortion is the wrong choice, that the homosexual lifestyle is sinful but can be abandoned, or that families are happier if the mother stays home with the children.

Many Christian Right activists strongly object to Weyrich and Thomas's call to withdraw from partisan politics, however. They continue to hope that George W. Bush and a Republican Congress will enact important elements of their agenda and appoint strict conservatives to the all-important Supreme Court. Moreover, the Republican Party has extended its control over state legislatures, and Christian conservatives now hold more seats and key leadership posts in the Congress. This suggests a broader question: Could the Christian Right win?

Can the Christian Right Come to Power?

Those who most fear the Christian Right wonder if its elites could ever seize power and control American politics, perhaps someday ruling by force, as the Nazis did in Germany. Such fears are almost certainly unfounded. Most leaders of the Christian Right are committed to the democratic process and strongly supportive of the American political system (Lienesch, 1994; Reed, 1994a). Although some Christian Right activists would like to restrict the civil liberties of their political opponents, only a few isolated extremists would abolish elections and seek to rule by force.[8]

Others worry that Christian Right activists might win control of the Republican Party and perhaps gain control of the political system through democratic means and enact their entire policy agenda. This is also unlikely. The American political system was designed specifically to prevent any single faction from dominating politics. The shared powers of the presidency, the Congress, and the U.S. Supreme Court provide many avenues to thwart the policy program of any one political group. Even in 2004, with a sympathetic president and sympathetic majorities in the House and Senate, the Christian Right has made little progress on its core agenda. The Republican Party is internally divided on most of the issues on the Christian Right agenda. Moreover, the Supreme Court can overturn laws, and state and local governments would retain the authority to legislate policy on education, gay rights, and abortion. The American system would prevent any organized group from imposing its will on a majority opposed to its agenda.

This means that liberals' worst nightmares of an American theocracy are probably just nightmares. But it does not mean that the Christian Right cannot affect public policy in the United States. Social movements can profoundly affect social and political life without ever "taking over" the political system.

Consider the profound changes to policy and government brought about by the civil rights and feminist movements in a relatively short period. In the early 1960s, blacks could not vote in many southern counties, eat in many restaurants, swim in many swimming pools, or stay in many hotels. There were separate drinking fountains for blacks and whites, and a black section in the back of the bus. Today racism persists, but racial discrimination by businesses is greatly diminished, and blacks have won elected offices from county boards to city mayors to the governorship, hold seats in the U.S. House and Senate, sit on the Supreme Court, and hold key cabinet positions.

Similarly, the feminist movement of the 1960s and 1970s radically altered social relations in the United States. Although women remain disadvantaged in many aspects of society, they now constitute more than half of the graduating classes in major law schools and have achieved positions of power in politics, business, and other areas of society. Retiring Justice Sandra Day O'Connor was arguably the most influential justice on the Supreme Court during her tenure, and Democratic Congresswoman Nancy Pelosi will likely become Speaker of the House if her party gains a majority in the next election. Sexism, like racism, still persists, but women have many more life choices today than they had in the 1950s.

To evaluate the impact of the civil rights, feminist, and Christian Right movements, imagine that Rip Van Winkle had fallen asleep during the GOP nominating convention of 1960 and wakened during the 1996 GOP presidential convention. He would not have been surprised by the conservative Christian rhetoric—indeed he would have been somewhat surprised to hear some Republicans speak openly of supporting abortion rights. He would have been quite startled, however, to watch the moderate GOP delegates enthusiastically welcoming an African American military leader, Colin Powell, and later that week to see the social conservatives responding with equal fervor to a black congressman, J. C. Watts. And he would have been very surprised to see the keynote address given by a woman who served in the House of Representatives, while her husband held their child on his lap in the audience. Clearly, the civil rights and feminist movements have transformed society in a much more profound way than the Christian Right. The 1996 GOP convention provides an exceptional opportunity to make these contrasts, but the 2004 convention would have similarly astounded Rip.

To determine whether the Christian Right could possibly have such a great impact on American society, it is first necessary to consider just what the movement has accomplished to date. There has been continuous Christian Right activity in the United States for more than twenty-five years, and it is useful to assess just how successful these efforts have been.

On the core issues of the Christian Right agenda, there has been only marginal success. States are now free to impose procedural restrictions on access to abortion, such as requiring teenagers to notify their parents and women to wait twenty-four hours before obtaining an abortion, and there is a national law restricting a specific abortion procedure that must still be approved by the Supreme Court. Although some states have made abortion more difficult to obtain, many have not. Moreover, even where access to abortion has been made more difficult, ultimately any adult woman who is determined to obtain an abortion and has the resources to travel to places where abortions are performed may still do so. These restrictions strike pro-choice Americans as an intolerable infringement on their reproductive liberties, but America is far from the ban on all abortions that most Christian Right activists seek.

Gays and lesbians are also more integrated into American public life and protected from discrimination. Many large companies now offer benefits to the partners of gay employees, and many television shows and movies have depicted gay and lesbian characters in positive or sympathetic light. The Supreme Court struck down the remaining state sodomy laws that ban sexual activity by gay and lesbian couples in the privacy of their home. In 2000, the Vermont Supreme Court created a legal partnership for gay and lesbian couples, and in 2005 the Connecticut legislature followed suit. In 2003, the Massachusetts Supreme Court granted gay couples the right to marry. In 2005, the Massachusetts state legislature voted down an effort to overturn that decision by amending the Massachusetts constitution to bar same-sex marriage. In 2005, the California state legislature passed a bill that would have legalized same-sex marriage, but Governor Schwarzenegger vetoed the bill. Other states have passed laws that have extended protections to gay couples, although they fall far short of allowing civil unions. The incredible success of movement activists in passing thirteen state constitutional amendments by referendum in 2004 points to the ability of the movement to mobilize on this issue. Nevertheless, overall, gays and lesbians have far more rights in 2005 than they did in 1978, when the Moral Majority was formed.

Prayer is still barred from public schools, although this does not prohibit students from offering a quiet personal prayer before lunch or reading their

Bibles in study hall. Public school curricula remain secular, and evolution is taught in biology classes across the country, although not all classes teach it, and not all present it as an accepted theory. Sex education is taught in most communities, and although that curriculum generally encourages abstinence, in most states it also teaches teenagers how to minimize their chances of sexually transmitted disease or pregnancy.

Moreover, after twenty-five years of preaching in the wilderness, the Christian Right has not persuaded Americans of the wisdom of its policies. Overall, there has been liberalization on many social issues, especially evaluations of homosexuality. However, in recent years there has been a small but significant decline in liberal attitudes on school prayer and abortion. Figure 5.1 shows the percentage of Americans who approve of Supreme Court decisions that bar prayer and Bible readings from classrooms, who oppose any restriction on abortion and on pornography for adults, and who believe that homosexual relations are always acceptable, according to data from the General Social Survey (Davis and Smith, 2004). We begin our comparison in 1978 and in a few cases 1977, corresponding to the years that the latest wave of Christian Right activity began, and continue through 2004, the latest year in which the General Social Survey was administered.

Between 1977 and 2004, the portion of the population who think that homosexual relations is not wrong at all has doubled from 15 percent to 30 percent, and the percentage who think that pornography should be legal for adults has increased slightly from 56 percent to 61 percent. The portion who favor allowing abortion for any reason at all has increased from 38 percent to 46 percent in 1994, before declining to 41 percent in 2004. And the portion who favor the Supreme Court ruling banning officially sanctioned prayer in public schools has increased from 34 percent in 1977 to 45 percent in 1998, before declining to 36 percent in 2004.[9]

For two issues, school prayer and pornography, attitudes in the late 1970s (when the Christian Right formed) and in 2004 are essentially unchanged. On abortion, there is a small but statistically significant increase in support for abortion under all circumstances. And public attitudes on homosexuality and gender roles have undergone a dramatic and significant shift. When asked whether homosexuals should be allowed to teach in colleges and universities, 51 percent of the public approved in 1978, but fully 80 percent did so in 2004. On gender roles, 66 percent of the public agreed that it was better if the woman tended the home while the man worked outside the home in 1977, but only 37 percent agreed in 2004.

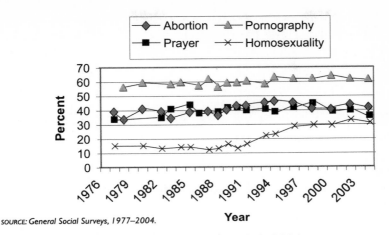

SOURCE: *General Social Surveys, 1977–2004.*

FIGURE 5.1   Social Issue Liberalism, 1977–2004

Some Christian conservatives would respond to figure 5.1 by saying that they have stemmed the tide of liberal attitude change, and recent downturns in support for legal abortion and pornography and increases in support for school prayer might support that claim. It is, of course, impossible to know how these attitudes would have changed without the active involvement of the Christian Right. Moreover, it is hard to know how much recent trends in figure 5.1 might reflect a response to the 9/11 attacks, when Americans showed a small but significant increase in religious observance. What is clear, however, is that after twenty-five years, the Christian Right has not succeeded in convincing the public to adopt more conservative attitudes.

The concentrated efforts of the Christian Right to overturn restrictions on religious practice have had some real success, and it is on this issue that the movement is most likely to make real gains in the future. In 1994 President Clinton spoke of the need to allow religious expression in the public schools and directed the Department of Education to clarify this position for local schools. As a result of lobbying by the Christian Right and the threat of lawsuits from the movement's legal arm, many communities and school districts have become more accommodating to religious expression by conservative Christians. The Supreme Court has ruled that student religious groups deserve equal access to the use of school property. In other areas where the Christian Right has made claims that rules restricted freedom of religion, society has generally been supportive.

At the state and local level, Christian Right activity has had a greater impact on public policy. This is perhaps most apparent in the field of education; various curricula and programs have been revised or eliminated because of organized protests by parents, including the teaching of modern scientific thinking in biology, geology, and astronomy. In some cities, gay rights laws have been overturned, and abortion is more difficult to obtain today in many states than it was in 1978. In 2004, the Virginia state legislature made it a double felony to kill a pregnant woman. After much lobbying by Christian Right groups, they also removed language from a bill that would have instructed school health officials to inform students who have been raped about the availability of legal emergency contraception. Thus a school guidance counselor who learns that a student has been raped can suggest that she consult a doctor but cannot tell her of a legal drug that could terminate her pregnancy.

Perhaps more important is the impact the Christian Right has had in framing the policy agenda, as noted by political scientist Kenneth Wald:

> It is difficult to identify any substantive public policy that has been implemented primarily because of the Christian Right. Rather, the mobilization of conservative Christians has affected the agenda of American politics, promoting some issues from obscurity to a central place on the national agenda. We would probably not be arguing about school prayer, tuition vouchers, and other proposals had the Christian Right failed to materialize.[10]

The Future of the Christian Right Agenda

Of course, Christian Right activists seek to do more than affect the policy debate—they wish to alter public policy, to change the direction of America, and to redeem it from what they see as its sinful path. Where are they likely to have success in the future?

The biggest question in 2005 as we write this third edition is the future of the U.S. Supreme Court. Many critical decisions have been decided by a slim majority of the Court, and Christian conservatives are hopeful that new Bush appointees to the Court will help to reverse key decisions that they oppose. Foremost on most minds is *Roe v. Wade,* which established abortion as a privacy right, so that no national, state, or local law could bar an adult woman from obtaining an abortion in the first two trimesters of pregnancy. If *Roe* were overturned, states would be free to ban or severely restrict abortion, and some states have laws in place that will automatically ban all abortions within the state if *Roe* is overturned.

Some states that have such laws in place, however, might find that they would be less popular once women actually confronted the total loss of the abortion option. Many more states would impose restrictions on abortion, limiting the circumstances under which women might obtain them. Even if *Roe* is not entirely overturned, it might be limited in ways that allow greater national and state restrictions on abortion. If the court overturned or restricted *Roe,* there would follow intense battles over regulation in all states and many localities. But some states would not ban abortions, and adult women would still be free to travel to those states to obtain abortions.[11]

The Court could also overturn *Lawrence and Garner v. Texas* which overturned state laws banning sodomy, and perhaps a handful of states (most notably Texas and Virginia) would reinstate their sodomy laws if allowed to do so. It might also revisit various church-state cases, including recent cases limiting public displays of the Ten Commandments on public land and allowing for public prayer at football games and high school graduations. With new justices, the Court might even allow states to require that biology teachers present intelligent design as an equally plausible scientific theory along with the theory of evolution.

The confirmation of John Roberts and the nomination of Samuel Alito to the Supreme Court raise the possibility that some of these decisions may be revisited. Both judges appear to be more supportive of Christian Right policies than Sandra Day O'Connor. With more than three years to go in his second term, Bush has the potential to replace other justices and perhaps mold a Court far more friendly to Christian Right policies. But in November 2005, President Bush's popularity reached new lows, and other GOP leaders such as Bill Frist and Tom DeLay were damaged by ethics charges. Whether conservative Republicans can win a long and drawn-out fight to reshape the Court remains to be seen.

The proposed constitutional amendment to ban same-sex marriage faces the hurdles designed by the Founding Fathers to make the Constitution difficult to change. The failure of popular proposed amendments such as the Equal Rights Amendment and the amendment to ban the burning of the American flag is clear evidence that momentary passions are not enough to change the Constitution. But many more states might bar such marriages in referenda and state constitutional amendments, and the Supreme Court might uphold the Defense of Marriage Act, which would allow such states to refuse to recognize gay marriage. In this event, a lesbian couple married in Massachusetts would not be considered married in Texas if they moved there or even took a vacation there.

On other gay rights issues, however, public opinion is moving so rapidly in a liberal direction that the Christian Right seems certain to lose ground. Indeed, it seems likely that other states will allow same-sex marriage in the future and that majorities of voters in those states will support the policy.[12] On gay rights and gender role issues, the public is far more liberal than Christian Right activists, and younger Americans are more liberal than the older cohort they are replacing.

Thus it seems that the core agenda of the movement—to ban abortions, to restrict homosexual activity, to return religion to the classroom, and to restore traditional family structures where women stay home to care for children—is unlikely to succeed. However, the movement has the potential to make progress in some of these policy areas as President George W. Bush's appointees take their seats in the U.S. Supreme Court.

The Christian Right as a Social Movement

The Christian Right has paradoxically been the most successful social movement in influencing elections and party politics over the past century and the least successful in influencing policy and culture. The labor movement, the civil rights movement, the women's movement, and even the gay and lesbian rights movement have created far greater change in politics and society than the Christian Right, for all of the movement's political mobilization.

Each of these more successful movements had as its primary goal the amelioration of real social and economic discrimination against its movement constituency. Blacks and women, for example, were denied jobs, promotions, housing, credit, and access to political office. Such discrimination clearly ran against American notions of fairness and equal opportunity, and the movements ultimately have helped reduce this discrimination. When these groups complained to society that they were treated unfairly, ultimately whites and men agreed with the charge.

Although the Christian Right claims that evangelicals face real discrimination, at best they face cultural, not economic, bias. Christians are not being denied jobs, promotions, housing, credit, or the chance to run for higher office—indeed the president of the United States, the majority leader in the

House of Representatives, and the Senate majority leader are all evangelicals. Moreover, despite the heated rhetoric of Christian Right direct mail and e-mails, conservative Christians are free to worship in America as they choose and are in no danger of losing that right. In a country that is overwhelmingly Christian, many Americans regard claims that Christians face serious bias as unbelievable.

The Christian Right has been successful when it has pointed to real discrimination in America. Some misguided school principals have interfered with student religious freedom because they misinterpreted Supreme Court rulings, and the movement has made great strides in protecting student rights. The U.S. Supreme Court ruling that the University of Virginia should provide funds to student religious publications if it funds other kinds of student publications is a case in point. The Christian Right has also been somewhat successful in its advocacy for a greater public acknowledgment of religion in America.

The Christian Right has also succeeded in playing the role of the "Christian Anti-Defamation League," responding quickly and forcefully to real and perceived slights in the media and public life. For example, in December 1995 a poet who regularly contributed to National Public Radio was forced to apologize for his comments after Ralph Reed quickly denounced his remarks. Just as the civil rights movement succeeded in making racist jokes unacceptable in polite company and the feminist movement banished sexist and off-color jokes, so the Christian Right seeks to bar demeaning humor aimed at conservative Christians.

At some point evangelicals may succeed in making the point that popular culture has few positive depictions of the lifestyles of a quarter of the American public. In 1999 black Americans justifiably protested the heavily white fall lineup on the major television networks, but evangelical Christians were far more underrepresented. Television in recent years has featured a few angels and some characters who took religion seriously, but sympathetic portraits of born-again Christians are nonexistent. They are more likely to be ridiculed, as they were in various episodes of *Seinfeld* and *The Simpsons* in the 1990s and in the 2004 movie *Saved*. Thus far, however, conservative Christians have been more interested in creating their own parallel cultural outlets—their own television shows, movies, music, and even comic books (Bates, 2002).

In all of these areas, the Christian Right has had some success and will probably continue to do so in the future. But the core of the Christian Right agenda is not just about allowing conservative Christians to practice their religion and avoid public ridicule; it is about legislating morality. The Christian Right seeks to legislate policies that affect the behavior of others—their sexual relationships, their access to abortion, their ability to read what they choose. Because these behaviors lie in what some have called the "sphere of privacy," social change is much more difficult to achieve. Blacks and women were able to achieve much by calling on Americans to confront their own discriminatory behavior. The Christian Right asks people not just to stop discriminating against Christians but to live their lives according to its version of morality and religion. This is a much harder sell.

Premillennialists in the New Millennium

In 2005 the Christian Right stands at the crossroads. Its future is far murkier than when the first edition of this book appeared ten years ago. It is possible that the Christian Right will continue to institutionalize, that groups will be revitalized by the fight against same-sex marriage, and that the movement will continue to recruit young, talented leaders committed to the long haul who will not go gently into that good night in response to temporary setbacks. It is also possible that the movement will fragment, with some retreating from politics to build alternative institutions, and others remaining as activists in the Republican Party.

In part, the future of the movement depends on whether pragmatists or ideologues dominate the movement. If the ideological wing of the Christian Right comes to dominate the movement, leading it to take relatively extreme positions with little room for compromise, the Christian Right probably will continue for a time to have a strong core of activists. Relations between the movement and Republican Party regulars will remain strained, for candidates who adopt the positions of the ideological wing of the movement usually lose general elections. Moderate Republicans outnumber ideological Christian Right activists, so eventually the moderate wing of the party will win. Disheartened by its inability to control party nominations or platforms, the Christian Right may offer some independent candidates, but a steadfastly ideological movement would probably fade away.

It is also possible, however, that the pragmatic wing of the movement will dominate and the Christian Right will pursue normal politics like many social movements. It will offer candidates for public office who will sometimes win; like other interest groups, it will press its demands on governments and will sometimes succeed. The social movement will solidify into more permanent organizations that must bargain with others at the pluralist table of American politics.

If the Christian Right moderates win, it is likely that the activist core of the movement will become even more disenchanted with politics. Some activists will tire of laboring in the political vineyards for little reward and will leave politics altogether. Others will remain active and become socialized into the norms of bargaining and compromise. If the Christian Right is to become an active part of American pluralism, its leadership will need to facilitate that socialization process, and this means reducing perceptions of threat that drive the intolerance of movement activists.

Ironically, the more the Christian Right succeeds, the more heated the opposition to the movement becomes. Historically, groups that are losing in the political arena are able to ask for greater sacrifice from their members and their ability to raise funds and mobilize voters increases. Should *Roe* be overturned, the pro-choice movement would likely be energized and would be effective in lobbying in many states. At that point, the ability of pragmatic movement leaders to bargain and compromise would be critical to the success of the movement.

Ted Jelen (1990) has argued that support for the Christian Right waxes and wanes in a cyclical fashion. As cultural minorities become visible and make demands for social justice, Christian Right movements arise to enforce conventional morality. Yet the movements inevitably fail because of the religious prejudice of the various elements of the movement, and religion again becomes a private matter. Jelen's account seems to fit nicely the rise and fall of the fundamentalist movements of the 1920s, 1950s, and 1980s, but if the movement collapses again it will not be from religious particularism but from the failure of the electoral strategy to lead to the movement's policy goals. Most likely, the Christian Right will become institutionalized as a permanent fixture in American politics—a significant collection of interest groups and national, state, and local party factions.

Conclusion

In this book we have explored two radically divergent visions of the Christian Right: In the first it is an intolerant, uncompromising movement that would deprive women, gays and lesbians, and others of their rights; in the second it is a defensive movement that would protect conservative Christians from a hostile society and government. As in most heated political debates, the truth appears to lie somewhere in between these two positions. Ultimately the Christian Right probably poses only a limited threat to basic American civil liberties because it is unlikely to gain access to sufficient political power to enact legislation and because many activists hold conflicting values of intolerance and democratic government. And although the agenda of the Christian Right is in some ways defensive, the movement also asks Americans to adopt policies that would affect the lives and liberties of many citizens.

Is the movement good or bad for America? The answer for each person depends partially on the individual's reactions to the agenda of the Christian Right. For someone who supports restrictions on abortion and on civil rights protections for gays and lesbians and who supports school prayer and the teaching of creationism, the Christian Right appears to be a very good thing. For someone who opposes those policies, the movement appears to be a threatening, hostile force.

It is important to go beyond these political calculations, however, and assess the positive and negative things the movement has accomplished. Because these judgments are ultimately normative, we conclude on a personal note. With one of us holding some sympathy for Christian Right policy and one opposed to most of the movement's agenda, we both support the free exercise of religion for conservative Christians and all other Americans and believe that Christian conservatives deserve a place in the political process. And we both believe that Christian Right activists must respect the rights of other groups, including those they fear.

There are several positive aspects to the involvement of the Christian Right in American politics. The mobilization of previously apolitical evangelicals and fundamentalists into politics constitutes a useful broadening of the electorate and of the politically engaged public. America's pluralist system works best when all important groups are represented in policy negotiations, and the Christian Right's constituency has a unique set of policy concerns that should be part of the policy debate. The careful monitoring of the rights of religious expression in public schools has also been a positive result, for in a few communities Christian children have been prohibited from engaging in religious activities that do not disrupt the school curriculum. Moreover, the efforts by the Christian Right to counter negative stereotypes in news and popular media have been generally helpful, although claims that anyone who opposes the movement exhibits anti-Christian bias are disingenuous and distort the image of cultural liberals as badly as the media may distort the lives and values of Christian conservatives.

Probably the most important benefit of the Christian Right has been its insistence that America consider basic moral and religious values as it crafts public policy. Often policy debates in America are artificially devoid of any discussion of values, and the Christian Right deserves some credit for the rediscovery of their importance in the 1990s. Moreover, because many Americans are deeply religious, it is odd to deny the role of religious values in policy debates, and the Christian Right has gone far toward legitimizing the inclusion of these values in the larger discussion of America's agenda. If the Christian Right forces America to consider its core values and to connect those values to public policy, it will have been a positive force.

The values the Christian Right brings to the debate are but one set of religious values, of course, and we hope that others will engage movement participants in a discussion of competing values, such as social justice, equality, and personal liberation. A political scientist, Clarke Cochran, responded to a paper by Ralph Reed at a conference in the 1990s by noting: "A lot of issues that Christians should be supporting, such things as gun control, justice in health care, protecting the vulnerable widows and orphans (to use Biblical language), dignified work for people, and property for the common good (from the Catholic natural law tradition) never appear because . . . the Christian Coalition . . . has been captured by the conservative ideological position."[13] Cochran's analysis is just one example of the useful debate that could be undertaken on the religious values that underlie public policy.

Yet we also see some negative aspects to Christian Right involvement in American politics. The harsh, uncompromising moral certitude of many Christian Right activists often does not further the policy debate but rather precludes it. For many activists, there is no room for debate because they see their policy preferences as the will of God. One activist in Virginia told one of us in no uncertain terms that a flat tax was biblical policy, and therefore there was no room for discussion. Such certitude actually discourages the inclusion of religious values in the policy debate, for it brands alternative values as illegitimate and encourages others to steer clear of religious argument.

The heated rhetoric of Christian Right direct mail exacerbates this problem by telling contributors that an alliance of liberal groups may take over America, strip them of their basic religious rights, teach their children Satan

worship and witchcraft, and implement other almost unspeakably evil policies. It is small wonder that many Christian Right activists fear their political enemies and consider them a danger to the republic. Liberal groups also
contribute to this climate of cultural conflict by portraying conservative
Christians as jack-booted thugs who would overturn American democracy.
The tone of political discourse would be improved if both sides would calm
down a bit.

Moreover, the failure of many Christian Right activists to support basic
civil liberties is troubling. When movement leaders write that gays and lesbians, feminists, liberals, and secular citizens should not be permitted to
teach in schools, they invite their followers to take action against teachers
in school districts across the country. We know teachers who have been
confronted by movement activists in harsh and unfair ways. At the fringe of
the movement, some write that America has no room for anyone but
Christian conservatives.

The lasting legacy of the Christian Right will depend critically on
whether pragmatists or ideologues come to dominate the movement, on
how those new leaders choose to mold the movement, and on the willingness of their followers to be so molded. If pragmatic leaders dominate,
counsel the virtues of bargaining and compromise, and encourage their activists to think of their political antagonists as reasonable citizens with basic
rights, the movement may ultimately prove to be a constructive voice in the
policy debate. If ideological leaders warn darkly of the dangers of the forces
of liberalism and stir up hatred toward gays and lesbians, feminists, secularists, and others with whom they do not agree, the movement will constitute
a divisive force in America that threatens the lifestyles and civil liberties of
many citizens.

If Christian conservatives choose to follow the suggestion of Cal Thomas
and Ed Dobson to pull back from partisan political action and to instead
engage the culture in a debate and discussion of the religious and moral underpinnings of public policy, it is possible that the movement will have its
greatest, and most positive, impact. Because of the partisan nature of the
current incarnation of the movement, there has been more shouting than
discussion, and both sides have ended up adopting more extreme positions
in an effort to mobilize voters. Between the shouting voices there is room
for a quieter discussion, where both sides might be surprised that they have
some common ground.

Discussion Questions

Chapter 1

1. How do terms such as "Christian Right," "religious Right," "pro-family movement," and "Christian conservative" differ in their meaning? What are the advantages and disadvantages of each term?

2. What is a social movement? How does this label fit the Christian Right? What are examples of other social movements?

3. Why is the Christian Right controversial?

4. How do American religious diversity, civil religion, and constitutional context affect your assessment of the Christian Right?

Chapter 2

1. What have been the common themes of different waves of Christian Right activity? How have these various manifestations of the Christian Right differed?

2. Why do fundamentalists object to teaching evolution in public schools? Do parents have a right to see that their children are exposed only to ideas of which they approve, or does society have the right to expose children to different ideas as part of the educational process? Would it be fair to teach both evolution and creationism in science classes, or would that constitute teaching religion as though it were science?

3. How do fundamentalists, evangelicals, pentecostals, and charismatics differ? Why are these differences important to individuals within these traditions?

Chapter 3

1. Consider two theses: (a) The various groups of the contemporary Christian Right compete with one another for members, confuse their constituency by taking different policy positions, and foster rivalries. They constitute a weakness for the movement; (b) the various groups of the contemporary Christian Right are an advantage to the movement because they allow activists to choose among several groups based on their issue positions and thereby attract a wider audience. Which thesis do you think is true and why?

2. Some writers classify the pro-life movement as part of the Christian Right, but this book does not. What are the arguments for each point of view?

3. How does the Christian Right seek to influence government? How do these strategies and tactics differ from those of the civil rights movement or the feminist movement?

4. What are the advantages and disadvantages to the Republican Party that result from its alliance with the Christian Right? What are the advantages and disadvantages to the Christian Right from this alliance?

Chapter 4

1. Explain how mobilizing evangelicals and other conservative Christians into politics might provide a more balanced policy debate.

2. Why do you think Christian Right activists are less supportive of basic civil liberties than other activists? Does this lack of support pose a danger to democracy? How might Christian Right leaders help to increase support for civil liberties among their activist core?

3. Consider the policy agenda of the Christian Right. Why do Christian Right supporters believe that theirs is a defensive agenda, and why do the movement's opponents believe that it is an offensive agenda?

4. Opposition to gay marriage has broadened the Christian Right's constituency. Do you think cooperation among white and black evangelicals, Catholics, and conservative Jews is likely to carry over into other policy issues?

5. Is the Christian Right good or bad for America? Does the movement enhance democracy by mobilizing a new group into the policy debate, or does it threaten democracy and civil liberties?

Chapter 5

1. Will the Christian Right be able to expand its base among white evangelicals? What are its prospects for attracting Catholics, mainline Protestants, and African Americans?

2. What are your predictions for the Christian Right's relationship with the Republican Party in the 2008 presidential election?

3. What are the advantages and disadvantages to a strategy of moderation by the Christian Right? What would the movement gain and what would it lose by adopting this strategy?

4. In what ways has the Christian Right affected public policy in America? In what ways has it changed the terms of the debate?

Glossary

accommodationist   Person who believes that the First Amendment permits the government to support all religions so long as it does not discriminate among religions. Accommodationists welcome public displays of religious symbols and practice.

Alliance Defense Fund   Christian Right organization committed to working through the courts to ensure religious freedom and defend the traditional family structure.

Alliance for Marriage   A research and educational organization that seeks to promote traditional marriage more broadly.

American Center for Law and Justice   Legal organization of the contemporary Christian Right, associated with Pat Robertson and spearheaded by Jay Sekulow. The ACLJ files lawsuits on behalf of Christians who believe they have faced discrimination.

American Civil Liberties Union   Organization devoted to protecting civil liberties for all Americans, usually through legal action. The group has defended religious liberties of unpopular groups and sought to maintain a strong separation between church and state.

American Council of Christian Churches   Militant fundamentalist organization, formed in 1941 by Carl McIntyre. The ACCC denounced communist infiltration in society and in mainline Protestant churches and provided resources to the anticommunist groups of the 1950s.

American Family Association   Organization of the contemporary Christian Right, originally known as the National Federation for Decency, headed by Donald Wildmon. The AFA focuses primarily on monitoring sex and violence on television and on countering anti-Christian stereotypes on television. It organizes consumer boycotts of the sponsors of offending programs.

Bible Crusaders of America   Antievolution organization of the 1920s. The BCA was well funded, linked to Baptist churches, and active primarily in the South.

Bible League of North America   Organization formed in 1902 that, through arguments and publications, fought the teaching of evolution.

born-again experience   Experience common in evangelical churches in which an individual repents of his or her sin, accepts Christ as his or her personal savior, and is redeemed by grace. Often an emotional experience, accompanied by a sense of release.

Center for Reclaiming America   A Christian Right organization founded in 1996 by Dr. D. James Kennedy. It is an outreach of Coral Ridge Ministries and primarily offers grassroots training to Christian activists.

charismatic   Term used to refer to a religious movement and to certain religious doctrines. Charismatics worship with ecstatic spiritual gifts, including speaking in tongues, faith healing, and being slain in the Spirit. The charismatic movement transcends denominational boundaries, with charismatic caucuses in most denominations and inter-faith charismatic gatherings in most major cities.

Christian Anti-Communism Crusade Anticommunist organization of the 1950s, which used radio and traveling schools of anticommunism to spread its message. The organization continued into the late 1990s.

Christian Coalition Most prominent Christian Right organization in the 1990s, at that time headed by Pat Robertson. In 2005, the organization led by Roberta Combs was largely defunct at the national level, though state affiliates were still active.

Christian Crusade Anticommunist organization of the 1950s.

Christian preferentialist Individual who takes an accommodationist position on the establishment clause of the First Amendment and a communitarian position on the free exercise clause. A Christian preferentialist seeks a more open display of Christian symbols and faith but is less willing to allow displays of other American religions.

Christian reconstructionism Also known as dominion theology and theonomy, this doctrine teaches that American law and politics should be structured along the lines of Old Testament law.

Christian Voice Christian Right organization founded in the late 1970s by Robert Grant with the help of Pat Robertson. The Christian Voice was known for its lobbying and ridiculed for its voters guides, which nonetheless served as the precursors for more sophisticated contemporary efforts.

Church League of America Anticommunist organization of the 1950s.

Citizens for Excellence in Education Organization of the contemporary Christian Right, headed by Robert Simonds. CEE opposes the teaching of secular humanism and witchcraft in schools and opposes programs to establish national education standards, such as outcomes-based education.

civil religion A set of beliefs about the relationship between God and country, generally centering on a special relationship. In America, civil religion is evident in the frequent references to religious images in public life.

communitarian (First Amendment) View that religious liberties can be limited by community norms. Communitarians generally disapprove of religious exemptions from otherwise valid laws and hold that the free exercise clause bars government from directly prohibiting religious observance but not from limiting such observance if the law has a secular purpose.

Concerned Maine Families Organization of the contemporary Christian Right that sought to pass a referendum in Maine in 1995 that would have barred local jurisdictions from passing laws forbidding job discrimination against gays and lesbians.

Concerned Women for America Organization of the contemporary Christian Right, headed by Beverly LaHaye. CWA is composed primarily of women and takes a special interest in women's issues.

Contract with the American Family Political document by the Christian Coalition that includes ten policy goals.

Creation Care The term used by the National Association of Evangelicals to explain their commitment to the environment.

creationism   The belief that the world, its flora and fauna, were created by God and that he made humans at that time. Creationists explicitly reject the theory of evolution. Most believe that the world was created in six days in the relatively recent past.

Defenders of the Christian Faith   Antievolution organization of the 1920s, active primarily in the Midwest.

Discovery Institute   A conservative think-tank in Seattle, Washington, that is one of the most prominent advocates of intelligent design.

dispensationalism   Doctrine that God has dealt with humans under different covenants or dispensations at different times in history. Although accounts vary, many dispensationalists believe that the first covenant was the period of innocence in the Garden of Eden, which ended with Eve and the apple; the second was mankind on its own, which ended with the flood of Noah; the third was chastened humanity, which ended with the Tower of Babel; the fourth was God's promise to Abraham, which ended with the captivity in Egypt; the fifth was the covenant with Moses; the sixth was the period of grace ushered in by Jesus; and the seventh will be the millennium, a thousand-year period of perfect peace.

Eagle Forum   Antifeminist organization headed by Phyllis Schlafly. Eagle Forum was organized to fight the Equal Rights Amendment in the 1970s and now focuses on opposition to feminism, to the teaching of secular humanism, and to legal abortion.

establishment clause   Phrase in the First Amendment that is source of controversy regarding separation of church and state: "Congress shall make no law respecting an establishment of religion."

evangelical   Term used to refer to a religious movement, to specific denominations, and to religious doctrine. Evangelicals believe in the importance of personal salvation through Jesus Christ, usually through a born-again experience, in the inerrancy of the Bible, and in the importance of spreading the gospel.

Family Research Council   Organization of the contemporary Christian Right, headed by Tony Perkins. The FRC was once the political arm of Focus on the Family, although the two groups are now separate for tax reasons. The FRC specializes in providing detailed research on policy issues.

Flying Fundamentalists   Arm of the Defenders of the Christian Faith that dispatched squadrons of speakers to antievolution rallies in the Midwest. In 1926 the Flying Fundamentalists appeared in more than 200 cities in Minnesota alone.

Focus on the Family   Primarily a Christian media ministry and organization of the contemporary Christian Right, headed by James Dobson. The organization's political arm is named Focus on the Family Action.

free exercise clause   Phrase in First Amendment that is source of controversy regarding religious liberty: "Congress shall make no law . . . prohibiting the free exercise [of religion]."

fundamentalist   Term used to describe a religious movement, specific denominations and churches, and religious doctrine. Fundamentalists believe in the importance of remaining separate from the world, in the literal truth of the Bible, and in the importance of personal salvation.

glossolalia Commonly known as "speaking in tongues." Religious practice in which individual speaks in no known human language. Some individuals believe they speak in the language of angels; others think they are worshiping in their own private language with God.

Home School Legal Defense Association Organization that defends rights of homeschooling parents, most of whom are Christian conservatives. The HSLDA is headed by Michael Farris.

intelligent design The belief that the earth was created by an intelligent being, not necessarily the God spoken of in Genesis.

libertarian (First Amendment) Individual who believes that free exercise of religion should not be limited. Libertarians generally hold that religious liberty should supersede secular law and that laws that have the effect of limiting the religious practice of one or more groups should have religious exemptions.

Marriage Amendment Project A coalition of more than fifty Christian Right organizations that work together to pass amendments to state constitutions that would bar same-sex marriage. They ultimately seek to pass an amendment to the federal constitution.

menorah Jewish candelabrum displayed during Hanukkah.

Moral Majority Premier Christian Right group of the 1980s, headed by Jerry Falwell. The Moral Majority established paper organizations in all states but was primarily a direct-mail organization that received substantial media attention.

National Association of Evangelicals Organization of evangelical denominations, formed by neoevangelicals in 1942 and active today.

neoevangelicalism Term used to describe religious movement and religious doctrine. Neoevangelicals rejected the militant separatism of the fundamentalists and encouraged an engagement with the modern world.

Ohio Campaign to Protect Marriage A state organization led by Phil Burress that coordinated efforts to bar same-sex marriage in Ohio in 2004.

Old Time Gospel Hour Jerry Falwell's televised sermons from the Liberty Baptist Church in Lynchburg, Virginia.

Operation Rescue Antiabortion group that specializes in blockading abortion clinics. Members try to prevent women from entering the clinics by physically blocking their path and by harassing them verbally. The organization attracts members of Christian Right groups but also a few pro-life liberals.

Oregon Citizens Alliance Organization of the contemporary Christian Right that continues to attempt to amend the Oregon constitution to allow job discrimination against gays and lesbians and to condemn homosexuality.

party faction Identifiable group within a political party that fields its own candidates for intraparty nomination contests and usually has an identifiable ideology as well.

pentecostal (pentacostalism) Term used to describe religious movement, specific denominations, and religious doctrine. Pentecostals believe in the second blessing of the Holy Spirit and in worship that includes ecstatic practices such as speaking in tongues. Unlike charismatics, pentecostals are found in specific denominations.

People for the American Way Organization founded by Norman Lear to oppose the Christian Right.

postmillennialism   The doctrinal belief that the millennial kingdom will occur before Christ comes again. The implication of the doctrine is that political action may improve the world and hasten the millennium.

premillennialism   The doctrinal belief that the millennial kingdom will occur after Christ comes again. Premillennialists believe that the condition of the world must worsen until Christ comes again. The implication of the doctrine is that political action is somewhat futile.

pro-family   Term preferred by some Christian Right groups to describe their movement.

religious nonpreferentialist   Individual who takes an accommodationist position on the establishment clause of the First Amendment and a libertarian position on the free exercise clause. A religious nonpreferentialist seeks a more open display of Christian and other religious symbols and practices.

Religious Roundtable   Christian Right group from the 1980s.

Scopes trial   Also known as the "Great Monkey Trial," the trial of John Scopes for teaching evolution in Dayton, Tennessee, embarrassed fundamentalists and led them to retreat from politics, but it also led textbook publishers to retreat from including evolution in biology texts.

secular humanism   Philosophy that centers on human values and denies the influence of supernatural forces such as gods. Although the American Humanist Association has a membership of around 5,000, Christian Right activists depict secular humanism as a militant religious system that wants to destroy Christianity. In fundamentalist circles, secular humanism is a very broad, vague concept.

separationist   Person who believes that the First Amendment establishment clause mandates that government not become entangled in religion in any way and remain neutral between religion and secularism.

separatism   Doctrinal belief of fundamentalists that Christians should remain apart from the world.

700 Club   Pat Robertson's television program, which features interviews with guests of varied religious backgrounds, an African-American cohost, and political commentary by Robertson. The *700 Club* provided the financial nucleus of Robertson's 1988 presidential campaign.

social conservatives   Americans who take conservative positions on issues such as abortion, gay rights, and school prayer.

social gospel   Doctrine in the early twentieth century that the church should focus its efforts on helping alleviate social problems.

stealth candidates   Candidates who hide their ties to the Christian Right until after the election. Although stealth candidacies were once encouraged, most Christian Right groups now advise their activists to acknowledge their connections with the movement if asked but to concentrate their campaigns on other issues.

Traditional Values Coalition   Organization of the contemporary Christian Right, headed by Louis Sheldon. TVC focuses primarily on opposing laws that protect gays and lesbians from job discrimination.

voter guides   Materials distributed by Christian Right and other groups providing information on the policy positions of candidates. If voter guides are produced by tax-exempt groups, they must be nonpartisan.

World's Christian Fundamentals Association   Religious group formed in 1919 to provide structure to the fundamentalist religious movement. The WCFA provided resources for the formation of the antievolution groups of the 1920s.

Notes

Chapter 1

1. Focus on the Family member update, February 15, 2005, from Tom Minnery, Vice President.

2. Whether "family values night" at the GOP convention hurt the Republicans is the subject of some debate. See Cromartie, 1994; Abramowitz, 1995.

3. Personal communication via e-mail, September 1994.

4. Although most movement leaders explicitly include Jews in their discussion of the American religious tradition, others do not. Mississippi Governor Kirk Fordice attracted praise and rebuke when he refused to change his statement that the United States was a Christian nation to a claim that it was a Judeo-Christian nation. The statement was made to GOP governors in November 1992.

5. Jerry Falwell speaking at the Christian Coalition's Road to Victory Conference, September 24, 2004, Washington, D.C. (attended by one of the authors).

6. See the case studies in Green, Rozell, and Wilcox, 2006; see also Wilcox, Green, and Rozell, 1995.

7. Quoted in "GOP ally's threat seen cause for party concern; Dobson vows to pull out 2.1 million members," *Washington Times*, February 17, 1998.

8. For an overview of public attitudes on these issues, see Jelen and Wilcox, 1995.

9. "Equal Rights Initiative in Iowa Attacked," *Washington Post*, August 23, 1995, p. A15.

10. All movement leaders now eschew stealth tactics, although many opponents remain convinced that school board candidates frequently attempt to disguise their ties to the movement.

11. Personal interview, November 2004. The analogy was in reference to the national movement's decision to initially forego the ban on civil unions at the federal level to focus on a ban of same-sex marriage.

12. Vision America, at http://www.visionamerica.us/cwofreg.asp, accessed September 7, 2005.

13. Statement by William J. Bennett, Press Conference on Religious Bigotry in Virginia Politics, October 25, 1993.

14. See especially the publication "The Freedom Writer," published by the Institute for First Amendment Studies, Great Barrington, Massachusetts.

15. Quoted in *Atlanta Journal and Constitution*, December 14, 1994.

16. A prominent exception is A. James Reichley (1985), who argued that theistic-humanist religions provide the proper values to mold a good society.

17. "Among Wealthy Nations . . . U.S. Stands Alone in its Embrace of Religion." The Pew Research Center for the People and the Press. December 19, 2002. http://people-press.org/reports/display.php3?ReportID=167, accessed September 7, 2005.

18. The Williamsburg Charter survey, conducted in 1988, indicated that more than 85 percent would vote for candidates from all religious traditions but only a third would support an atheist, even if the person were from their party and shared their political views.

19. "GOP the Religion-Friendly Party, But Stem Cell Issue May Help Democrats," Pew Research Center and the Pew Forum on Religion & Public Life, August 24, 2004. http://pewforum.org/docs/index.php?DocID=51, accessed October 14, 2005.

20. Data are from National Election Study, 2004. The National Election Study includes a separate question to filter out those who do not attend church at all, and this results in lower estimates than single-question measures. Gallup reported that 32 percent attend church weekly in 2005, with 44 percent attending in the last seven days. http://poll.gallup.com/content/default.aspx?ci=1690&pg=2, accessed October 15, 2005.

21. General Social Survey, 2000–2004. Davis and Smith, 2004.

Chapter 2

1. These doctrinal differences have important implications for the policy positions of evangelicals. Guth et al., 1995, have shown that premillennialists are less likely to support environmental protection. If Christ will soon come again, why worry about a little pollution? On the other hand, postmillennialists may support environmental legislation, arguing that God created the snail darter and it therefore should be present during the millennium that ushers in the kingdom of heaven.

2. See Acts 2:1–23.

3. There is some dispute among pentecostals as to just how many blessings exist. For many, speaking in tongues is part of a third blessing, but for the Assemblies of God it is part of a second blessing.

4. Speaking in tongues generally involves one or more members of a congregation speaking in what the nonbeliever would deem nonsense syllables. Two somewhat different explanations are usually offered by those within the tradition: They are speaking the "language of the angels," or they are speaking different private languages that exist between God and his believers. Being "slain in the Spirit" generally involves falling to the floor, often after the loss of consciousness. In charismatic and pentecostal services, strong men identify those who are likely to be slain and move to catch them as they fall.

5. The biblical account of the Pentecost in the second chapter of Acts describes the apostles speaking in tongues, so that members of the polynational audience all heard the sermon in their native language. For fundamentalists, this gift was given in the early days of the church to further its evangelical mission. The "tongues" were real, earthly languages.

6. For a detailed discussion, see Furniss, 1963.

7. For a detailed account of the bills, see Furniss, 1963. See also Hunter, 1987.

8. Some continued to exist, however. The Christian Anti-Communism Crusade was still mailing literature as late as 1990.

9. The church now has 22,000 members. For more information, see http://www.trbc.org/.

10. Quoted in Harrell, 1988, p. 140.

11. The Michigan process was a complex, multistage affair, and there was no real counting of delegates after the first stage. But journalists and political professionals polled delegates for the second stage who claimed Robertson was comfortably ahead of Bush. Eventually, however, the Bush forces joined with those who backed Jack Kemp and managed to seize control.

12. For an interesting account of the Robertson campaign, see Hertzke, 1993.

13. For a well-argued example, see Bruce, 1988.

14. Anticommunism played its least important role in the Robertson campaign, although Robertson's claim of secret missiles in Cuba hearkened to the earlier, more conspiratorial accounts of communism.

15. Quoted in Rozell and Wilcox, 1996.

16. For the biblical referents to the term "born again," see John 3:5–8; 1 Peter 1:23. For many evangelicals, the born-again experience is a sudden one, marked by an emotional release. Evangelicals in this tradition can usually recite the date and circumstances when they were reborn. For others, it is a gradual process.

17. The "other evangelicals" category is quite heterogeneous. It includes moderate neo-evangelicals, Anabaptists from peace churches, and members of Holiness churches.

18. This is especially a problem in the South, where most respondents claim to be born again.

19. For example, surveys show a relatively high portion of churchgoers call themselves fundamentalists, yet many of these do not support any fundamentalist doctrine.

20. See, for example, Emerson and Smith, 2000.

Chapter 3

1. Michael Gerson, "A Righteous Indignation," *U.S. News and World Report*, May 4, 1998, cited in Apostolidis, 2000.

2. There is some disagreement among scholars as to whether the Eagle Forum is a Christian Right organization. Schlafly is Catholic, as are many women in the organization, and the group did base much of its opposition to the ERA on antistatist appeals that the government should not interfere in the relationship between men and women. But much of the organization's literature links its antifeminism to biblical and other religious arguments.

3. Groups that have taken such positions include the now-defunct Just Life political action committee (Bendyna, 1993) and Common Concern (Maxwell, 1994).

4. There is obviously no biblical warrant for opposition to gun control, but in the South many Christian conservatives speak of the "God-given right to carry a gun." Bates (1993) reported that Christian conservative parents who objected to what they perceived

to be antibiblical passages in a school text listed among the objectionable passages one that endorsed gun control.

5. For a detailed account, see Lunch, 1995.

6. Virginia's sodomy laws at the time prohibited homosexual relations and some kinds of sexual relations among heterosexuals as well. Although the U.S. Supreme Court overturned state sodomy laws in 2003, Virginia's legislature passed another sodomy statute at the urging of Christian Right groups. The new state law cannot be enforced, however.

7. Robert O'Harrow Jr., "Christian Group's Push Felt in Move Against Gay Paper," *Washington Post,* October 1, 1993, p. D2.

8. Burl Gilyard, "Fake Wobegon," *New Republic,* September 12, 1994, p. 20.

9. In the mid–1990s, approximately a third of the members of the state central committee were Christian Right supporters, a third were moderates who opposed the Christian Right, and a third were neutral toward the movement. A majority of the neutral members were strong conservatives who worked with Christian conservatives, which gave the Christian Right a working majority on the committee (Rozell and Wilcox, 1996). Although there have been no surveys of the state committee since this study, a majority of the committee still supports Christian Right positions.

10. Jim Toler, "Local GOP Shifts Toward the Right," *Fredericksburg Free Lance Star,* March 29, 1994, pp. 1, 3.

11. Cited in Hertzke, 1993, p. 149.

12. http://www.citizenreviewonline.org/may2004/platform.htm.

13. Surveys show that although most Americans want their president to have strong religious beliefs, many are quite leery of voting for a minister. See Jelen and Wilcox, 1995.

14. Ultimately, however, Robertson lost because voters did not like him or his message.

15. This is not always true; in 1986, when a moderate Republican, Ed Zchau, ran against the incumbent, Alan Cranston, for one of California's U.S. Senate seats, an independent Christian Right candidate pulled enough votes to deny Zchau the victory.

16. For example, the guides listed Robb as favoring taxpayer funding of obscene art and North as opposing it. Yet Robb had voted for the controversial Helms amendment to cut the budget of the National Endowment for the Arts and to restrict federal funding of offensive art. The guides said that Robb opposed voluntary school prayer when he clearly was on record as favoring it.

17. For an account of the earlier PACs, see Wilcox, 1988a.

18. See Ann E. Marimow, "Conservatives Ascendent in Charles Schools," *Washington Post,* September 16, 2005, A1.

19. Lottery referenda generate interesting coalitions. Christian Right activists oppose lotteries because gambling is sinful, whereas liberal churches and citizens oppose them because they are a revenue source that draws disproportionately from the poor.

20. Moen, 1990. But Moen correctly noted that Christian Right issues were not highlighted in Reagan's State of the Union addresses and that his endorsement of the agenda was not especially ringing.

21. David Kirkpatrick, "In Secretly Taped Conversations, a Portrait of a Future President," February 20, 2005, at http://www.nytimes.com/2005/02/20/politics/20talk.html?pagewanted=1&oref=login, accessed March 6, 2005.

22. Religious groups have also become far more active in filing amicus briefs. For an overview of legal activity by religious groups, see Ivers, 1990; 1992.

Chapter 4

1. The John Birch Society was secular only in comparison with the explicitly fundamentalist Right. It had strong constituencies among fundamentalists and conservative Catholics. See Grupp, 1969.

2. See, for example, the essays in Schoenberger, 1969.

3. Pat Robertson's writings echo some of these more eccentric theories; see especially *The New World Order.*

4. Among large donors to GOP presidential candidates in 2000, for example, members of Christian Right groups rated Jews some 12 degrees warmer than those who were not members of Christian Right groups. Among donors of smaller amounts, Christian Right group members rated Jews 8 degrees warmer than non-members.

5. For a description of how churches can dominate social networks, see Ammerman, 1987.

6. The source of these data, and others pertaining to political contributors, comes from a mail survey conducted by Alexandra Cooper, John Green, Mark Rozell, and Clyde Wilcox in early 2001.

7. In fact, some researchers have argued that membership in any group that seeks to alter public policy to benefit all citizens is in one sense irrational. From an economic perspective, it is far more logical for individuals to be "free riders," in the hope that the group succeeds without investing their own time and money. It is highly unlikely that ten hours a week or $25 a year will make any difference in the success of the group, and citizens will benefit from the policies enacted whether or not they have contributed to the group's efforts. Yet many citizens are active in political organizations and give their time and money even when they believe that theirs is a lost cause. Many enjoy interacting with others who share their views, and others feel motivated to help pursue their policy goals because of a sense of obligation or because they derive great pleasure from their occasional political victories.

8. See, for example, "The Two Faces of the Christian Coalition," a pamphlet published by People for the American Way.

9. See, for example, Verba and Nie, 1972.

10. Fully 80 percent agreed with at least one of the statements. The figures were somewhat lower among donors of larger amounts.

11. Exodus 22:18.

12. Thanks to John Green for providing these data.

13. Political scientist John Green has argued instead that Christian Right elites would be less likely to protect civil liberties but not more likely to limit them.

14. It is worth noting, however, that even non-Christian Right activists among Republican donors were not a terribly tolerant lot.

15. Family Research Council, March 9, 1994, p. 2.

16. Direct mail solicitation received by one of the authors.

17. The Catholic church does not permit abortions to save the life of the mother, but most Protestants in the movement would allow this exception while setting strict limits on doctors to certify that there is a real and present danger.

18. Coburn's comments came during a debate on *Meet the Press*. See http://www .pbs.org/newshour/updates/ok_debate_10–5.html. Accessed September 19, 2005.

19. But recent trends in abortion attitudes have shown a modest retreat in pro-choice sentiments. The 2004 General Social Survey showed the lowest level of pro-choice attitudes since 1972, although pro-choice respondents still outnumbered those who would ban all abortions.

20. Transcript of ABC *Nightline* program, "God and the Grassroots," November 4, 1993.

21. "People and Events," *Church and State,* April 1988, p. 14.

22. For an account of a Christian school associated with a fundamentalist church, see Ammerman, 1987.

23. "Homosexual Behavior & Pedophilia," at http://us2000.org/cfmc/Pedophilia.pdf.

24. Pat Robertson noted on the *700 Club* on February 26, 1987, "As a seventeen-, sixteen-year-old, the maximum sex urges running through a young boy, and you give him pictures . . . positive homosexual and lesbian relationships with pictures and the whole thing . . . that's going to get his juices coursing through him, and he's going to be looking for sex part-ners as fast as he can."

25. For a detailed discussion, see Morken, 1994.

26. Interestingly, this was the position of the first wave of gay rights activists, although many now believe that sexual orientation is fixed by genes or socialization.

27. Interestingly, many Christian Right activists favor repealing the earned income tax credit for poor families, which would lower the incomes of poor families and by the same logic force more women into the labor force.

28. This does not mean, of course, that Christian conservatives advocate spousal abuse. Indeed, Christian conservatives counsel men to offer great respect and support for their wives and advise wives to obey their husbands. Some Christian Right leaders object to spousal abuse laws because they believe they could be misused or provide a wedge for greater government interference into the privacy of families.

29. Sources for these data are the General Social Survey (GSS) and the American Na-tional Election Studies (NES).

30. Indeed, one Christian Right activist told one of us that when Ned Flanders died on *The Simpsons,* the number of evangelicals on TV was cut in half.

31. Cited in Shupe, 1989, p. 25.

32. Cited in Neuhaus, 1991.

33. Family Research Council, at http://www.frc.org/get.cfm?c=EC_RESEARCH, ac-cessed October 17, 2005.

34. Matthew 19:23–24. Many scholars and activists argue that the Christian Right sup-port for tax policies that benefit affluent families, and for cuts in spending on programs that benefit poor families, to be inconsistent with biblical teachings. See, for example, Wal-lis, 2005.

35. Sojourners, at http://www.sojo.net/index.cfm?action=action.home, accessed October 17, 2005.

Chapter 5

1. Cited in Lienesch, 1994, p. 243. Presumably Robertson's birthday party that year will require some very careful planning and may draw a very large crowd.

2. "Public Divided on Origins of Life: Religion a Strength and Weakness for Both Parties," survey conducted by the Pew Research Center for People and the Press and the Pew Forum on Religion and Public Life, July 2005, at http://pewforum.org/publications/surveys/religion-politics–05.pdf, accessed October 18, 2005.

3. Survey of 2000 presidential nomination contributors, by Alexandra Cooper, John C. Green, Mark J. Rozell, and Clyde Wilcox.

4. Survey conducted of Virginia GOP delegates to 1993 and 1994 nominating conventions and of delegates to other state conventions in 1995 and 1996. Data collected by John C. Green, Mark J. Rozell, and Clyde Wilcox.

5. Author analysis of National Election Study data, 2004.

6. "For the Health of the Nation: An Evangelical Call to Civic Responsibility," at http://www.nae.net/images/civic_responsibility2.pdf.

7. Many activists quote with approval 2 Timothy 4:7, "I have fought a good fight, I have finished my course, I have kept the faith."

8. There are some Christian reconstructionists who are willing to dominate society by force, but they constitute the fringe of the movement.

9. The precise wording of the GSS question reads, "The United States Supreme Court has ruled that no state or local government may require the reading of the Lord's prayer or Bible verses in public schools. What are your views on this—do you approve or disapprove of the court ruling?" 1. Approve 2. Disapprove 3. Don't know

10. Personal communication via e-mail, October 10, 1995.

11. It is possible that Congress might try to limit interstate travel to obtain abortions through its power to regulate interstate commerce, but such a law would likely be quite unpopular, and probably unconstitutional as well.

12. In the summer of 2005, one of us taught a public policy seminar to a group of college student interns. At one point, students all predicted when, if ever, the first state legislature would vote to allow same sex marriage. The earliest prediction in the class was within five years; in fact, California did it just one month later.

13. Cited in Cromartie, 1994, p. 36.

References

Abramowitz, Alan. 1995. "It's Abortion, Stupid: Policy Voting in the 1992 Presidential Election." *Journal of Politics* 57:176–186.

Adorno, T. W., Else Frenkel-Brunswik, Daniel J. Levinson, and R. Nevitt Sanford. 1950. *The Authoritarian Personality.* New York: Harper and Row.

Ammerman, Nancy Tatom. 1987. *Bible Believers: Fundamentalists in the Modern World.* New Brunswick, NJ: Rutgers University Press.

Andolina, Molly W., and Clyde Wilcox. 2000. "The Paradoxes of Popularity: Public Support for Bill Clinton During the Lewinsky Scandal" (with Molly Sonner). In Mark J. Rozell and Clyde Wilcox (eds.), *The Clinton Scandal and the Future of American Government.* Washington, DC: Georgetown University Press.

Apostolidis, Paul. 2000. *Stations of the Cross: Adorno and Christian Right Radio.* Durham, NC: Duke University Press.

Baker, Peter, and Dan Balz. 2005. "Conservatives Confront Bush Aides." Washington Post, October 6, p. A1.

Barber, Benjamin R. 1984. *Strong Democracy: Participatory Politics for a New Age.* Berkeley: University of California Press.

Barkun, Michael. 1994. *Religion and the Racist Right.* Chapel Hill: University of North Carolina Press.

Barrett, Greg. 1999. "Why James Dobson's $120 Million Ministry Is a Household Name." *Detroit News,* May 3, p. A12.

Bartels, Lynn. 2004. "GOP Assailed for Defeat; Jeffco Republican: Party 'Prostituted' Itself on Vouchers." *Rocky Mountain News,* November 16, http://rockymountainnews.com/drmn/election/article/0,1299,DRMN_36_3331828,00.html. Accessed March 30, 2005.

Bates, Stephen. 1993. *Battleground.* New York: Henry Holt.

_____. 1995. "The Christian Coalition Nobody Knows." *Weekly Standard,* September 25.

_____. 2002. "The Jesus Market: Christianity May Be Struggling in the Public Square, but It's Prospering in the Public Bazaar." *Weekly Standard,* December 16. http://www.weeklystandard.com/Content/Public/Articles/000/000/001/988ovwyu.asp?pg=1 Accessed October 18, 2005.

Bendyna, Mary. 1993. "Just Life Action." In R. Biersack, P. Herrnson, and C. Wilcox (eds.), *Risky Business: PAC Decisionmaking in Congressional Elections.* Armonk, NY: M. E. Sharpe.

_____. 1995. "Catholics and the Christian Coalition." Presented at the annual meeting of the Association for the Sociology of Religion, Washington, DC.

Bendyna, Mary, John C. Green, Mark J. Rozell, and Clyde Wilcox. 2000. "Catholics and the Christian Right: A View from Four States." *Journal for the Scientific Study of Religion* 39:321–332.

Berry, Jeffrey M., Kent E. Portney, and Ken Thomson. 1993. *The Rebirth of Urban Democracy.* Washington, DC: Brookings.

Blakeman, Bruce W. 1996. "Report of Survey of Concerned Women of America Members and of Randomly Selected Women." Concerned Women of America.

Blaker, Kimberly. 2003. *The Fundamentals of Extremism: The Christian Right in America.* Plymouth, MI: New Boston Books.

Blumenthal, Sidney. 1994. "Christian Soldiers." *New Yorker* 70, July 18, pp. 31–37.

Brin, David. 1994. *Otherness.* New York: Bantam Books.

Broder, David S. 1995. "Christian Group Flexes Newfound Muscles." *Washington Post,* September 10, pp. A1, A24.

Brown, Clifford W., Jr., Lynda W. Powell, and Clyde Wilcox. 1994. Presidential Contributor Study. Computer data file.

————. 1995. *Serious Money: Fundraising and Contributing in Presidential Nomination Campaigns.* New York: Cambridge University Press.

Brown, Steven. 2004. *Trumping Religion: The New Christian Right, the Free Speech Clause, and the Courts.* Tuscaloosa: University of Alabama Press.

Bruce, Steve. 1988. *The Rise and Fall of the New Christian Right: Conservative Protestant Politics in America, 1978–1988.* Oxford: Oxford University Press.

Bruce, Steve, Peter Kivisto, and William Swatos Jr. 1994. *The Rapture of Politics: The Christian Right as the United States Approaches the Year 2000.* New Brunswick, NJ: Transaction Press.

Bush, George W. 1999. *A Charge to Keep: My Journey to the White House.* New York: William Morrow.

Buss, Doris, and Didi Herman. 2003. *Globalizing Family Values: The Christian Right in International Politics.* Minneapolis: University of Minnesota Press.

Campbell, David, and Carin Larson. 2006. "Religious Coalitions For and Against Gay Marriage." In Craig Rimmerman and Clyde Wilcox (eds), *The Politics of Same-Sex Marriage.* Chicago: University of Chicago Press.

Cleary, Edward, and Allen Hertzke (eds.). 2006. *Representing God at the Statehouse: Religion and Politics in the American States.* Lanham, MD: Rowman & Littlefield.

Cole, Stewart. 1931. *The History of Fundamentalism.* Westport, CT: Greenwood Press.

Conger, Kimberly H., and John C. Green. 2002. "Spreading Out and Digging In: Christian Conservatives and State Republican Parties." *Campaigns and Elections* 23 (1):59.

Conger, Kimberly H., and Donald Ratcheter. 2006. "Iowa: In the Heart of Bush Country." In John C. Green, Mark J. Rozell, and Clyde Wilcox (eds.), *The Values Campaign? The Christian Right in the 2004 Election.* Washington, DC: Georgetown University Press.

Conover, Pamela, and Virginia Gray. 1981. "Political Activists and Conflict over Abortion and ERA: Pro-Family vs. Pro-Woman." Presented at the annual meeting of the Midwest Political Science Association, Chicago.

Cook, Elizabeth Adell, Ted G. Jelen, and Clyde Wilcox. 1992. *Between Two Absolutes: Public Opinion and the Politics of Abortion.* Boulder, CO: Westview.

_____. 1993. "Generational Differences in Attitudes Toward Abortion." In M. Goggin (ed.), *Understanding the New Politics of Abortion.* Beverly Hills, CA: Sage.

_____. 1994. "Issue Voting in Gubernatorial Elections: Abortion and Post-Webster Politics." *Journal of Politics* 56:187–199.

Cooperman, Alan, and Thomas B. Edsall. 2004. "Evangelicals Say They Led Charge for the GOP." *Washington Post,* November 8, p. A1.

Cromartie, Michael (ed.). 1994. *Disciples and Democracy: Religious Conservatives and the Future of American Politics.* Washington, DC: Ethics and Public Policy Center.

Dao, James. 2004. "Flush with Victory, Grass-Roots Crusader Against Same-Sex Marriage Thinks Big." *New York Times,* November 23, p. A28.

Davis, James Allan, and Tom W. Smith. 2004. General Social Surveys, 1972–1994. National Opinion Research Center, University Of Chicago. Computer data file.

Deckman, Melissa M. 2004. *School Board Battles: The Christian Right in Local Politics.* Washington, DC: Georgetown University Press.

Dillon, S. 1993a. "Catholics Join Bid by Conservatives for School Boards." *New York Times,* April 16.

_____. 1993b. "Fundamentalists and Catholics." *New York Times,* November 14, p. 6.

Dodson, Debra L. 1990. "Socialization of Party Activists: National Convention Delegates, 1972–1981." *American Journal of Political Science* 34:1119–1141.

Duin, Julia. 2005. "Christian Coalition Falls on Lean Days." *Washington Times,* October 13. http://www.washingtontimes.com/national/20051013-121940-9083r.htm. Accessed October 17, 2005.

Edsall, Thomas B. 1995. "Robertson Urges Christian Activists to Take Over GOP." *Washington Post,* September 10, p. A24.

Ellison, Christopher G., Samuel Echevarría, and Brad Smith. 2005. "Religion and Abortion Attitudes Among U.S. Hispanics: Findings from the 1990 Latino National Political Survey." *Social Science Quarterly* 86, 1:192–208.

Emerson, Michael O., and Christian Smith. 2000. *Divided by Faith: Evangelical Religion and the Problem of Race in America.* Oxford: Oxford University Press.

Falwell, Jerry. 1981. *The Fundamentalist Phenomenon.* Garden City, NJ: Doubleday.

Farrell, John Aloysius, and Anne C. Mulkern. 2005. "Dobson seen as driven, divisive—As respect rises, worries surface: The evangelical leader's resounding plunge into politics has stirred both Democrats and the GOP." *Denver Post,* April 27, p. A1.

Farris, Michael P. 1992. *Where Do I Draw the Line?* Minneapolis: Bethany House.

Finke, Roger, and Rodney Stark. 1992. *The Churching of America, 1776–1992.* New Brunswick, NJ: Rutgers University Press.

Furniss, Norman. 1963. *The Fundamentalist Controversy, 1918–1931.* Hamden, CT: Archdon Books.

Gamble, Barbara S. 1995. "Putting Civil Rights to a Popular Vote." Unpublished mauscript.

Georgianna, Sharon Linzey. 1988. Moral Majority Survey. Computer data file. Collected at Indiana University.

_____. 1989. *The Moral Majority and Fundamentalism: Plausibility and Dissonance.* Lewiston, NY: Edwin Mellon Press.

Gimpel, James G. 1994. *Risky Business? PAC Decisionmaking in Congressional Elections.* Armonk, NY: M. E. Sharpe.

Goodstein, Laurie. 1999. "Coalitions's Woes May Hinder Goals of Christian Right." *New York Times,* August 2, www.nytimes.com.

Green, John C. 1995. "The Christian Right and the 1994 Elections: An Overview." In M. Rozell and C. Wilcox (eds.), *God at the Grassroots: The Christian Right in the 1994 Elections.* Lanham, MD: Rowman & Littlefield.

_____. 2000. "The Christian Right and the 1998 Elections: An Overview." In John C. Green, Mark J. Rozell, and Clyde Wilcox (eds.), *Prayers in the Precincts.* Washington, DC: Georgetown University Press.

Green, John, Kimberly Conger, and James Guth. 2006. "Agents of Value: Christian Right Activists in 2004." In John C. Green, Mark J. Rozell, and Clyde Wilcox (eds.), *The Values Campaign? The Christian Right in the 2004 Election.* Washington, DC: Georgetown University Press.

Green, John C., and James L. Guth. 1988. "The Christian Right in the Republican Party: The Case of Pat Robertson's Contributors." *Journal of Politics* 50:150–165.

Green, John C., James L. Guth, Lyman A. Kellstedt, and Corwin E. Smidt. 1990–1991. Survey of Religious Activists, 1990–1991. Computer data file. Collected at the University of Akron.

_____. 1992. National Survey of Religion and Politics, 1992. Computer data file. Collected at the University of Akron.

_____. 1994. "Uncivil Challengers? Support for Civil Liberties Among Religious Activists." *Journal of Political Science* 24:25–49.

Green, John C., James L. Guth, and Clyde Wilcox. 1995. "The Christian Right in State Republican Parties." Presented at the annual meeting of the Midwest Political Science Association, Chicago.

_____. 1998. "The Social Movement Meets the Party: The Christian Right in the GOP." In Anne Costain and Andrew S. McFarland (eds.), *Social Movements and American Political Institutions.* Lanham, MD: Rowman & Littlefield.

Green, John C., Lyman Kellstedt, Corwin Smidt, and James L. Guth. 1992. "National Survey of American Evangelicals." Ray C. Bliss Institute of Applied Politics and Survey Research, University of Akron.

Green, John C., Mark J. Rozell, and Clyde Wilcox (eds.). 2006. *The Values Campaign? The Christian Right in the 2004 Election.* Washington, DC: Georgetown University Press.

Grove, Steve. 2004. "Reading, Writing & Right-Wing Politics." *Boston Globe,* August 15, p. D1.

Grupp, Fred. 1969. "The Political Perspectives of the John Birch Society Members." In R. Schoenberger (ed.), *The American Right Wing.* New York: Holt, Rinehart, and Winston.

Guth, James L. 1983. "The Politics of the Christian Right." In A. Cigler and B. Loomis (eds.), *Interest Group Politics.* Washington, DC: CQ Press.

Guth, James L., John C. Green, Lyman A. Kellstedt, and Corwin E. Smidt. 1995. "Faith and the Environment: Religious Beliefs and Attitudes on Environmental Policy." *American Journal of Political Science* 39:364–382.

Guth, James L., and Lyman A. Kellstedt. 1999. "Religion on Capitol Hill: The Case of the House of Representatives in the 105th Congress." Presented at the Biennial Meeting of Christians in Political Science, Calvin College, Grand Rapids, MI.

Hacker, Hans J. 2005. *The Culture of Conservative Christian Litigation.* Lanham, MD: Rowman & Littlefield.

Hadden, Jeffery K., Anson Shupe, James Hawdon, and Kenneth Martin. 1987. "Why Jerry Falwell Killed the Moral Majority." In M. Fishwick and R. Browne (eds.), *The God Pumpers: Religion in the Electronic Age.* Bowling Green, OH: Popular Press.

Haider-Markel, Donald P., and Kenneth J. Meier. 1996. "The Politics of Gay and Lesbian Rights: Expanding the Scope of the Conflict." *Journal of Politics* 150:47–62.

Hale, John. 1995. "Mainers Face Off on Gays." *Bangor Daily News,* October 28, p. 14.

Harden, Blaine. 2005. "The Greening of Evangelicals; Christian Right Turns, Sometimes Warily, to Environmentalism." *Washington Post,* February 6, p. A1.

Harrell, David E. 1988. *Pat Robertson: A Personal, Religious, and Political Portrait.* San Francisco: Harper and Row.

Hedges, Chris. 2005. "Soldiers of Christ II: Feeling the Hate with the National Religious Broadcasters." *Harper's Magazine,* May.

Hertzke, Allen. 1988. *Representing God in Washington: The Role of Religious Lobbies in the American Polity.* Knoxville: University of Tennessee Press.

_____. 1993. *Echoes of Discontent: Jesse Jackson, Pat Robertson, and the Resurgence of Populism.* Washington, DC: CQ Press.

Hula, Kevin W. 2005. "Dolly Goes to Washington: Coalitions, Cloning, and the Role of Inter-Group Trust." In Paul S. Herrnson, Ronald G. Shaiko, and Clyde Wilcox (eds.), *The Interest Group Connection: Electioneering, Lobbying, and Policymaking in Washington,* 2nd edition. Washington, DC: CQ Press.

Hunter, James Davison. 1987. "The Evangelical Worldview Since 1890." In R. Neuhaus and M. Cromartie (eds.), *Piety and Politics.* Washington, DC: Ethics and Public Policy Center.

_____. 1991. *Culture Wars: The Struggle to Define America.* New York: Basic Books.

Ivers, Gregg. 1990. "Organized Religion and the Supreme Court." *Journal of Church and State* 32:775–793.

_____. 1992. "Religious Organizations as Constitutional Litigants." *Polity* 25:243–266.

Jacobs, Mike. 1995. "A Tale of Two Cities: Christian Right Activism in the New York City and Vista, California, School Districts." Unpublished manuscript.

Jacoby, Mary. 1999. "What Has She Done to the Christian Coalition?" *St. Petersburg Times,* October 3, p. A1.

Jelen, Ted G. 1990. *The Political Mobilization of Religious Belief.* New York: Greenwood.

_____. 1991a. "Religion and Democratic Citizenship: A Review Essay." *Polity* 23:471–481.

_____. 1991b. *The Political World of the Clergy.* New York: Praeger.

_____. 2004. *Sacred Markets, Sacred Canopies: Essays on Religious Markets and Religious Pluralism.* Lanham, MD: Rowman & Littlefield.

Jelen, Ted G., and Clyde Wilcox. 1995. *Public Attitudes Toward Church and State.* Armonk, NY: M. E. Sharpe.

Jorstad, Erling. 1970. *The Politics of Doomsday.* Nashville, TN: Abingdon Press.

Kellstedt, Lyman. 1989. "The Meaning and Measurement of Evangelicalism: Problems and Prospects." In T. Jelen (ed.), *Religion and Political Behavior in the United States.* New York: Praeger.

Kirkpatrick, David. 2005. "In Secretly Taped Conversations, a Portrait of a Future President." *New York Times,* February 20, p. 1.

Kirkpatrick, David D., and Albert Salvato. 2005. "In Telecast, Frist Defends His Effort to Stop Filibusters." *New York Times,* April 25, p. A14.

Koeppen, Sheilah. 1969. "The Radical Right and the Politics of Consensus." In R. Schoenberger (ed.), *The American Right Wing.* New York: Holt, Rinehart, and Winston.

Larson, Carin. 2006. "An Uphill Climb: The Christian Right and the 2004 Election in Colorado." In John C. Green, Mark J. Rozell, and Clyde Wilcox (eds.), *The Values Campaign? The Christian Right in the 2004 Election.* Washington, DC: Georgetown University Press.

Larson, Carin, David Madland, and Clyde Wilcox. 2005. "Religious Lobbying in Virginia: How Institutions Can Quiet Prophetic Voices." In Edward Cleary and Allen Hertzke (eds.), *Representing God at the Statehouse: Religion and Politics in the American States.* Lanham, MD: Rowman & Littlefield.

Larson, Carin, and Clyde Wilcox. 2005. "Sowing on Rocky Soil: The Christian Right on College Campuses." Paper presented at the University of Maryland.

———. 2006. "The Faith of George W. Bush: The Personal, Practical, and Political." In Mark J. Rozell and Gleaves Whitney (eds.), *Religion and American Presidents.* New York: Palmave/McMillan.

LaRue, Jan. 2005. "The Nomination of Harriet Miers to the U.S. Supreme Court." Concerned Women for America, memorandum to constituents, October 10. http://www.cwfa.org/articles/9148/LEGAL/scourt/, accessed October 15, 2005.

Levy, Leonard W. 1986. *The Establishment Clause.* New York: Macmillan.

Lewis, Gregory B., and Jonathan L. Edelson. 2000. "DOMA and ENDA: Congress Votes on Gay Rights." In Craig A. Rimmerman, Kenneth D. Wald, and Clyde Wilcox (eds.), *The Politics of Gay Rights.* Chicago: University of Chicago Press.

Liebman, Robert C. 1983. "Mobilizing the Moral Majority." In R. Liebman and R. Wuthnow (eds.), *The New Christian Right: Mobilization and Legitimation.* New York: Aldine.

———. 1995. "New Perspectives on the New Christian Right." Presented at the annual meeting of the American Sociological Association, Washington, DC.

Lienesch, Michael. 1994. *Redeeming America.* Chapel Hill: University of North Carolina Press.

———. 1995. "Mobilizing Against Modernity: The World's Christian Fundamentals Association and the Fundamentalist Movement." Presented at the annual meeting of the American Political Science Association, Chicago.

Lunch, William. 1995. "Oregon: Identity and Politics in the Northwest." In M. Rozell and C. Wilcox (eds.), *God at the Grassroots.* Lanham, MD: Rowman & Littlefield.

Malbin, Michael. 1978. *Religion and Politics: The Intentions of the Authors of the First Amendment.* Washington, DC: AEI Press.

Marsden, George. 1980. *Fundamentalism and American Culture.* New York: Oxford University Press.

Maxwell, Carol J. C. 1994. "Meaning and Motivation in Pro-Life Direct Action." Unpublished Ph.D. dissertation, Washington University, St. Louis, MO.

Mill, John Stuart. 1862. *Considerations on Representative Government.* New York: Harper and Brothers.

Miller, Warren E., Donald Kinder, Stephen Rosenstone, and the National Election Studies. 1952–2004. American National Election Study, 1952–2004. Computer file. Center for Political Studies, University of Michigan.

Millsaps, Rhett. 1999. "Loving the Sinner and Hating the Sin: The Emerging Ex-Gay Movement in Christian Right Politics." Unpublished manuscript.

Moen, Matthew. 1989. *The Christian Right and Congress.* Tuscaloosa: University of Alabama Press.

_____. 1990. "Ronald Reagan and the Social Issues: Rhetorical Support for the Christian Right." *Social Science Journal* 27:199–207.

_____. 1992. *The Transformation of the Christian Right.* Tuscaloosa: University of Alabama Press.

_____. 1994. "From Revolution to Evolution: The Changing Nature of the Christian Right." In S. Bruce, P. Kivisto, and W. Swatos (eds.), *The Rapture of Politics.* New Brunswick, NJ: Transaction Press.

_____. 1995. "The Christian Right in the Twenty-First Century." Presented at the annual meeting of the Northeastern Political Science Association, Newark, NJ.

Morken, Hubert. 1994. "'No Special Rights': The Thinking Strategy Behind Colorado's Amendment #2 Strategy." Presented at the annual meeting of the American Political Science Association, New York.

Murphy, Caryle, and Hamil R. Harris. 2004. "Thousands Rally on the Mall to Protest Same-Sex Marriage." *Washington Post*, October 16, p. B1.

Neuhaus, Richard. 1991. "The Theonomist Temptation." *First Things* 35:151–155.

Noll, Mark, and Carolyn Nystrom. 2005. *Is the Reformation Over? An Evangelical Assessment of Contemporary Roman Catholicism.* Grand Rapids: Baker Academics.

Numbers, Ronald N. 1992. *The Creationists.* New York: Alfred A. Knopf.

Nunn, C., H. Crockett, and J. A. Williams. 1978. *Tolerance for Nonconformity.* San Francisco: Jossey-Bass.

O'Hara, Thomas J. 1989. "The Civil Rights Restoration Act: The Role of Religious Lobbies." Presented at the annual meeting of the American Political Science Association, Atlanta.

Penning, James M., and Corwin E. Smidt. 2006. "A War on the Home Front? The Christian Right in the 2004 Elections." In John C. Green, Mark J. Rozell and Clyde Wilcox (eds.), *The Values Campaign? The Christian Right in the 2004 Election.* Washington, DC: Georgetown University Press.

People for the American Way. 1995. "The Two Faces of the Christian Coalition."

Persinos, John F. 1994. "Has the Christian Right Taken Over the Republican Party?" *Campaigns and Elections*, September: 21–24.

Peterson, Kavan, and Mark K. Matthews. 2005. "Evangelical Law Firm at Front of Culture War." Stateline.org., June 18. http://www.stateline.org/live/ViewPage.action?siteNodeId=136&languageId=1&contentId=38432. Accessed June 22, 2005.

Quebedeaux, Richard. 1983. *The New Charismatics II.* New York: Harper and Row.

Randolph, E. 1993. "In NY School Board 'Holy War,' Vote Is Split but Civics Triumph." *Washington Post,* May 22, p. A5.

Reed, Douglas S. 1998. "I Can Play That: Social Movement Repertoires and State Constitutional Politics." Presented at the annual meeting of the American Political Science Association, Boston.

Reed, Ralph. 1994a. *Politically Incorrect: The Emerging Faith Factor in American Politics.* Dallas: Word Publishing.

_____. 1994b. "What Do Religious Conservatives Really Want?" In Michael Cromartie (ed.), *Disciples and Democracy.* Washington, DC: Ethics and Public Policy Center.

Reichley, A. James. 1985. *Religion in American Public Life.* Washington, DC: Brookings.

Ribuffo, Leo. 1983. *The Old Christian Right.* Philadelphia: Temple University Press.

Robertson, Pat. 1992. *The New World Order.* Dallas: Word Publishing.

Rozell, Mark. 2002. "The Christian Right in the 2000 GOP Presidential Campaign." In Mary C. Seegers (ed.), *Piety, Politics, and Pluralism.* Lanham, MD: Rowman & Littlefield.

Rozell, Mark J., and Clyde Wilcox (eds.). 1995a. *God at the Grassroots: The Christian Right in the 1994 Elections.* Lanham, MD: Rowman & Littlefield.

Rozell, Mark J., and Clyde Wilcox. 1995b. Virginia Delegate Survey. Computer data file. Collected at Georgetown University.

_____. 1996. *Second Coming: The New Christian Right in Virginia Politics.* Baltimore: Johns Hopkins University Press.

_____. 1997. *God at the Grassroots, 1996: The Christian Right in the 1996 Elections.* Lanham, MD: Rowman & Littlefield.

_____. 2000. "Virginia: Prophet in Waiting?" In John C. Green, Mark J. Rozell, and Clyde Wilcox (eds.), *Prayers in the Precincts.* Washington, DC: Georgetown U Press.

Sandeen, Ernest. 1970. *The Roots of Fundamentalism.* Chicago: University of Chicago Press.

Schoenberger, Robert. 1969. *The American Right Wing.* New York: Holt, Rinehart, and Winston.

Shupe, Anson. 1989. "The Reconstructionist Movement in the New Christian Right." *Christian Century* 106:880–882.

Sigelman, Lee, Clyde Wilcox, and Emmett Buell. 1987. "An Unchanged Minority: Popular Support for the Moral Majority in 1980 and 1984." *Social Science Quarterly* 68:876–884.

Simon, Stephanie. 2005. "Grooming Politicians for Christ; Evangelical programs on Capitol Hill Seek to Mold a New Generation of Leaders Who Will Answer Not to Voters, but to God." *Los Angeles Times,* August 23, p. A1.

Smidt, Corwin. 1980. "Civil Religious Orientations Among Elementary School Children." *Sociological Analysis* 41:25–40.

Sniderman, Paul M., Richard A. Brody, and Philip E. Tetlock. 1991. *Reasoning and Choice: Explorations in Political Psychology.* New York: Cambridge University Press.

Sprengelmeyer, M. E. 2005. "Salazar Regrets Antichrist Barb." *Rocky Mountain News,* April 28. http://www.rockymountainnews.com/drmn/state/article/0,1299,DRMN_21_3735539,00.html. Accessed October 17, 2005.

Stouffer, Samuel A. 1955. *Communism, Conformity, and Civil Liberties.* New York: Doubleday.

Suczek, Yohanna M. 1995. "Christ, the Internet, and You." Unpublished manuscript.

Sullivan, Robert. 1993. "An Army of the Faithful." *New York Times Magazine,* April 25, pp. 32–35, 40–44.

Suro, Roberto, Richard Fry, and Jeffrey Passel. 2005. "Hispanics and the 2004 Election: Population, Electorate, and Voters." Pew Hispanic Center, June 27. http://pewhispanic.org/files/reports/48.pdf. Accessed October 16, 2005.

Thomas, Cal, and Ed Dobson. 1999. *Blinded by Might: Can the Religious Right Save America?* Grand Rapids, MI: Zondervan.

Tocqueville, Alexis de. 1945. *Democracy in America,* edited by P. Bradley. 2 vols. New York: Vintage Books.

Verba, Sidney, and Norman Nie. 1972. *Participation in America: Political Democracy and Social Equality.* Cambridge, MA: Harvard University Press.

Wald, Kenneth J. 1992. *Religion and Politics in the United States,* 2nd ed. Washington, DC: CQ Press.

Wald, Kenneth J., Dennis Owen, and Samuel Hill. 1988. "Churches as Political Communities." *American Political Science Review* 82:531–549.

Wallis, Jim. 2005. *God's Politics: Why the Right Gets It Wrong and the Left Doesn't Get It.* San Francisco: HarperSanFrancisco.

Warren, Mark. 1993. "New Patterns of Politicization: Implications for Participatory Democratic Theory." Presented at the annual meeting of the American Political Science Association, Washington, DC.

_____. 1996. "Deliberative Democracy and Authority." *American Political Science Review* 139:96–115.

_____. 2000. *Democracy and Association.* Princeton: Princeton University Press.

Wesskopf, Michael. 1993. "'Gospel Grapevine' Displays Strength in Controversy over Gay Ban." *Washington Post,* February 1, p. A10.

White, Gayle. 2001. "Evangelical power couple; Authors Tim and Beverly LaHaye, with scores of books between them, rank as four-star generals to many conservative Christians." *Atlanta Journal-Constitution,* July 7, p. 1B.

Whitley, Tyler. 1994. "GOP Factions Square Off at Local Level." *Richmond Times-Dispatch,* April 30, pp. A1, 8.

Wilcox, Clyde. 1987. "Popular Support for the Moral Majority in 1980: A Second Look." *Social Science Quarterly* 68:157–167.

_____. 1988a. "Political Action Committees of the New Christian Right: A Longitudinal Analysis." *Journal for the Scientific Study of Religion* 27:60–71.

_____. 1988b. "American Religion and Politics in Comparative Perspective." Presented at the annual meeting of the World Congress on Sociology, Madrid.

_____. 1992. *God's Warriors: The Christian Right in 20th Century America.* Baltimore: Johns Hopkins University Press.

_____. 1995. *The Latest American Revolution?* New York: St. Martin's.

_____. 2002. "Wither the Christian Right: The Elections and Beyond." In Stephen J. Wayne and Clyde Wilcox (eds.), *The Election of the Century and What It Tells Us About the Future of American Politics.* Armonk, NY: M. E. Sharpe.

_____. 2005. "Religious Dreams and Political Realities: Religion and Social Movements in the United States." Paper presented at the conference, Faith-based Radicalism: Christianity, Islam, and Judaism Between Constructive Activism and Destructive Fanaticism, September 14–25, University of Antwerp, Antwerp, Belgium.

Wilcox, Clyde, Paul Brewer, Shauna Shames, and Celinda Lake. 2006. "'If I Bend This Far I Will Break?' Public Opinion on Same Sex Marriage." In Craig Rimmerman and Clyde Wilcox (eds.), *The Politics of Same-Sex Marriage*. Chicago: University of Chicago Press.

Wilcox, Clyde, Matthew DeBell, and Lee Sigelman. 1999. "The Second Coming of the New Christian Right: Patterns of Popular Support in 1984 and 1996." *Social Science Quarterly* 80: 181–192.

Wilcox, Clyde, John C. Green, and Mark J. Rozell. 1995. "Faith, Hope, and Conflict: The Christian Right in State Republican Politics." Presented at the annual meeting of the American Sociological Association, Washington, DC.

Wilcox, Clyde, and Ted G. Jelen. 1990. "Evangelicals and Political Tolerance." *American Politics Quarterly* 18:25–46.

Wilcox, Clyde, Ted G. Jelen, and Sharon Linzey. 1991. "Reluctant Warriors: Premillennialism and Politics in the Moral Majority." *Journal for the Scientific Study of Religion* 30:245–258.

_____. 1995. "Rethinking the Reasonableness of the Religious Right." *Review of Religious Research* 36:263–276.

Wilcox, Clyde, Linda Merola, David Beer. 2006 "The Gay Marriage Issue and Christian Right Mobilization." In John C. Green, Mark J. Rozell, and Clyde Wilcox (eds.), *The Values Campaign? The Christian Right in the 2004 Election*. Washington, DC: Georgetown University Press.

Wilcox, Clyde, Mark J. Rozell, and Roland Gunn. 1996. "Religious Coalitions in the New Christian Right." *Social Science Quarterly* 77:543–559.

Wilcox, Clyde, and Robin Wolpert. 2000. "Gay Rights in the Public Sphere: Public Opinion on Gay and Lesbian Equality." In Craig A. Rimmerman, Kenneth D. Wald, and Clyde Wilcox (eds.), *The Politics of Gay Rights*. Chicago: University of Chicago Press.

Williamsburg Charter. 1988. Surveys of Church-State Attitudes. Computer data file. Williamsburg, Virginia.

Wills, Garry. 1990. *Under God: Religion and American Politics.* New York: Simon and Schuster.

Wimberly, Ronald C. 1976. "Testing the Civil Religion Hypothesis." *Sociological Analysis* 40:59–62.

Wolfinger, Raymond E., Barbara Kaye Wolfinger, Kenneth Prewitt, and Sheilah Rosenhack. 1969. "America's Radical Right: Politics and Ideology." In R. Schoenberger (ed.), *The American Right Wing*. New York: Holt, Rinehart, and Winston.

Zwier, Robert. 1984. *Born-Again Politics: The New Christian Right in America.* Downer's Grove, IL: Intervarsity Press.

Index